w/n

A STUDY OF TINDALE'S GENESIS
COMPARED WITH THE GENESIS OF COVERDALE
AND OF THE AUTHORIZED VERSION

BY

ELIZABETH WHITTLESEY CLEAVELAND

ARCHON BOOKS

1972

LIBRARY OF CONGRESS CATALOGING IN PUBLICATION DATA

Cleaveland, Elizabeth Whittlesey.
   A Study of Tindale's Genesis.

   Originally presented as the author's thesis, Yale, 1910.
   Reprint of the 1911 ed., which was issued as no. 43 of Yale studies in
English.
   1. Tyndale, William, d. 1536. 2. Coverdale, Miles, Bp. of Exeter,
1488-1568. 3. Bible. O. T. Genesis. English—Versions. I. Title.
II. Series: Yale studies in English, 43.
PR2384.T9Z6 1972   222'.11'052   72-341
ISBN 0-208-011269

First published 1911. Reprinted 1972 with permission of Yale University
Press, Inc., in an unaltered and unabridged edition as an Archon Book by
The Shoe String Press, Inc., Hamden, Connecticut 06514. *Printed in the
United States of Ameria*

TO THE MEMORY OF
MY FATHER,
ELISHA WHITTLESEY CLEAVELAND, M. D.

CONTENTS

PREFACE

There are years in a nation's life marked as epochs, and there are just as truly books that mark a new era in a nation's development, recording a rebirth of intellectual activity or indicating a revival of spiritual life. As the progress of a nation is too often traced by bloodstained milestones, where the wrestling with angels—or with fiends—has been until the dawn of a day of triumph, so it is with the blood of the reformer that a new era of intellectual or of spiritual life must be opened: a martyr's blood shall be the sacrificial oblation. One may precede and make inevitable the other; one may follow remotely as the indirect outcome of the other. Rarely, however, are a great spiritual change and a political revolution so brought together that one is immediately attendant upon the other, so closely connected, indeed, that the two are really one, each being the consummation of a long series of events that through years have been slowly riving the mountains of prejudice and superstition to open this highroad of a new life.

Thus closely identified are the English Reformation and the beginning of England's greatness as a world-power. The breaking away from old forms, the rending asunder of established institutions of government, the great intellectual and spiritual awakening that came to Britain with the reception by Henry VIII of the Bible in the language of the people, were followed or accompanied by those events of progress which so unified the kingdom as to make it a power to be reckoned with in the world's changes.[1]

To trace, however, the rise of England's greatness from the foundations laid in ' a tyrant's strenuous efforts to defend his own position,'[2] is not the purpose here. Nor is it the purpose of this work to show how the world-power of the English language lies in its inherent strength; how it was protected during the years of the Norman usurpation; conserved in the great literary monuments of the nation's vernacular; brought again to activity in Chaucer; polished, refined, enlarged by Spenser, Ben Jonson, Shakespeare, and Milton. But it is the purpose to show, in some measure, the debt of the language to the translation of the Bible by one who sought to make the Bible ' a book for the plough-boy,' for simple folk; that their lives should be made purer by its precepts, more unified by the teachings of the Old Testament, more lovely by the Sermon on the Mount, more holy by the strong admonitions of the Epistles.

This scholar, in the early sixteenth century, resolved ' that our Bible should be popular '—a book for the people—' and not literary; that it should speak in a simple dialect; and that by its simplicity it should be endowed with permanence,'[3] and, we may add, with power. This determination was manifest in other English scholars who thwarted the earlier issue of the Bishop's Bible, because Gardiner strove to make it a book for scholars by retaining Latin words in place of the familiar Anglo-Saxon. In Tindale's version,

---

[1] *Cambridge Modern History* 2. 472.

[2] *Cambridge Modern History* 2. 472.

[3] B. F. Westcott, *History of the English Bible* p. 165, second edition of 1872.

one can almost detect the choosing of a word or of an expression that shall be familiar to those Gloucester farmers among whom the translator's early years were spent, that rude folk for whom he avowedly began and carried on his work.

Yet in this endeavor to put the Word of God into the speech of the peasant, there is nowhere any descent to what is common; the simplicity is ever dignified. This must be so if even Sir Thomas More brings no charge of vulgarity against him. He lifted the rude language of the rude people to his own strong dialect, the grand simplicity appealing to high and low alike. ' When the king had allowed the Bible to be read in the churches, immediately several poor men in Essex bought the New Testament, and on Sunday sat reading it in the lower end of the church; many would flock about to hear the reading.' [1] And it was Cranmer himself who wrote to Cromwell begging him ' to read it [Matthew's Bible], and to exhibit it to the king,' [2] and to obtain from Henry ' a license that the same may be sold and read of every person,' ' until such time that we, the bishops, shall set forth a better translation '; adding with honest appreciation of its worth, ' which, I think will not be till a day after doomsday.' [3]

Although Tindale's Bible, under the translator's name, was never authorized by king nor by parliament, it was Tindale's Bible, called ' Matthew's Bible ', that was first sanctioned by the king (1537), and ordered ' to be sold and read of every person.' [4] And it was Matthew's Bible, and therefore Tindale's, that fur-

---

[1] Westcott, *History of the English Bible*, p. 83, second edition of 1872.

[2] Foxe's *Acts and Monuments*.

[3] Moulton, p. 133.

[4] Dore, p. 33.

nished the basis for Cranmer's, or the Great Bible, authorized in 1539 to be placed in every church and in every bishop's hall.[1] To show that it was Tindale's and not Coverdale's translation that was made the basis of the Authorized Version of 1611, is another purpose of this study.

This comparison will show at a glance the changes made by Coverdale, and how many were adopted by the Authorized Version. It will show, too, the limited influence that any other version could have had on the Authorized Version. That Coverdale was familiar with Tindale's version, there can be no doubt. ' Dr. Whittaker maintains that the ' five translations' used by Coverdale can have been no other than the Latin Vulgate, the Latin of Pagninus, the German of Luther, a Dutch translation of Luther, and a German translation of the Vulgate,'[2] all of which resolve themselves to three. Moulton believes that Tindale's should be considered as one of the five, for he holds as authentic the tradition that Coverdale worked in Hamburg[3] with Tindale, and in this way became familiar with Tindale's translation as early as 1530.[4]

That Coverdale was an independent worker, and not a servile copyist, is evident from his characteristic style. Though more diffuse in general, he is often much more concise. When Tindale says, ' The name of the city was,' etc., Coverdale says, ' The city was,' etc., or ' The city was called,' etc. Final *e* in many words, if pronounced, would give a certain rhythmic effect to Coverdale's diction.

[1] Smythe, p. 100. See Dore, pp. 83, 84.
[2] Moulton, pp. 105, 106.
[3] Foxe's *Acts and Monuments* 5. 120, edition of 1838.
[4] Moulton, pp. 54, 98, 108.

Whole phrases, however, similar to or almost iden-
tical with Tindale's, will be noted in Coverdale's Genesis.
Moreover, there is in Coverdale a following of the
unusual chapter-division found in Tindale, and not
used in the Bishop's Bible: so, between chapters 26
and 27, the division is made after verse 33 of chapter 26,
thus carrying verses 34 and 35 into chapter 27; between
chapters 31 and 32, verses 1 and 2 of chapter 32 are
placed with chapter 31; and between chapters 49 and
50, the division places the first verse of chapter 50
with chapter 49.

Genesis is chosen for this study, because that book,
obviously the first work done on the Pentateuch, and
so the first done on the Old Testament, represents ' the
last formal contribution on a very large scale to the
English Bible'[1]; and because it was not the first work
done by Tindale in translation. To this work the
author came after experience in translating, after the
completion of the New Testament. Hence he came
with a clearer vision of his work, of its difficulties, and
of its importance, even though one commentator
remarks, 'Before he began, he had prepared himself
for a task of which he could apprehend the full difficulty.'[2] That this book, like the others, was in the
later edition 'newly correctyd and amendyd,' does not
detract from the value of this first edition for our study
of it. Strangely enough, quotations in dictionaries
for illustration and for comparison are taken from all
books of Tindale's Bible except Genesis—notably from
Numbers and from the New Testament. More often
than from Tindale, the citations are from the Authorized
Version or from Coverdale; not infrequently from

[1] Demaus, pp. 245, 246.
[2] Westcott, *History of the English Bible*, second edition of 1872,
p. 164.

Matthew's Bible. All these are, as history clearly shows, dependent upon Tindale.

The editions used for this study are: Tindale, the verbatim reprint of 1530, edited in 1884 by the Rev. J. J. Mombert; Coverdale, the edition of 1535, reprinted in 1835; the Authorized Version, the version of 1611, reprinted in 1833. The New English Dictionary has, in all cases, been relied upon as far as that dictionary is at the present time available.

In the Alphabetical Index, words are arranged, generally, in the following order: 1. The first occurrence of the word with like forms through all, if there are such. 2. Variations occurring more than once, in the order of their occurrence, preference being given to those having only one variation. 3. Variations occurring only once, in the order of their occurrence.

Special attention is not given to the different spellings of an auxiliary or of an accompanying word in Coverdale or in the Authorized Version: *shall, shal; a certain man, a certaine man* etc. Certain compounds are treated as single words: *out of, according as, as concerning,* etc., and are so arranged in alphabetical sequence. Forms in *u* for *v* are generally used with no consideration of difference; but preference is usually given to the form that occurs most frequently.

The † marks a notable difference in translation, but in a passage too long to be transcribed.

From the Alphabetical Index have been omitted the articles *a* and *the*, and the personal pronouns.

I wish to express my sincere thanks to Professor Albert S. Cook for patient enthusiasm during the long months spent in the preparation of this work; and to members of the staff of Yale University Library for unfailing courtesy.

A portion of the expense of printing this book has been borne by the Modern Language Club and by the English Club of Yale University from funds placed at their disposal by the generosity of Mr. George E. Dimock of Elizabeth, New Jersey, a graduate of Yale in the Class of 1874.

E. W. C.

NEW HAVEN,
January 1911.

INTRODUCTION

I. A DISCUSSION OF WORDS PECULIAR TO TINDALE OR USED BY TINDALE IN A PECULIAR SIGNIFICANCE

Adam, 11. 5: The LORde came downe to see the cyte and the toure which the children of Adam had buylded. C.[1] has *mē* (men) and AV. has *men*. This word used by T. for *men* is retained from the Hebrew. *NED.* fails to note the fact that T. uses this word for *men* and that, therefore, the word was long retained in its Hebraic meaning, quite apart from its use by Shakespeare and later writers as signifying an 'unregenerate condition or character.'

Apparell, 2. 1: Thus was heave & erth fynished wyth all their apparell. C. has, 'with all their hoost', and AV. translates, 'and all the host ot them.' A gloss in T. notes, 'apparell, *the heavenly bodies.*' No meaning is given in *NED.* that can be construed as signifying *number collectively*, as *host*, nor as in any way pertaining to heavenly bodies. *NED.* gives as one meaning, 'appendages of a house,' in the way of glory or beauty, as is the rendering in the Vulgate: i. e., *ornamentum.*

Appoyntment, 9. 13: I will sette my bowe in the clouds, and it shall be a sygne of the appoyntment made betwene me and the erth. A gloss gives, 'appointment, covenant.' In 9. 15, 16, 17, the word used is *testament*, with a like gloss, 'testament, covenant.' *NED.* gives the definition

---

[1] C. = Coverdale; **AV.** = Authorized Version; T. = Tindale; *NED.* = New English Dictionary.

of this word as, 'an agreement, pact, contract,' obsolete;
cites *Paston Letters* as the earliest use (1440); the latest
use quoted is Defoe's, from *The English Tradesman*
(1745). No mention is made of T.s use. Vulgate gives,
'erit signum foederis.'

Asene, 41. 31 : the plenteousness shal not be once asene in
the land by reason of that hunger. This form is probably
from the obsolete verb *asee*, a variant of *isee, ysee*, from
OE. *gesēne*.

A sonder, 1. 7 : And God sayd : let there be a fyrmament
betwene the waters, ād let it devyde the waters a sonder.
NED. does not record just this form in the list of variant
spellings, but gives *asonder* (not as two words) : it does,
however, cite its use in quotation from C : Erasm.
Par. Gal. 1. 15 : But me called he a sonder to be his
preacher. Again, in illustrating partitive preposition *a* in
combination, it is C. (1535) that is quoted : Acts 1. 18 :
brast a sonder in the myddes.

Bisse, 41. 42 : and arayed him in a raymēt of bisse. It is
interesting to note the apparent difficulty over this word.
It is undoubtedly from the Latin *byssus*, 'flax.' The Vulgate
has in this passage, 'stola byssina.' In the table of words
appended to Genesis, the translator comments : 'Bisse :
fyne white, whether it be silke or linen.' The word was
evidently 'a mere name to which English writers attached
no certain meaning except that of fineness and value,'
(*NED*). In Luke 16. 19 : T. translates the word *fyne raynes* ;
Wyclif, *biys (or white silke)* ; the Genevan Bible, *fyne lynen* ;
the Rheims Bible, *silke* ; Bishop's, *fine white* ; C., *linen* ;
Matthew's, *fine bysse*.

Bothe, 7. 21 : extended to more than two objects in sequence :
bothe birdes, catell and beasts. *NED.* notes this use as
early as Chaucer (1386), *Knight's Tale,* l. 1440 : 'To whom
bothe heuene and erthe, and see is sene,' and down
through Shakespeare, Bunyan, Coleridge, De Quincey;
but T.s use is not cited. Shakespeare, in *Venus and
Adonis* 747, uses four nouns : 'Both favour, savour, hue,
& quality.' Lord Berners (1528), *Froissart,* uses five :

'Bothe prelates, bysshoppes, abbottes, barownes, and knyghtes.'

Brede, 35. 16: when he was but a feld brede from Ephrath. This is equal to *breadth*; in North of England dialects its use is still common. This combination, *feld brede*, is not given in *NED.* AV. has, 'a little way.'

Bring. This word is used with the meaning now given to *take*, i. e., to carry in *going*; *bring* to-day is confined to the use with the notion of coming. 37. 28: and sold him [Joseph] vnto the Ismaelites. . . . And they brought him into Egipte, 37. 32: they sent that gay coote & caused it to be brought vnto their father, 43. 11: take of the best frutes of the lande in youre vesseles, and brynge the man a present.

    NED. notes the singular dialectic use of this word with the signification, *to convoy, escort, accompany*; this meaning might have the notion of *going*. But in one example cited, *Merlin* (1450): 'He brought the on the wey hiderwarde a great part,' the word *hiderwarde* gives the sense of *coming*.

Brode, 30. 42: so the last brode was Labās, and the first Iacobs. *NED.* notes: 'of cattle or large animals [brood] is obsolete.' This word is given as being in use about 1250, but is not cited later than 1387.

Buryall, 47. 30: burie me in their buryall. This word for burying-place was used as early as 1250, and as late as 1612. C. (1535) is quoted, from Nehemia 2. 5. The OE. form was *byrʒels*, and was last used in this form in the late 15ᵗʰ century.

Buttelar, 41. 9: This form of the now common *butler* was not infrequent in the 16ᵗʰ century; no citation from T. is made, however, in *NED.*

Come on, as an expletive, 11. 3, 4, 7: Come on, let us make brycke; Come on, let us buylde us a cyte; Come on, let us descende and myngell thiere tongue. *NED.* does not note just this use of the word *come*; i. e., as an expletive without any sense of challenge. The *Century Dictionary* records it as a colloquialism, in which use it

is often heard to-day. Neither dictionary quotes T. Halliwell makes no record of this use.

Curtesie, 43. 11: brynge the man a present, a curtesie
bawlme, and curtesie of honey. *NED.* defines the word
courtesy in this use as *a mannerly* or *moderate quantity*.
Palgrave's use (1530) is the earliest noted; C.s (1535),
Kings 17. 20. The last noted use is in 1627. AV. says,
'Take a little balme.'

Either, with present sense of *both*. 2. 25: they were ether
of them naked. C. and AV. both render this passage:
'They were both naked'; 40. 5: And they dreamed,
ether of them in one nyghte; both the butlar and the
baker. C. translates: 'They dreamed, both the butlar
and the baker, every mā his own dream.' AV. has,
'They dreamed a dreame both of them, each man his
dreame.' 41. 13: And he declared oure dreames to vs
acordynge to ether of oure dreames; C. and AV. omit
this phrase. The original sense of this word in OE. and
ME. is *each of two*. OE. *ǣghwæðer* = either, each,
both, and is so used here, even though it assumes its
disjunctive meaning, *one or other of two*, as early as the
14th century. This latter meaning belonged to OE.
awðer, ME. *oþer*. This disjunctive use in Modern English
is that most frequently used, the first being considered
ambiguous. C. is quoted, Ezekiel 40. 48: By the walles
also were pilers, on ether side one.

Enhabiter, 50. 11: When the enhabiters of the lande sawe
the moornynge. Inhabiter (enhabiter) is noted in *NED.*
as an archaic variant for inhabitant. Wyclif (1388) uses
enhabiters, Genesis 24. 13, where T. uses *men*: 'The douȝtris
of the enhabiters of this citee.' The Great Bible (1539)
uses *enhabitours,* Jeremiah 33. 5. The use of *inhabiter*
is found from Wyclif through Raleigh to Christina
Rossetti, with this meaning of *people*. The latest use
is noted in 1884, in '*Salmonidæ Westmoreland*': 'This
species [salmon] is not an inhabiter of our rivers,' and
probably marks the revival of the old word with a new
signification.

Every with **betwyxte,** 32. 16: Betwyxte euery drooue. No such use is recorded in *NED.*; every use of *betwyxte* or of *between* demands more than the one expressed. With all meanings of *every* the sense of the singular, of the individual, is maintained, and there is no sense of duality, necessary to the meaning of *betwyxte* or of *between*. Nor if *every* is taken in its distributive sense, does it assume the meaning of *one and another* involved in the use of this preposition.

Faintie, fayntie, 'faint', 25. 29: Iacob sod potage & Esau came from the feld & was faītie & sayd to Iacob: let me sypp of ỹ redde potage, for I am fayntie. *NED.* does not recognize this spelling. The word was dialectic in counties of northern and western England, meaning all that the adjective *faint* may mean.

Fared, meaning 'to deal with, to treat,' 16. 6: And because Sarai fared foule with her, she fled from her. The same expression is cited in *NED.* from *Knight de la Tour* (1450). T.s 2 Corinthians 5. 11 is quoted for its use with this meaning. The more frequent modern use is with the impersonal *it*; 'it fared ill with him.'

Fawte, 41. 9: I do remember my fawte this day. This was a common form in the 14th and 16th centuries, and was retained in dialectic use in the 18th and 19th centuries. During the 18th century, however, the *l* was not sounded, though inserted after the French usage; e. g., Pope:

> O born in sin, and forth in folly brought!
> Works damn'd or to be damn'd (your father's fault)!
>
> *Dunciad* 1. 226.

and Goldsmith:

> Yet he was kind; or if severe in aught,
> The love he bore to learning was in fault.
>
> *Deserted Village.*

Feders, 7. 15: all maner off foules whatsoeuer had feders. This form in *d* instead of *th* is curious in so late universal use as T. makes of it, though it was common in the 14th and 16th centuries (*NED.*). Lydgate (1430)

uses it: 'of his good fame she gan the feders pull.'
(Bochas, I. XII.). C. does not use the form, nor does
Shakespeare, and it must have been dropping out of use
in T.s time. In 1. 21: and all maner of federed foules
in their kyndes. The plural *feðera* was in OE. used for
wings; and C. has in 2 Samuel 22. 11: He appeared
vpon the fethers of the wynde. The nearest form recorded
as dialectic use is *fed bed* for feather bed (Halliwell).

Foule, 16. 6: because Sarai fared foule with her, she fled
from her. This is used as an adverb, and with the final
e of the adverb added to the adjective form. *NED.*
says: 'After the 14th century, the adverb was not distin-
guished in form from the adjective.' The sense here
is *harshly, severely*; the meaning given in *NED.* is different.
It is *unseemly, ugly*. 'To fare foule is to behave in an
unseemly way.' Chaucer is quoted from *Rom. Rose*
(1366): 'Frounced foule was hir visage.' The latest use
cited is 1450.

Good, meaning 'property' 14. 12: they toke Lot also . . .
and his good and departed. In OE. Luke 12. 18 (about
1000), is the expression: 'Ic secge minre sawle eala sawel
þu hæfst mycele god.' Many instances of this singular
form are cited, even down to Browning, in *Guardianship*
(*Red Cott. Nt. Cap. Cnty.*): 'Of earthly good for heavenly
purpose.' T.s use is not noted in *NED.* In 14. 22,
however: 'Gyue me the soulles, and take the goodes
to thy selfe.' This interchange of forms is not infrequent.

The letter **J.** This form occurs for the first and only time
in T.s Genesis in 41. 39: Pharao sayde unto Joseph. In
AV., while it is not the usual form, it occurs several
times: as, 5. 32; 6. 10; 7. 13, Japheth; 10. 16, Jebusite;
10. 25, 26, Joktan; 36. 40, Jethreth. In 22. 14 the small *j*
is found: Abraham called the name of the place Jehouah-
ijreh. Yet *NED.* says: 'It was not till the 17th century,
that the device of the two forms, *i* and *j*, for vowel and
consonant, was established, and the capital *J* was introduced.' 'The J, j types were not used in the Bible of
1611.' In German typography, almost from the first,

a tailed form was used for the initial consonant; 'but this was by no means generally established till later.' Louis Elzevir, printer at Leyden (1595–1619), is generally credited with making this distinction, as with that of W and V, 'which was followed by the introduction of U and J among capitals, by Lazarus Zetzner of Strasburg in 1619.' In England, an attempt to differentiate these letters 'was made by Richard Day, after 1587, in the lower case, but no capital J or U.' They were not generally established till after 1630. Samuel Johnson in his dictionary did not discriminate. (*NED.*)

Kepe, 37. 13, meaning 'to feed the flocks': do not thy brethern kepe in Sichem? C. uses the same expression, but AV. has 'feed the flock'; and T. has in 37. 16: 'Where they kepe shepe.' *NED.* gives no such specific use of the word, i. e., without the object named. This is equivalent to the New England dialectical use of *pasture*, or *feed*: 'Where do you pasture now?' meaning, 'Where do you allow your cattle to feed?'

Lucke, 30. 12: Then sayde Lea: good lucke, and called his name Gad: C. says: 'This is good lucke,' and AV.: 'And Leah said, A troupe commeth.'

Luckely, 39. 23: the LORde made it come luckely to passe. C. translates: 'made it come prosperously to passe'; AV. renders it: 'and that which he did, the LORD made it to prosper.'

Luckie, 39. 2: And the LORde was with Ioseph, and he was a luckie felowe. C. uses the same expression; but AV. says: 'And the LORD was with Ioseph, and hee was a prosperous man.' Whether or not this word came into English as a gambling term from the German, it must have been adopted early enough to have gained a very respectable place early in the 16th century, for in all these uses it has the sense of *good* only, and that quite removed from the element of chance. In 1502, we find in *Arnolde Chron.*: 'God Almyghty yeue you parte of his saluacion and make you lukky.' Of the adverb, instances are cited from Erasmus, *Par. Matt.*, under date of 1548. T.s use of this word *luckie* is cited in illustration of that form and use of the derivative.

Lustie, 25. 8: Abraham . . . fell seke ād dyed, in a lustie age. A marginal note gives *good.* C.s use of the word is quoted in *NED.* to illustrate the exact meaning here, i. e., full of healthy vigor. Proverbs 17. 22: A merry herte maketh a lusty age. See 3. 6: it was a good tree to eate of and lustie unto the eyes. A marginal note gives the explanation: 'affording pleasure.'

Mischefe, 6. 12: the erth was corrupte in the syghte of god, and was full of mischefe. *NED.* quotes the same use from C. in 6. 5, where T. has *wekednesse.* T.s use is not noted.

Move, 'breed abundantly' 8. 17: let them moue, growe ād multiplye vppon the erth. C. gives: 'Be ye occupied vpon the earth, growe and multiplye vpon the earth'; and AV. has: 'may breed abundantly.' The nearest definition found for the word *move* to cover this use is 'to be stirred or excited,' as relating to the passions. Here undoubtedly the meaning is to breed.

Occupie, 'to traffic, to trade, to do business,' 42. 34: So will I delyuer you youre brother agayne, and ye shall occupie in the lande. This is an obsolete sense of the word; used by T., Luke 19. 13, where the RV. has *trade.* This citation is not found. The meaning here is quite different from that of 9. 7 or 46. 34, in both of which places it has the passive form, and signifies: 'be engaged in labor.' Foxe uses the word with this signification: 'Without loss of time in his own business and occupying.'[1] In 34. 21, is found: 'Will dwell in the lāde and do their occupatiō therein,' where the noun clearly has the significance of *business.*

Oke, 12. 6: vnto the oke of More. The word here translated *oke* is in AV. rendered *plaine.* In the Hebrew are five words that have been rendered *oak,* of which only two are held to have certainly this meaning. As the AV. translates this *plaine,* and as that seems to interpret

[1] Anderson 1. 144.

the meaning, this may be an example of the erroneous or disputed renderings. C. is quoted (*NED.*) as using this term in 35. 4. There he follows T., but in 12. 6 he translates the word *oke grove*. Moulton[1] makes the evidence that the books from Joshua to Chronicles are from the same hand as the Pentateuch depend upon the rendering of certain Hebrew words; the word here translated *oke* is one of these words. Brown, *Hebrew and English Lexicon*, p. 18, renders by 'Terebinth.'

Once, meaning 'now,' 2. 23: Then sayd Adā this is once bone of my boones, and flesh of my fleesh. AV. has *now*. T. adds a marginal note: 'once, *now* (a *Saxon idiom*).' *NED.* quotes T. (1526), 1 Corinthians 15. 6, for *at once*; this seems to be the earliest recorded use of *c* instead of *s* in this word; earlier forms are in *es, is, us, ez*. The meaning of *now* for *once* is not recorded at all, nor is it found in Wright's *Dialect Dictionary*. It is probably translating the German *einmal*, used in this sense.

Perauenture, 11. 4: 'perauenture we shall be scatered abrode over all the erth.' This archaic form is from the OF. *per* + *auenture*, 'by chance' (*NED.*). In the 15th century it began to be conformed to the Latin spelling, which in the 16th century superseded the earlier form. The fact that T. uses it almost to the exclusion of the Latin form would indicate the general use in the 16th century.

Popular, 30. 37: Iacob toke roddes of grene popular, hasell, & chestnottrees. *NED.* does not record any such form of the word, nor do Halliwell and Wright, nor does Wright in the *Dialect Dictionary* (*popple* = poplar, various species of *populus*). Wyclif renders the word *popil*. T. probably follows closely the derivation. The tree is of the genus *Populus*. AV. *poplar*; Vulgate, *populus*.

Rennagate, 4. 12: A vagabunde and a rennagate shalt thou be vpon the erth. This word is defined in *NED.* as 'an apostate from any form of religious faith,' 'one who deserts a party, person, or principle in favor of another.' The meaning here is, from the gloss, a *wanderer*, but

[1] P. 128.

with the added notion of being an *outlaw*; and this signification is allowed for *renegado*, a newer word credited
for first use to Beaumont and Fletcher (1611); but this
is earlier by nearly a century than Beaumont and Fletcher.
Wyclif translates the word *vagaunt,* i. e., a wanderer.

Ryd, rydd, 37. 21, 22: 'he wēt aboute to ryd him out of
their handes.' 'he wolde haue rydd him out of their
handes:' The participial form is not given among regular
grammatical forms in *NED.*, even though it is used there
in the illustrative quotation. The meaning 'to deliver, to
set free', is marked as 'rare, but common in the 16th
Century.' C. is quoted, Isaiah 47, 14: no man may ryd it.

Scace, 27. 30: Iacob was scace gone out frō the preseance
of Isaac his father. C., *scace*; AV., *scarce*. This form,
apparently dialectic, is not noted by Wright in his *Dialect
Dictionary*, nor by Palmer in *Corrupted Words*. Halliwell, however, in the *Archaic and Provincial Dictionary*
mentions its use by Lydgate (1375–1461). C. repeats
this form, but AV. has the spelling *scarce*. It is interesting
to note this very early dialectic use of a word now common
in New England dialect, together with its variant *scurce*.

Slee, 42. 37: Slee my two sonnes, yf I bringe him not to
the agayne. This is a form retained from the OE. strong
verb *slēan*, to slay; it is the second person singular of
the imperative mood (made by dropping the *an* of the
infinitive, according to the rule for strong verbs (§ 367,
p. 255, *OE. Grammar*).

Sotyller, 3. 1: The serpent was sotyller than all the beasts
of the felde. This spelling justifies the pronunciation of
to-day. It is remarkable that the new spelling, that is,
the word-form showing its root-value is preserved. The
Century Dictionary quotes the Bible, the AV., and
spells the word *subtil*. The use of the word as a verb,
sotiled, is in Piers Plowman (x. 214); so too in *Holy
Rood* (E.E.T.S.), p. 162, *subtyll*. In the older forms,
the *b* was silent, having been inserted in simulation
of the original Latin *subtilis*. In 27. 35 is the noun:
'thy brother came with subtilte.' The Vulgate, however,

uses for 3. 1, *callidior cunctis*; and for 27. 35, *frau-dulenter*.

Sowe, 1. 11: grasse that sowe seed. This is an unusual sense for the word *sow*, the accepted notion being to *scatter*. This signification is *to produce* or *to yield*. Webster gives the sense *to propagate*, which may be accepted for this use; and quotes Chaucer. This meaning, *to propagate*, is found in Beaumont and Fletcher, *Maid's Tragedy* 3. 1.

Soythsayers, 41. 8: he sent and called for all the soyth-sayers of Egypt. This old word, coming as it does from the Gothic, presents, as here found, a unique form. According to the *Century Dictionary*, Webster, Worcester, Wright's *Dialect Dictionary*, and Halliwell's *Provincial Dictionary*, no such form is known.

Sprete, 41. 8: When the mornynge came, his sprete was troubled. This dialectic form is probably from Lancashire, but there has the meaning of ' a shrew.' The same word is found in *Nominale MS.*, 15th century, with the sense of *a soul, a spirit.* Cf. the modern *sprite*.

Ah syr, 3. 1: The serpent sayd vnto the woman. Ah syr, that God hath sayd, ye shall not eate of all maner trees in the garden. A marginal note suggests ' ah surely.' The use here is evidently in the sense of remonstrance or of objection. C. says: 'Yee, hath God sayde indeed,' etc., and AV. has: ' Yea, hath God said,' etc. This use of *sir* or *syr* in addressing a woman is not unusual before the 17th century. The *Century Dictionary*, however, does not quote T.

Totehill, 31. 48: and this totehill which the lorde seeth (sayde he) be wytnesse betwene me and the when we are departed one from a nother. AV. has *Mizpah*. The *Century Dictionary* gives the derivation from ME., 'a lookout-hill; any high place of observation.' The quotation is from Mandeville, *Travels*, p. 312. Wright, however, does not note it in the *Dialect Dictionary*.

Tyllman, 25. 27: Esau became a conynge hunter & a tyll-man. Wright records no such word, neither *tilman* nor *tillman,* in the *Dialect Dictionary.* The *Century Dictionary* has the form *tillman,* and quotes from Palladius (E.E.T.S., p. 149). Worcester records the word; Webster does not.

Vnrighte, 16. 5: Thou dost me vnrighte. A marginal note gives *wrong.* The *Century Dictionary* records this word with the meaning *wrong, injustice.* The uses cited are: Chaucer, *W.B.T.,* 237, and Freeman's *Norman Conquest,* v, 108. It is interesting to find it in common use in T.s time. Perhaps from the German *unrecht,* which is found here: Du thust *unrecht* an mir.

Voyde, 1. 2: The erth was voyde and emptie. AV. says: 'without form and void'; while RV. translates: 'was waste and void.' This is from the OF. *voide,* meaning *empty.* A quotation is given from *Merlin:* 'The voyde place at the table that Ioseph made,' where it has the sense of *empty.*

Waxe, 9. 7, with the meaning of *multiply*: See that ye encrease, and waxe. This meaning of *multiply* is not given in the *Century Dictionary,* in Webster, nor in Worcester. This is either a different use of the word, or it is used figuratively with the idea of growing greater. In 18. 12, the participial form is used in another sense, but in the usual one: 'I am waxed old.'

Wife, meaning *woman,* 38. 20: And Iudas sent the kydd ... for to fetch out his pledge agayne from the wifes hande. The meaning in OE. and ME. is of *woman* only. Chaucer and Tennyson are quoted to illustrate this use, with the added sense of one in humble station. T. uses the word as meaning not one in humble station, but perhaps as a term of reproach or of contempt.

Yer, 45. 28: 'I will goo and se him, yer that I dye. A marginal note is: 'yer, *before.*' This form for *ere* was found as early as the 16th and 17th centuries. T. uses this form in John 1. 15, in the sense of *earlier*: 'He that commeth after me, was before me because he was yer than I.'

Yet, 40. 8: Interpretynge belongeth to God but tel me yet. Perhaps translating Ger. *doch*: *doch* erzählet mir's.

Ys, 4. 1: 'wyth ... ys wife.' This form for the personal pronoun *his* is found in the 13 th, 16 th, and 17th centuries; in *Chron. Gr. Friars* (1556) is: 'He was dyscharged ys byschopryge and all hys bondes'; in Robert of Gloucester (1297) is: 'He let a moneþ of þ ʒer clepye aftur ys owne name'; and in *Harl. Misc.* (1609) is found: 'Man can receive is birth but from one place.'

II. GRAMMAR.

In considering the peculiarities in Grammar found in Tindale's Genesis, it seems best to group them by parts of speech rather than by an alphabetical arrangement.

Nouns and Pronouns in Syntax.

Many nouns have been considered in the discussion of 'peculiar words'; there remain only a few to be reviewed.

Singular noun with plural adjective.

V. chaunge, 45. 22: vnto Ben Iamin he gaue .iii. hundred peces of syluer and .v. chaunge of rayment. This word retains even now the same form in the plural as in the singular, with the application to raiment, or garments. The earliest use recorded (*NED.*) is in the Bible of 1611, Judges 14. 12: thirtie chaunge of garments.

All thynge, 9. 3: so geue I yow all thynge; 9. 12: betwene all lyvynge thing that is with yow for ever; 24. 8: aboue all thinge. This use, unknown to OE., seems to have begun with *thing*'s having a singular and plural alike. *All thing* is a northern dialectic form for *everything*.

An hundred yere olde, 11. 10, 11, 12, etc.: an hundred yere olde; Sē lyved . . . v. hundred yere, etc. This word *yere* is from the OE. *gēar*, year (singular and plural alike), and the ME. *yer*, with its plural *yere*. This is the form used by Tindale, but he uses the same for the singular, 8. 13: the syxte hundred and one yere and the fyrst daye of the fyrst moneth. The form became fixed as a singular, forming its plural in *s*, with its variant *yeares*: as, 15. 14: And they shall make bondmen of them and entreate them evell .iiii. hundred yeares.

The possessive form in *s* without the apostrophe, and with the apostrophe.

As in all writers before the 17th century no apostrophe is used with the possessive case. This is the original genitive form for the masculine and neuter strong OE. substantives. The apostrophe is used consistently since the 17th century—appearing even in Shakespeare, *Romeo and Juliet*, and *Macbeth*—marking the elision of the inflectional ending. It was not, however, placed consistently before the *s* in the singular, and after the *s* in plurals ending in *s*; as, 'warriour's arms, or arms of the warriours'; 'the stone's end, or the end of stones'; for 'the warriours's arms; stones's end.'[1] In T.s Genesis is found one instance of the use of the apostrophe, 31. 33: 'Thā wēt Labā in to Iacob's tēte.'

Selfe for *selves*, 30. 40: And he made him flockes of his own by thē selfe. The only explanation of this is that the plural being signified in the first part of what is really a compound, the need for its repetition in the second is not felt. Hence, the inflection is given to one part only. Many examples of this will be found in compound nouns and in combinations not compounded; as, courts-martial, three-foot rule. No similar form, however, is found. Neither Mætzner nor Halliwell mentions it.

Mine with noun expressed.

Myne office, 24. 40: thā shalt thou bere no perell of myne oothe; 41. 13: I was restored to myne office.

Her as a possessive of *it*, 40. 10: and in the vyne were .iii. braunches, . . . and her blossōs shott forth. The original possessive form for this pronoun was *his*, from the OE. nominative form *hit*. About 1600, we find *it's*, which gradually assumed the form *its*. The earlier possessive was expressed by the use of the preposition *of*; as, T.s Genesis, 7. 22: all that had the breth of liffe in the nostrels of it. We find this expression also for the masculine pronoun, 8. 21: from the very youth of him.

---

[1] Greenwood, *English Grammar*, p. 64 ff. (printed in 1729).

Numerals.

No difference is noted in recording values, and numerals are therefore omitted; but here are noted various unusal forms used by Tindale for expressing numbers:—

18. 28 : .xl. and .v
17. 17 : nynetie
        24 : nynetie . . . and .ix.
 6. 3 :   and hundred and .xx.
23. 1 :   an hundred and .xxvii
 8. 3 :   an hundred and .L
 5. 28 : and hundred .Lxxxii.
14. 14 : .iii hundred & .xviii.
11. 17 : foure hundred and .xxx.
 5. 30 : .v. hundred, nynetie and v.
 7. 6 :   .vi. hundred.

Verbs.

Many verbs have been treated under unusual word-forms. Here will be considered unusual verb-forms—participial forms, mood- and tense-forms, including unusual infinitives and subjunctives.

Awake, wake.

These two verbs, or this one verb under different forms, are extremely interesting from their interchanged forms, and from the dispute arising as to the meaning and correct use of the forms. In T. we find, 41. 7, 'Pharao awaked'; 41. 21 : 'I awoke'; 28. 16 : 'Iacob was awaked out of his sleep.' For *awake*, then, we have past *awaked* and *awoke*; for the participle, *awaked*.

There are three verbs now having really the same meaning in current use: *awake, awaken*, and *wake*. The endeavor to confine the first to intransitive use, and the last to transitive use, is quite unfounded in derivation or in usage; indeed, the participle form *awaked* instead of *awakened* is now considered archaic (see *NED.*). The different forms in *awake* as well as in the simple *wake* came from the blending of two early verbs. The form-history from *awacan*,[1] an OE. strong, intransitive verb, is complicated with the sense-history of *awæccan* (or *aweccan*, ME. *awecche*),[2] an OE. transitive and weak verb.

The first verb *awacan* = 'to awake into being, to arise, to be born.' The second *awæccan* = 'to arouse, to raise up' (like Latin *excitare, suscitare, resuscitare*).

The verb *awacan*, even in OE., began to be treated as a weak verb; and from it comes the later modern English *awaken*, weak, and transitive as well as intransitive. After a little the original relation of *awoke* to the intransitive *awacan* was obscured, and it was treated as a varying form of the weak transitive *awæccan*.

The strong participle was early in the 13th century re-duced to *awake*, and became merely an adjective (mostly predicative). All forms are now used either transitively or intransitively, though the strong form *awoke* is preferred for the past action, and the weak *awakened* for the participle.

Axe.

Axe, 34. 12; *axed*, 37. 15; *axeth*, 32. 17.

This form, now only dialectic and that in the remote inland towns or in Ireland where old forms are found petrified, was in general use until nearly 1600; it comes from *āscian*, by metathesis. Its first changed form was *ācsian*.

Begot.

Had begot.

This is used many times. *NED.* gives this as an early form for the participle of *beget*, but does not cite any use of it as a participle.

Brente.

38. 24: brynge her forth ād let her be brente.

Our present verb *burn, burnt, burnt*, with its older variant *burned, burned*, is the offspring of two old forms: First, the intransitive strong verb *brinnan*, by metathesis *birnan*; sec-

---

[1] Principal parts: āwacan, āwóc, āwacen.
[2]   „   „   āwæccan, āweahte, āweaht.

ond, the OE. *bœrnan,* by metathesis from *brenan.* These two
verbs, distinct in OE., became confused in the ME. period.
Brenne, brent, were the most common forms in late ME. and
even to the 16th century, when they somewhat abruptly
gave place to *burn, burnt.* Spenser, however, as late as 1596
uses the form *brent*: 'The fire which them to ashes brent.'
Faery Queen 1. 9. 10. In the 13th and 14th centuries is
found the infinitive *brennen.* It is recorded in the Shropshire
dialect as late as 1796, and Mrs. Gaskell uses it in dialect,
in *Sylvia's Lovers,* 1863 : 'It were a good job it were brenned
down.' T. uses the infinitive *bren* in Luke 1. 9.

Had corrupte.

6. 12: God loked vpon the erth, ād loo it was corrupte:
for all flesh had corrupte his way vppon the erth.

This is from the Latin *corrumpere*; when the verb was
introduced, it came in as *corrump,* with the past following
the Latin forms. The English forms then would have been
corrump, corrupte, corrupte. Very soon *corrupte* as the infinitive superseded *corrump,* but held for some time *corrupte,*
besides *corrupted,* for its participle. Wyclif (1382, earliest
use noted) uses *corrupted,* but still holds to *corrump* for the
infinitive: 'I shal corrumpe hir vyneȝeerd and hir fijge tree,'
Hosea 2. 12. In 1489, Caxton uses *corromped.* Compare, for
a like change, the vulgar 'drownded,' and 'attackted.' While
T. is quoted (*NED.*) as using *corrupte,* it is to illustrate the
present form; and no example is given of this form in past
or participle.

Digged.

The verb *dig* was originally a weak verb, having come
into the language, probably, from the French *diguer.* It took
its strong past in the 16th century (*NED.*), but the Bible
of 1611 retained this weak form; and Johnson in a review
of Blackwell[1] uses this form (1755). As late as 1778 the form
is found,[2] and in *The Trifler* (1789, No. 43, 549). For earlier
examples of this form, C. is quoted more than once in those

[1] Review of Blackwell's *Mem. Crt. Augustus* (*Wks.* 10. 185).
[2] Bp. Lowth, *Trans. Isa., Notes,* 313.

references where T. uses the form; T. not at all in OT., but one is taken from Romans 11. 3.

Dwelled.

This is the form generally used by T. for past and for participle. It is, however, varied by *dweld* and *dwelt*.

Forgeten.

41. 30: all the plenteousnes shalbe forgeten in the lande of Egipte.

In *get* is found the participle *geten* used in the 14th to 16th centuries; in the 13th to 14th centuries there was a like infinitive form; in the 15th century this is found for a past form. In 1540, *Howers of the Blessed Virgin*: ‘They shall be registered so they shall not be forgetten; in 950, *Lindisfarne Gospels*, Mark 10. 21: an ðe is forʒeten, and Chaucer uses ‘was foryeten.’

Interpretate.

40. 16: When the chefe baker sawe that he had well interpretate it.

This is the participle *interpretatus* of the Latin verb *interpretare*. There were at first two forms from this Latin verb, introduced between the 14th and 17th centuries; they were *interpret*, with its participle *interpreted* (Wyclif (1382) uses this *interpretid*), and the variant participial form *interpretate*, taken more directly from the verb; the second verb is *interpretate*, with the participle *interpretated*. This verb was introduced later than *interpret*, but at the same time as the participle *interpretate*.

41. 8: but there was none of them that coude interpretate vnto Pharao; 40. 22: euē as Ioseph had interpretated vnto thē.

This form was used (1522) in a letter of Bishop Fox; and as late as 1763, we find *interpretating*; and the form in the infinitive again as late as 1866.

Kepte.

41. 35: and there let them kepte it.

No such form is possible from the OE. verb *cēpan*. Is this a misprint of the form *kepe*?

Late.

24. 18: she hasted and late downe her pytcher.

This form of the past of *let* is recorded in the 15th century in Scotland. The use is not noted with this spelling.

47. 19: the form *latest = lettest* is found: Wherfore latest thou vs dye before thyne eyes?

This is not recorded among existing forms. The nearest is *lat* in the third singular of the 13th century. No authority is cited. This form is found in C.

Layde, reflexive.

28. 11: And toke a stone of the place, and put it vnder his heade, and layde him down in the same place to slepe.

Layd is found as a participle from the 16th to 18th centuries and as a past form as early as 1375; but this reflexive use is not common.

Lyen.

34. 7: he had lyen with.

This participial form is found from the 14th to 18th centuries; in *Merlin* (1450), and in De Foe (1722) *The Plague*: It had lyen much longer.' C. makes the same translation, but AV. uses 'in lying with.'

Lyne.

26. 10: myght lightely haue lyne.

This participial form also appears in the 14th and 15th centuries, and even in 1300 in *Cursor Mundi*, and Heywood (1624), *Gunaik* II. 67: 'Oft in one shade the hare and hound hath lyne.' C. and AV. both follow this translation.

Lyfte.

7. 18: ād it [the ark] was lifte up from of the erth.

13. 10: And Lot lyft vp his eyes and beheld all the contre aboute Iordane.

This is the old past and participle of the verb *leftyn*. The form *lifted*, however, was used as early as 1300 (*Cursor Mundi*). In T. *lyfted* is used three times: 22. 13; 27. 38; 40. 20.

Make, had make.

2. 19 : And after ẏ the LORde God had make of the erth all maner beastes of the felde.

OE. *macian* had the past participle ȝemacod about the 12th and 13th centuries, *imaked* in the 12th and 13th centuries, and in the 14th century is recorded the form *imake*. This form *had make* is probably a survival of *imake* weakened to *make*. Under the definition, 'to bring into existence,' the only quotation from the Bible is from Wyclif's Psalm 103 : There sparewis shal make nestis. In 3. 1, is : which the LORde God had made; also in 8. 6, is : which he [Noe] had made.

Satt, reflexive.

24. 61 : And Rebecca arose & hir damsels, & satt thē vp apō the camels.

This use of the pronoun unstrengthened by *self* is found early in OE. It is noted from Robert of Gloucester to Longfellow; and Southey uses this very form : 'They sate them down beside the stream.'[1] This in modern grammar is considered pleonastic, and often rejected. It is the remains of the old reflexive dative, and is used with many verbs of rest 'admitting a notion of motion.' In this use may be included such phrases as *I fear me*, *I doubt me*, and in Genesis 6. 7 : it repenteth me.[2]

Sende.

26. 9 : 'And Abimelech sende for Isaac & sayde.'

This is the old past form of the OE. verb *sendan*, coming down to the ME. in this form. In 26. 31, is : and Isaac sent thē awaye.

Perfect infinitive for the present infinitive.

22. 10 : toke the knyfe to haue killed.

34. 19 : 'he came in ... for to haue slept.'

The infinitive never indicates time of action, but merely names an activity *going on* or in a *state of completion* at

[1] Mætzner, 2. 64.
[2] Mætzner, 2. 64, 65, 66.

the time of the predicate verb. Mætzner, however, discusses this above mentioned use under the '*subjective* supposition not realized, and thought of as not realized.'[1] This is not an old use; the oldest examples cited are from Marlowe and Shakespeare.

Subjunctive forms.

1. Present in expressing a wish for the future.

9. 2: The feare also and drede of yow be vppon all beasts of the erth.

27. 28, 29: God geue the of ẙ dewe of heavē. . . . People be thy servauntes. Be lorde ouer thy brethrē, and thy mothers children stoupe vnto the. Cursed be he ẙ curseth the.

2. Perfect for action to be completed in the future expressed by *tyll* and *vntyll*.

19. 22: I can do nothynge tyll thou be come in thyder.

42. 15: ye shall not goo hence vntyll youre yongest brother be come hither.

3. Perfect instead of present in future meaning with *lest*.

26. 7: he feared to calle her his wife left the mē of the place shulde haue kylled him for hir sake.

4. Past perfect for past meaning.

26. 9: I thought ẙ I mighte peradventure haue dyed for hir sake.

5. Perfect for past in undecided thought, or conjecture, of fear.

31. 30: I was afrayed, & thought that thou woldest haue takē awaye thy doughters frō me.

38. 11: for he feared lest he shulde haue dyed also, as his brethren did.

The first expresses *wish for the future*, and is, therefore, put in the present subjunctive form instead of the future indicative; as it would be if a statement of fact had been made, or a determination on the part of the speaker for enforced action had been expressed.

[1] 3. 59.

In the second, the entire thought of activity is controlled by *completed action* of the *future*, an action in the present *uncertain*.

In the subjunctive there was, in its earliest and strongest days, little determination of time; but its 'sphere of action' depended, as in the infinitive, upon the time of action indicated by the predicate verb. Under this rule for *tense* use, the author meant, in the third, fourth, and fifth examples, what would have been expressed by the past subjunctive forms, *should kyll, might dye, wouldest take.* This is an illustration of the subjunctive feeling towards these acts already passed, in time of speaking, beyond realization; and, therefore, the thought of *non-realization* is uppermost, and must be expressed by *completeness* of activity.[1]

Adjective or Adverb.

Evelfauored and leane fleshed, 41. 3 : evill favored and lenefleshed; 41. 4 : the evill favored and lenefleshed kyne. The use of the adjective as an adverb modifying a participle is not common before the 16th century, though it is found as early as 1422, tr. *Secreta Secret., Priv. Priv.* Foxe and Taverner are quoted by *NED.* as using the form. T.s use is not noted. An early use of the word *lenefleshed* is attributed to C. (1535), and in this passage.

Adjective in double superlative.

Most hyghest, 14. 19 : he beynge the prest of the most hyghest God. Mætzner fails to treat of this emphatic superlative. Shakespeare's 'most unkindest cut of all' has long stood for an authority in this, and as a use without a parallel. *NED.* quotes as earliest use, Maunde. (1400), but Langland uses the same construction in Piers Ploughman.

Conjunctions.

Excepte, 31. 42 : And excepte the God of my father . . . . had bene with me; and several other uses (see 32. 26; 43.

---

[1] Mætzner 2. 72, 92, 117; 3. 59.

3, 5, 10; 44. 23, 26). This use as a conjunction is now almost superseded by *unless,* and by modern grammarians is wholly forbidden. *NED.* cites examples of its use from the 14th century to 1877, but does not quote T.

That with other connectives.

Before that, 27. 4: that my soull may blesse the before that I dye. The conjunction *that,* being in the most comprehensive sense the conjunction of the subordinate sentence, was once attached to almost all subordinating conjunctive words.[1] It is really the demonstrative pronoun *that,* which is combined with the preposition or the adverb, and so gives to it a conjunctional nature.[2] The omission of *that* in this use began as early as the 14th century.[3] The AV. takes this form from T. in John 1. 48: Before that Philip called thee, I saw thee. Cf. 33. 18, *after that,* and 3. 7, *how that.*

But and yf, 24. 40: But and yf ... they will not geue the one, thā shalt thou bere no perell of myne oothe. This compound conjunction is used for emphasis; *but* is the true conjunction, *and* is 'conjunction conditional strengthened by if,' although it is in itself equivalent to *if;*[4] as, 'and you please, for '*if* you please.' This *and* is sometimes weakened to *an,* Tennyson's *Enid* l. 1402: 'an if he live, we will have him of our band.' Other examples are found in Chaucer *L. G. W.* l. 1385, and in C's Matthew 5. 13, T.s Matthew 4. 48: But and yf that evill servaunt shall saye; and T.s Matthew 6. 14: For and yf; while in Genesis 24. 5 is found, 'what ād yf.'

And as a preposition.

And, 24. 16, 45: And it came to passe yer he had leeft spakynge, that Rebecca came out, . . . and hir pytcher apon hir shulder. This is possibly the OE. preposition *and* formerly governing a dative. *NED.* gives its use only about 1000, quoting Cædmon.

---

[1] Mætzner 1. 421.
[2] Mætzner 3. 389 ff.
[3] *NED.*
[4] Greenwood, *English Grammar* (1711), p. 163.

Double preposition, or the preposition followed by a pleonastic
  preposition.

4. 14: thou castest me out thys day from of the face of
the erth.   This is very different from ' the preposition followed
by a substantive notion.' [1]   *Out* is a part of the verb *cast
out*; *from* is the preposition strengthened by the pleonastic
of (off).   This double preposition form is of early occurrence in
modern English.   The earliest quoted use is from *Cursor Mundi*
(1425).   T.s Matt. 8. 30 is cited for earliest use of *off from*.
In the AV. Exodus 3. 5 occurs the form: Put off thy shoes
from off thy feet, which T. renders: ' put thi shooes off thi
fete.'   In 22. 10 is found: and layde him on the aulter aboue
apon the wodd; and 31. 17: sett vp . . . vpon.

From off: a translation of Heb. *mē'al*, where *mē*, con-
tracted from *min*, denotes separation, and *'al*, upon; hence
mē'al = from upon, from over, from by (Brown, *Heb. and
Eng. Lex.*, p. 758), ' when removal, motion, etc., from a
surface is involved.'   Cf. Fr. *de dessus*.

Agreement of the singular verb with a compound subject.

6. 5: the ymaginacion and toughtes of his hert was only
evell.   Constructions similar to this are to be met not only
in OE., but in Modern.English as well.   ' Hys brayn and
wŷt ys so febl,' ' Envye and aun yvel wil was in the Jewes '
(P. Ploughman, p. 338); ' Kingdom and power and glory
pertains ' (Milton, P. L. 6. 814); ' My hope and heart is with
thee ' (Tennyson); ' Poetry and eloquence . . . was assiduously
studied ' (Macaulay).   This use of the singular verb arises
from the notion of the combination of the several into a single
conception.[2]

Idioms.

The study of idioms alone makes an investigation of this
kind valuable, for some idioms found in Tindale give authority
to expressions holding to-day a disputed place; as, the preposition *a*, and the use of the preposition *of* with the adjective *all*.   While many idioms of the 16th century have

---

[1] Mætzner 2. 479.
[2] Mætzner 2. 150.

become wholly obsolete, many are seen to survive with their first strength.

And connecting two verbs, the latter of which would logically be an infinitive. 45. 28: 'I will goo and se him.' T's (1526) Acts 11. 4, is quoted in *NED.* as the earliest use of the signification of *and*: 'He began and expounde.' It was in the 16ᵗʰ century dialectic; it is now idiomatic, and is found in literary as well as in vulgar use.

At doores, 19. 6: Lot went out at doores. This idiom is used by Shakespeare; *King John* V. VII. 29: It would not out at windows, nor at doors.

Be as auxiliary of the perfect tense. 6. 13: the end of all flesh is come before me. 13. 14: after that Lot was departed from hym. 31. 22: was it told Labā ỹ Iacob was fled, etc. 'If a few grammarians permit to all intransitives the conjugation with *have* alone, rejecting that with *be*, they are in contradiction with the usage of the tongue, although it must be granted that in the course of time the formation with *have* has gained ground.'[1] Shakespeare uses this even with a transitive verb: The enemy is passed the marsh (*Richard III*, 5. 3) and Miracles are ceased (*Henry V*, 1. 1).

For because. Besides the combination of *that* with other connectives, as noticed under grammatical forms, this double conjunction is found, 38. 14: sat her downe at the entrynge of Enaim . . . for because she sawe that Sela was growne.

Get used reflexively. 22. 3: 'and rose vp and gott him to the place'; 26. 16: 'gett the frō me; 35. 1: get the vp to Bethell; 38. 1: Iudas . . . gatt him to a man called Hira of Odollam; 39. 12: he left his garment, . . . and goot him out; 42. 2: Gete you thither, and bye vs corne.

Imperative in se. 28. 6: se thou take not; 3. 17: se thou eate not therof; 4. 7: see thou rule it; 6. 20: male and female se that they be.

---

[1] Mætzner 2. 71.

Infinitive with **for.** 1. 20: & foules for to flee over the erth; 3. 6: a pleasant tre for to make wyse. This is an old idiom, reaching back to the OE., particularly with the idea of purpose; but it is rarely used out of vulgar speech after the 16th century. It is found, however, in Washington's *Journal* (1748), and in J. Q. Adams's *Letters* (1774).

Infinitive with **to** instead of the present participle or gerund. 11. 9: left of to bylde the citie.

Of. Certain grammarians forbid the use *of* with *all*; as, 'all of us are present,' maintaining that the correct form is 'we are all present,' or 'all we are present.' In T., however, this form is quite as frequently found as *all* without *of*. 8. 19: all of one kynde. C. and AV. follow the same use. While our present idiom is 'all manner of,' T., C., and AV. frequently omit this preposition. 1. 25: all maner wormes of the erth in their kyndes; 1. 29: all maner trees; 2. 20: all maner beastes of the felde. Mætzner [1] classes this as a construction in which the substantive operates like a preposition. 'He has left you all his walks on this side Tiber' (Shakespeare, *Julius Cæsar*). In popular speech to-day one hears 'on board a ship' for 'on board of a ship.' With this may be given the peculiar construction, 24. 10: .x. camels of the camels of his master, and had of all maner goodes of his master with him.

Omission of the article. 3. 18: In sorow shalt thou eate therof all dayes of thy life; 26. 8: it happened after he had bene there longe tyme.

Omission of *that.* 7. 23: they were destroyed from the erth: save Noe was reserved only.

Pleonastic forms:

From thence, 27. 45: Thā will I sende and fett the awaye from thence.

To, 19. 10: shott to the doore; 20. 18: The LORde had closed to, all the matryces of the house of Abimelech.

[1] 1. 244.

Subject. 4. 4: Abell, he brought also of the fyrstlynges
of hys shepe; 4. 22: Zilla she also bare Tubalcain.

So in measure of degree. 43. 34: fyue times so much as.

Survived datives. 3. 12: she toke me of the tree ād I
ate; 31. 9: thus hath God take awaye youre fathers
catell and geue thē me.

Virtual compounds, or phrases consisting of two nouns
in which the former has the function of an adjective.
44. 1: the bagge mouth; 29. 2: the well mouth.

III. TRANSLATIONS.

Passages showing notable difference in translation in the versions compared, not sufficiently emphasized in the comparison of words :—

4. 7 :

T. Notwithstondyng let it be subdued vnto the, ād see thou rule it.

C. Shal he then he subdued vnto the? and wilt thou rule him?

AV. And unto thee shall be his desire, and thou shalt rule ouer him.

4. 13 :

T. Cain sayd ... my synne is greater, than that it may be forgeven.

C. Cain sayde ... my sinne is greater, then that it maye be forgeuen me.

AV. Cain said ... My punishment is greater, then I can beare.

11. 6 :

T. Thys haue they begon to do, and wyll not leaue of from all that they haue purposed to do.

C. This haue they begonne to do, and wil not leaue of from all ẙ they haue purposed to do.

AV. This they begin to doe: and now nothinge will be restrained from them, which they haue imagined to doe.

16. 13 :

T. I haue of a suretie sene here the backe parties of him that seith me.

C. Of a suertye I haue sene the back partes of him that
    sawe me.

AV. Haue I also heere looked after him that seeth me.

18. 14:

T. In the tyme appoynted will I returne vnto the, as soone
    as the frute can haue lyfe, And Sara shall haue a sonne.

C. Aboute this tyme (yf I lyue) I wil come to the agayne,
    and Sara shal haue a sonne.

AV. At the time appointed will I returne vnto thee, according
    to the time of life, and Sara shall haue a sonne.

20. 16:

T. Beholde he shall be a couerynge to thyne eyes vnto
    all that ar with the and vnto all men and an excuse.

C. Lo, he shalbe vnto the a couerynge of the eyes, for
    all that are with the, and euery where, and a sure
    excuse.

AV. Behold, he is to thee a couering of the eyes, unto all
    that are with thee, and with all other: thus she was
    reproued.

21. 6:

T. And Sara sayde: God hath made me a laughinge stocke:
    for all ẏ heare, will laugh at me.

C. And Sara sayde: God had prepared a joye for me, for
    who so euer heareth of it, wyll reioyse with me.

AV. And Sara said, God hath made me to laugh, so that
    all that heare, will laugh with me.

27. 39:

T. Beholde thy dwellynge place shall haue of the fatnesse
    of the erth, & of the dewe of heauen fro aboue.

C. Beholde thou shalt haue a fat dwellinge vpon earth,
    and of ẏ dew of heauen from aboue.

AV. Behold, thy dwelling shall be the fatnesse of the earth,
    and of the dew of heauen from aboue.

27. 41:

T. The dayes of my fathers sorowe are at hāde, for I will
    sley my brother Iacob.

C.　The tyme wyll come shortly, that my father shal mourne, for I wil slaye my brother Iacob.

AV.　The dayes of mourning for my father are at hand; then will I slay my brother Iacob.

43. 30:

T.　His hert dyd melt apon his brother.

C.　The grounde of his hert was kyndled towarde his brother.

AV.　His bowels did yerne vpon his brother.

44. 20:

T.　The brother of the sayde lad is dead.

C.　His brother is deed.

AV.　His brother is dead.

47. 12:

T.　Ioseph made prouysion ... as yonge children are fedd with bread.

C.　He made prouysion ... with bred, euen as yonge children.

AV.　Ioseph nourished . . . with bread, according to their families.

49. 5:

T.　Weked instrumentes are their wepos.

C.　Their deedly weapons are perlous instrumentes.

AV.　Instruments of crueltie are in their habitations.

49. 6:

T.　In their selfewill they houghed an oxe.

C.　In their self will they houghed an oxe.

AV.　In their selfe will they digged downe a wall (*Marg.* 'Or houghed oxen').

49. 22:

T.　That florishynge childe Ioseph, that florishing childe and goodly vn to the eye: the doughters come forth to bere ruele.

C.　The fruteful sonne Ioseph, that florishinge sonne to loke vpon, the doughters go vpō the wall.

AV.　Ioseph is a fruitfull bough, euen a fruitfull bough by a well, whose branches runne ouer the wall.

49. 24 :

T.   Out of him shall come an herde mā a stone in Israel.

C.   Of him are come herdmen and stones in Israel.

AV. From thence is the Sheapheard, the stone of Israel.

49. 26 :

T.   After the desyre of the hiest in the worlde.

C.   After the desyre of the hyest in the worlde.

AV. Vnto the vtmost bound of the euerlasting hils.

ALPHABETICAL INDEX

containing every word used by Tyndale in the book
of Genesis; the word used by Coverdale in the same
passage; the word used in the Authorized Version
in the corresponding passage; the various spellings,
and the various verb forms.

a-able

	C	A
a 21. 9	*omit*	*omit*
35. 18	,,	in
abashed, were 45. 3	were so abashed	were troubled
abated., were 8. 11		
abated 8. 3	decreased	were abated
Abdeel 25. 13		
Abell 4. 2		Abel
Abel mizraim 50. 11	lamentacion of the Egipcians	
abhominacyon 46. 34	† abhoore	abomination
abhomynacyon 43. 32	abhominacion	,,
Abida 25. 4.		
abill 13. 6	able	able
See able		
Abimael 10. 28		
Abimelech		
20. 2 (23 times)		
20. 15	*omitted*	
able, be 15. 5	canst	
— am 31. 29	coude have	it is in the power of my hand

	C	A
able, be 33. 14	can	
See abill		
abode 8. 10		stayed
aboue 27. 39 (2 times)		
6. 16		*omit*
—, another, one 6. 16		lower, second, and third
22. 9		*omit*
48. 22	without	
24. 8	*omit*	,,
27. 34	exceadynge	,,
41. 40	more then	greater then
about 38. 30	aboute	vpon
aboute 35. 5 (2 times)		
—, which we have		
8. 11 (3 times)		*omit*
13. 10	rounde aboute	of
24. 11		euen
—, put 24. 65		couered
37. 34		vpon
38. 28		,,
39. 11	vpon	
41. 42		about
41. 48		,,
45. 1		by
46. 34	with	about
5. 29	vpon	because of
—, in 13. 17 (2 times)	thorow	through
— to, am 18. 17	will	*omit*
22. 13 (3 times)	*omit*	,,
Abraham, 17. 5		
(92 times)		
18. 7 (3 times)	he	
21. 4 (4 times)	*omit*	
18. 12 (2 times)	him	
23. 18	Abrahams	
—, of 24. 9	,,	

	C	A
Abraham, of 25. 7		Abrahams
26. 1	Abrahams	
Abrahams, 20. 18		
(9 times)		
17. 23	his	
21. 11	† Abraham	
26. 15		of Abraham
Abram, 11. 26		
(47 times)		
12. 6 (2 times)	he	
14. 20		hee
15. 6		he
16. 3	they	
12. 20	him	him
Abrams 11. 29		
(7 times)		
Abrech 41. 43	bow their knees	bow the knee
abrode 11. 9		
11. 4		abroad
28. 14	forth	,,
in 41. 45	out, for to vyset	out ouer
abyde 24. 55	tary	abide
29. 14		abode
accordinge, as 7. 16		as
—, as 27. 14		such as
accordynge as 33. 14	as	according as
See acord		
acordinge		
acordyng		
acordynge		
Achad 10. 10	Acad	Accad
Achbor 36. 38		
(2 times)		
acordinge as 27. 19	as	according as
—, as 30. 34	so as	,, to
— to 41. 40	acordinge to	,, vnto
acordyng vnto 43. 33	after	,, to

	C	A
acordynge to 6. 22 (3 times)	acordinge to	according to
— to 7. 5	*omit*	,, vnto
— to 18. 25	acordinge to	*omit*
— as 21. 1	,, as	as
— vnto 21. 23	the came	according to
— as 34. 12	acordinge as	,, as
— to these 39. 17	euen the same	,, to
— as 41. 54	wherof	,, as
— to 43. 7	as	according to
— vnto 43. 33	acordinge to	,, to
— as 44. 10	vnto	,, vnto
— as 50. 6	acordinge as	,, as
— as 50. 12	as	,, as
See accordinge accordynge		
actiuyte 47. 6		actiuitie
Ada 4. 19 (8 times)		Adah
Adam 3. 8 (8 times)		
2. 15 (2 times)	man	the man
2. 19 (4 times)	,,	
2. 22	,,	man
2. 22	him	the man
2. 25	the man	the man
3. 12 (3 times)		,, ,,
5. 4	*omit*	
5. 5.	his	
11. 5	men	men
Adama 10. 19 (3 times)	Adama	Adamah
a farr of 22. 4 (2 times)		afarre off
afrayd 3. 10	afrayed	afraid
afrayde 18. 15 (5 times)	afrayed	afraid
28. 17	afraied	afraid
afrayed 31. 31		,,
after 1. 26 (38 times)		
1. 27 (3 times)		in

	C	A
after that 2. 19	whan	*omit*
5. 3	like	
5.4 after (16 times)	therafter	
5. 30	after this	
6. 4 (2 times)	*omit*	
— the end of 8. 3	after	
— „ „ „ 8. 6		at the end of
— thys 12. 10 (2 times)	*omit*	*omit*
— that 13. 14	whan	after that
15. 1	it happened after	
20. 13	whan	it came to passe when
22. 1		it came to passe after
—, went 24. 61		followed
25. 11		it came to passe after
26. 8	whan	when
— that 30. 21		afterwardes
31. 36	vpon	
— this maner 32. 4	thus	thus
32. 18	behinde	behind
32. 20	behynde	„
— my name 32. 29	what my name	
— that 33. 18		when
35. 9	after that	„
— the deth of 36. 35	whan ... dyed	*omit*
— „ „ „ 35. 39	„ „	„
—, it came to passe	after	it came to passe
— that 38. 24		about ... after
— this maner 39. 10	soch wordes	*omit*
— „ „ 39. 10	thus	after this maner
41. 6	afterwarde	after them
41. 31	therafter	*omit*
— that 45. 15	afterwarde	
— the same maner	† him	after this maner

	C	A
after 45. 23		
48. 1		it came to passe after
48. 7	whan	as for me, when
48. 16		*omit*
49. 18	for	for
49. 26		vnto
afterward 10. 18	from whence	
25. 26	anone therafter	after that
26. 23	afterwarde	*omit*
29. 15	after that	,,
32. 20	after warde	
38. 30	afterwarde	
afterwarde 15. 14		afterward
agayne 4. 25		againe (31 times)
(31 times)		
8. 7 (26 times)		*omit*
18. 29	further	againe
20. 7 (2 times)	ageyne	*omit*
22. 5	againe	againe
29. 35	the fourth tyme	againe
33. 16	againe	*omit*
42. 37	againe	againe
46. 4	*omit*	,,
8. 11 (5 times)	,,	*omit*
See agene		
ageyne		
agaynst 39. 9 (2 times)		against
34. 30	against	,,
43. 25	ageynst	,,
14. 17	to mete	out to meete
19. 1	for to mete	to meet
29. 13	to mete	to meete
—, prevayle 32. 25	ouercome	preuailed against
33. 4	to mete	to meete
37. 18	*omit*	against
39. 9		

	C	A
agaynst 41. 36	in	against
42. 21	against	concerning
46. 29	vp to mete	vp to meet
See agenst		
ageynst		
age 15. 15 (8 times)		
43. 33	first byrth	birthright
44. 20		old age
agene 43. 21	agayne	againe
See agayne		
ageyne		
agenst 15. 10 (4 times)	agaynst	against
13. 13	,,	before
24. 65	,,	to meet
18. 2	to mete	to meete
agenste 14. 9	with	with
See agaynst		
ageynst		
ageyne 20. 7		*omit*
See agayne		
agene		
ageynst 32. 6	agaynst	to meet
See agaynst		
agenst		
agree to come with,	wyl folowe	will bee willing to
wyll 24. 5		follow
(2 times)		
Ahalibama 36. 2		Aholibamah
(6 times)		
Ah syr 3. 1	yee	yea
Ahusath 26. 26		Ahuzzath
Aia 36. 24		Aiah
Akan 36. 27	Ackan	
al 5. 14	whole	
7. 21	all	euery creeping
		thing

all 1. 26 (181 times)

	C	A
all maner 1. 25		every
(3 times)		
— maner of 1. 21		,,
(9 times)		
1. 26 (20 times)		,,
1. 29	all maner frutefull	euery
1. 29 (20 times)	whole	
1. 30 (3 ,,)	euery	euery
1. 31		euery thing
2. 4 (10 times)	*omit*	*omit*
2. 5	,,	euery
2. 6 (6 times)		the whole
2. 13 (2 ,,)	the whole	,, ,,
2. 16	all maner	euery
— maner 2. 20		all
2. 20		euery
3. 1		any
4. 21	they	
6. 2 (7 times)	*omit*	
7. 3	whole	
7. 8		euery thing
7. 11		al
— maner of 7. 14	*omit*	euery
7. 14	what so euer	
— the partes of 7. 19	the whole	the whole
— that 7. 22 (3 times)	what so euer	all in whose nosethrils
7. 23		euery liuing substance
8. 19 (3 times)		euery
— that 8. 19		whatsoeuer
8. 19	euery one	*omit*
8. 21		euery thing
— thynge 9. 3		euery thing
9. 15	all maner of	
—, of 14. 23		any thing
— places where 20.13	where so euer	euery place wither

	C	A
all men, vnto 20. 16	euery where	
21. 6	who so euer	
— thinge, but aboue	onely	onely
24. 8		
—, with 27. 41	withall	wherewith
— places whother, in	where so euer	in all places wither
28. 15		
28. 15		that which
30. 31 (3 times)		*omit*
30. 35		euery one
32. 21	same	*omit*
—, last of 33. 7	afterwarde	after
34. 15	as many as are	euery
— that 34. 24	as many as	
— maner 40. 17	all maner of	all maner of
— that, is 44. 20	alone	alone
— my life longe 44. 32		for euer
45. 1	euery man	euery man
allmightie 28. 3		
(3 times)		
See almightie		
almyghtie		
all to gether 46. 22		all
46. 25	*omit*	,,
all togither 46. 26	alltogether	,,
allwaye 6. 3		
30. 41	neuertheles	and it came to passe whenso-euer

almightie 49. 25
  See allmightie
    almyghtie
Almodad 10. 26
almondes 43. 11
almyghtie 17. 1
  See allmightie
    almightie

	C	A
alone 2. 18 (3 times)		
alowde 45. 2		
also 1. 16 (41 times)		
2. 8 (18 times)	also	*omit*
30. 6 (5 times)	*omit*	also
2. 9 (23 times)	„	*omit*
21. 7	morouer	.,
21. 26	nether	neither
24. 25	ynough	*omit*
24. 49	yet	„
38. 22	morouer	also
45. 19	† them	thou
50. 9	*omit*	both
altar 13. 18	altare	
Alua 36. 40		
Alvan 36. 23		
a lyve, to kepe 6. 16 (2 times)	maye lyue	to keepe aliue
43. 7 (5 times)	a lyue	aliue
45. 28	aliue	„
50. 20	*omit*	„
am 4. 9 (40 times)		
—, I 17. 4	it is I	as for me
— aboute to 18. 17	wil	*omit*
20. 13		he is
— at the poynte to 25. 32	must	
— deed 30. 1		I die
— I, happy 30. 13	well is me	
— contente 30. 34	let	would
34. 30		being
— content 46. 30	† let	let
Amalech 36. 12 (2 times)	Amaleck	Amalek
Amalechites 14. 7		Amalekites
Ammon 19. 38		
among 11. 6	amonge	*omit*

	C	A
amonge 3. 8 (5 times)		amongst
23. 4 (2 times)		with
23. 6 (5 times)		amongst
24. 37 (2 times)		of
6. 2	*omit*	,,
17. 12	thorow	among
17. 23	in	,,
36. 31	*omit*	ouer
40. 20	before	among
43. 33	amonge	at
Amorites 15. 16		
48. 22		Amorite
an ende 31. 45	for a piler or mark-stone	for a pillar
— hye 49. 9	vp hye	vp
Ana 36. 2 (8 times)		Anah
36. 2	*omit*	*omit*
Aner 14. 13 (2 times)		
angell 16. 7 (7 times)		angel
16. 9 (4 times)	angel	,,
angells 19. 1 (4 times)	angels	angels
angrie 40. 2 (2 times)		wroth
angry 4. 6	angrie	,,
angrye 18. 30 (2 times)	,,	angry
—, be 31. 35	be angrie	let it displease
anguysh 42. 21		anguish
another, 4. 25 (8 times)		
6. 16		*omit*
11. 3	*omit*	
11. 7		† one anothers
15. 10	the other	
25. 1		againe
30. 12		a second
31. 49	the other	
42. 28	*omit*	
43. 6	yet a	yet a
43. 7	,,	

	C	A
answerd 30. 31	sayd	said
See answered		
answere 41. 16		
—, coude 45. 3	coulde answere	could answere
—, shall 30. 33	shal testifie	
answered 18. 27		
(15 times)		
3. 12 (11 times)	sayde	said
21. 26 (3 times)		saide
21. 30 (21 times)		said
3. 10	said	saide
14. 22	sayde vnto	said to
42. 37		spake vnto
See answerd		
anoynteddest 31. 13	dyddest anoynte	annoyntedst
any 47. 6 (3 times)	*omit*	
31. 52	eny	*omit*
36. 31	,,	
anything, nether	nothinge	neither any thing
22. 12		
apeared 12.17 (5times)	appeared	appeared
35. 1	appared	,,
See apered		
appeared		
appered		
apere, made 30. 37	pylled	made appeare
See appere		
apered 26. 24	appeared	appeared
See apeared		
appeared		
appered		
apon 6. 17 (23 times)	vpon	vpon
6. 1 (4 times)	,,	on
6. 5 (2 times)	,,	in
8. 13	,,	from off
—, thought 19. 29	thought vpon	remembered
—, aboue 22. 9		vpon

	C	A
apon 24. 18	in	vpon
27. 16	aboute	„
28. 13	vpon	aboue
28. 13	„	wheron
31. 35	† after	vpon
—, loked 40. 6	sawe	looked vpon
43. 30	towarde	vpon
—, maye sett myne eyes 44. 21	wil se	
44. 29	*omit*	*omit*
47. 20	vpon	ouer
48. 7	by	by
48. 16	vpon	in the midst
49. 33	„	into
50. 1	*omit*	
See upon uppon		
apoynte 34. 11	appoynte	shall say
See appoynt		
apoyntment	couenaunt	couenant
See appoyntment		
apparell 2. 2	hoost	hoste
appeared 35. 9 (2 times)	apeared	
See apeared apered appered		
appere, may 1. 9	maye appeare	let appeare
—, shall 9. 14	shal „	shall be seene
See apere		
appered 8. 5	appeared	were seene
35. 7	„	appeared
See apeared apered appeared		
appoynt 30. 28		appoint
See apoynte		

	C	A
appoynted 18. 14	this	appointed
—, had 21. 2	† had spoken vnto him afore	had spoken to him
—, had 22. 3	had sayde vnto	had told
29. 21	*omit*	*omit*
47. 21	† became	remoued
—, was 47. 22	was appoynted	gaue
appoyntment 9. 13	my couenaunt	a couenant
apurns 3. 7		aprons
ar 20. 16 (6 times)	are	are
32. 18	† which sendeth	is
See are		
Aram 10. 22 (2 times)		
Aran 36. 28		
Ararat 8. 4		
aray to fyghte, sette in 14. 8	prepared to fight	ioyned battell
—, sette in 14. 15	† deuyded them	diuided himselfe against them
arayed 41. 42	clothed	
archer 21. 20		
arcke 6. 14 (5 times)		arke
6. 15 (3 times)	*omit*	„
8. 16 (2 times)	arke	„
See arke		
Ard 46. 16		
are 2. 4 (49 times)		
1. 9 (2 „)	*omit*	*omit*
6. 9 (6 „)	is	
36. 26 (3 times)	were	
1. 29	*omit*	is
2. 19		was
6. 3	is but	also is
7. 19	*omit*	were
8. 17		is
9. 5	is	*omit*
10. 29		were

	C	A
are 10. 32	is now	
19. 31	is	is
27. 41	wyll come	
30. 32	be	*omit*
31. 12	*omit*	
33. 5		*omit*
34. 22	*omit*	,,
34. 23	shal be	shall bee
36. 19	*omit*	
41. 25		is
— ye negligent 41. 27	gape ye	doe ye looke
46. 27	were	were
— abhominacyon	abhore	is abomination
46. 34	,,	,,
49. 12		shall be
See ar		
Areli 46. 16		
Arioch 14. 9		
arke 7. 7 (5 times)		
7. 9 (9 times)	arcke	arke
8. 19 (2 times)	,,	arcke
See arcke		
Arki 10. 17		Arkite
arme 24. 18	hande	hand
armes 49. 24		
Arodi 46. 16		
arose 19. 15 (2 times)		
2. 6		went vp
19. 28	rose	,, ,,
arose 19. 35	arose like wyse	
24. 61	gat hir vp	
Arphachsad 10. 24		
10. 22	Arphachad	Arphaxad
11. 11	*omit*	,,
art 3. 9 (22 times)		
13. 14	dwellest	
15. 15	*omit*	*omit*

	C	A
art 16. 13		*omit*
— a straunger 21. 23		hast soiourned
40. 14		shall be
arte 17. 8 (2 times)		
Aruadi 10. 18		Aruadite
aryse 21. 18 (2 times)		arise
28. 2 (3 times)	get the vp	,,
13. 17	arise	,,
35. 3	let vs get vp	,,
—, shall 41. 30	shal come	shall arise
43. 13	get you vp	arise
as 3. 5 (34 times)		
3. 8 (7 times)	*omit*	*omit*
2. 19		whatsoeuer
14. 17		after
18. 1		and
19. 15 (3 times)	whan	when
19. 16	whyle	while
21. 4 (3 times)	like as	
24. 22 (4 times)	whan	
26. 19	*omit*	and
31. 15 (3 times)		*omit*
32. 25	† in	
— we be 34. 15	like vnto us	
35. 22	that when	when
37. 25	in the meane season	*omit*
37. 28		then
38. 28		when
41. 38 (3 times)	*omit*	
43. 6	,,	
44. 2 (2 times)		according to
— one of 49. 16	as well as	
—, according 34. 12		
7. 16		as
27. 14		such as
27. 19	as	

	C	A
as 30. 34	as	according to
33. 14	there after as	
41. 54	wherof	
50. 12	as	
— concernynge		
5. 29	in	concerning
17. 20		as for
19. 21	in	concerning
41. 32	where as	and for that
—, euen 9. 3 (2 times)		
7. 9 (2 times)	as	as
40. 13	*omit*	*omit*
—, euen 40. 22	like as	as
(2 times)		
49. 26	*omit*	aboue
—, euen so 18. 5		
—, it were 3. 22		so as
21. 16	*omit*	*omit*
25. 25	as	**like**
— long as 8. 22	so longe as	while
— many as 17. 23		euery
— moch as 44. 1		
— moch as, for		
3. 17	for so moch as	because
—, in 19. 19		*omit*
23. 19	a reasonable	
—, for 41. 39	for so moch as	forasmuch as
— moch more 43. 12	other	double
—, so moch		euen to
14. 23		
43. 34	more then	
— pertaynyng to	vpon	from
assone as 50. 14	whan	after
as soone as 4. 8	whan	when
9. 24	,,	*omit*
18. 10	† aboute	according to
18. 33	whan	

	C	A
as soone as 24. 30	by the reason that	when
27. 30	whan	as soone as
39. 5	from the tyme forth that	from the time that
39. 18	whan	as
41. 15	,,	*omit*
as soone as 44. 3	whan	
44. 31	yf	when
as such 27. 4 (3 times)		
27. 46	as	
as though 33. 10		
19. 14	*omit*	as
27. 12 (2 times)		,,
40. 10	*omit*	
Asa 10. 19	Gasa	Gaza
Asbel 46. 21	Asber	
Ascenas 10. 3		Ashkenaz
asene, shal be 41. 31	shal be perceaued	shal be knowen
Aser 35. 26		Asher
See Asser		
ashamed 2. 55		
ashes 18. 27	aszhes	
aske, dost 32. 29	askest	doest aske
asked 24. 47 (5 times)	axed	
43. 7	enquered	
asketh 32. 17	axeth	
Asnath 41.45(2 times)		Asenath
a sonder 1. 7	a sunder	*omit*
asse 22. 3 (5 times)		
Asser 20. 13 (3 times)		Asher
See Aser		
asses 12. 16 (13 times)		
32. 15		ashes
Assirians 25. 18		Assyria
See Assyryans		
Assur 10. 11 (2 times)		Asshur
Assurim 25. 3		Asshurim

	C	A
Assyryans 2. 14	Assirians	Assyria
See Assirians		
Astarath Karnaim	Astaroth Karnaim	Ashteroth
14. 5		Karnaim
astoyned, was 27. 33	was amased	trembled
astoynyed, were	were afrayed	were afraid
42. 28		
at 13. 3 (15 times)		
11. 28 (3 „)		in
19. 1 (4 „)	in	
— all 22. 12 (3 times)	*omit*	*omit*
— all 26. 14 (2 „)		„
3. 24	before	
— that tyme 13. 7		then
— the doores, out		
15. 5	forth	forth abroad
19. 1	vnder	in
— hand 19. 15		here
21. 6	† with	with
— Berseba 22. 19	there	
— the poynte to		
25. 32	must	
— hand 27. 41	shortly	at hand
27. 43	in	to
29. 2	† of	out of
29. 2		vpon
30. 16		in the
31. 23	vpon	in
— your pleasure		
34. 10	open vnto you	before you
—, out 34. 24		out of
35. 4	besyde	by
37. 18		neere vnto
38. 5	*omit*	
38. 11	in	
38. 14	without	in
38. 21	„	openly by

	C	A
at 41. 1	after	
— the begynynge 41. 21	afore	at the beginning
— 44. 12	vnto	
45. 3	before	
45. 21	acordynge to	according to
— the ensample of these 48. 20	in the	in thee
49. 2		
See att		
Atad 50.10 (2 times)		
ate 3. 6 (15 times)		did eate
31. 54	had eaten	
43. 34	*omit*	*omit*
attayned, have 47. 9	attayneth	haue attained
att once, make redy 18. 6	make haist and mengle	make ready quickly
—, made redy 18. 7	madereadyatonce	hasted to dresse
See at		
audyence, in the 23. 10 (3 times)	that...mightheare	in the audience
44. 18	eares	eares
aulter 8. 20 (11 times)	altare	altar
aultere 12. 7	aulter	„
avayleth 37. 26	helpeth	profit is
avenged 4. 24		
Avith 36. 35		
awaked, was 9. 24 (2 times)	awaked	awoke
—, was 28. 16	„	awaked
aware, was 28. 16 (2 times)	knew	knew
away 31. 18 (2 times)	awaye	away
5. 24	awaye	*omit*
—, went 8. 5	wente awaye	decreased
—, send . . . 26. 29	let . . . departe	haue sent away
awaye 14. 15 (3 times)		*omit*

	C	A
awaye 15. 11		away
(13 times)		
20. 3 (3 times)	*omit*	*omit*
—, send . . . 24. 56	let . . . go	send . . . away
(2 times)		
—, put 21. 10	cast out	cast out
—, sent 26. 31	let . . . go	sent away
27. 45 (2 times)	*omit*	away
—, hath taken 31. 9	hath withdrawen from	hath taken away
31. 20 (2 times)	awaie	away
31. 31	away	by force
—, is 42. 33		is not
—, get 42. 33	go youre waye	be gone
44. 4	*omit*	off
48. 12	„	out
awne 15. 4 (3 times)	owne	
9. 6 (2 times)	„	*omit*
47. 24	*omit*	owne
awoke 41. 4 (2 times)	awaked	awoke
axe 34. 12	as ye wyll axe	aske
46. 33	saye	shall say
axed 37. 15 (2 times)		asked
25. 22	for to axe	to enquire
27. 24	sayde vnto	said
47. 8		said vnto
Ay 12. 8 (2 times)	Ay	Hai
ayleth 21. 17		aileth
ayre 1. 28		aire
1. 26 (6 times)	heauen	„
7. 23	heauen	heauen
Baal hanan 36. 38		
— Hanan 36. 39		
Babell 10. 10	Babel	Babel
11. 9		„
backe 16. 13	back	† after

	C	A
backe, his 18. 10		him
38. 29	in	
backward 9. 23	backwarde	
(2 times)		
9. 23	asyde	backward
bad 24. 50	euell	
43. 17		bade
43. 31	sayde	saide
badd 2. 17	euell	euill
12. 2	commaunded	had spoken vnto
See bade		
baddest 27. 19	saydest vnto	badest
bade 3. 11	commaunded	commanded
29. 22	bad	gathered together
See bad		
badd		
bagge 44. 1	sacke	sacke
bake, dyd 19. 3	baked	
bakemeats 40. 17	baken meates	bake-meats
baker 40. 1 (6 times)		
bare 4. 1 (48 times)		
bare 24. 36	hath borne	
25. 26	were borne	
38. 5	† had borne	
See beare		
bere		
Bared 16. 14		Bered
baren 11. 30 (3 times)	baren	barren
—, haue bene 31. 38	haue bene vnfrute-full	haue cast their yong
basket 40. 17 (2 times)	baszket	basket
baskettes 40. 16	baskettes	baskets
40. 18	baszkettes	,,
Basmath 26. 34	Basmath	Bashemath
(6 times)		
Bathuel 24. 47	Bethuel	Bethuel
Bathuell 24. 50	,,	,,

	C	A
bawlme 37. 25	balme	baulme
43. 11	„	balme
be 17. 1 (10 times)		
—, to 10. 8 (4 times)		
—, let 1. 3 (6 times)		
—, shal 2. 24 (32 times)		
—, shalt 4. 12 (4 times)		
8. 17 (3 times)		*omit*
9. 2		shall be
9. 11	shall come	
9. 15 (4 times)	*omit*	*omit*
9. 15	shall come	shall become
9. 25 (11 times)		bee
9. 26 (2 „)		shalbe
13. 8	are	bee
—, schulde 2. 18 (4 times)		
—, mayst 12. 2	shalt be	shalt be
—, wil, 17. 8 (7 times)		
—, let 1. 14		let bee
—, may 1. 15	maye be	*omit*
—, to 1. 29		shall be
3. 14 (2 times)		art
3. 17		is
6. 19	*omit*	shall be
—, shal 15. 1	*omit*	*omit*
15. 3 (2 times)	shal be	is
— able to, yf 15. 5	canst	
—, will 16. 12	shal be	will be
—, will 16. 12	*omit*	„ „
—, shal 17. 5		shall bee
—, wyll 17. 7		to bee
—, to 17. 7	that it maye be	for
—, though they 17. 12	that is	or bought with money of any

	C	A
be, may 17. 13	shall be	shall be
—, shall 17. 19	*omit*	for
—, ceased to 18. 11	wente no more	
—, shall 18. 18 (2 times)	shal be	shall be come
—, wilt 19. 9		will needs bee
— sure, shall 20. 7		know
— greavous, let 21.12	let displease	let be grieuous
—, maye 21. 30		
— without, shalt 24.8	art discharged of	shalt bee cleare from
—, let 24. 51 (2 times)	maye be	
— myghtier, shal 25. 23	shall ouer come	shal be stronger
— seruaunte, shalt 27. 40	shalt serue	shalt serue
—, mayst 28. 3		
— his wife, to 28. 9	to wife	
— keper, wyl 28. 15	wyll kepe	will keepe
—, shall 29.15	art	art
—, to 29. 24		for
—, shal 30. 28	that I shal geue	*omit*
—, let 30. 33	shal be	shalbe
30. 34	let be	might bee
—, angrye 31. 35		let displease
— iudge 31. 53		iudge
—, able to 33. 14	can	
—, as we 34. 15	like vnto us	
34. 16		will become
36. 12 (2 times)	are	are
—, king, shalt 37. 8		shalt reigne
—, may 41. 35	*omit*	let keepe
—, may 41. 36	maye be founde	shall be
—, shall 42. 16		shall be kept
42. 16	go aboute with	
42. 32 (2 times)	are	
—, must nedes 43. 11		must bee

	C	A
be, let 44. 9 (2 times)	wyll be	will be
—, shal 44. 10	let be	let be
— wroth 44. 18		let anger burne
44. 33	to be	*omit*
—, that there shuld 45. 1	stode	stood
—, shal 45. 20		is
45. 28	is	,,
46. 15	are	bee
— without 47. 16	are without	faile
— the chefest, shalt 49. 4		shalt excell
—, to 50. 13	for	for
beare, to 49. 15		
beare him company, to 2. 18 (2 times)		meet for him
—, shall 3. 18	shall beare	shall bring forth
—, maye 30. 3	bare	beare
See bare bere		
bearinge 30. 9	bearynge	bearing
bearynge 29. 35	,,	,,
See berynge		
beast 37. 20 (2 times)		
6. 7	beest	beast
See beste		
beastes 7. 2 (2 times)		
1. 24 (13 times)		beast
1. 28 (2 times)		liuing thing
2. 19	soules	creature
6. 20	beastes	cattel
7. 8	*omit*	beasts
7. 23	beast	cattell
18. 7	beastes	heard
31. 39	,,	beasts
44. 28	*omit*	*omit*
45. 10 (2 times)	greate catell	heards

	C	A
beasts 9. 2		
See beestes		
became 21.20 (5 times)		
4. 2 (2 times)	became	was
20. 12	is become	became
— ryche 30. 43	became ryche	increased exceedingly
because 2. 23		
(17 times)		
26. 7 (10 times)	for	because
16. 5 (3 times)	because	*omit*
because 11. 19	*omit*	,,
16. 6	whan	when
22. 16	that for so moch as	for because
31. 30	and	
31. 31	*omit*	
34. 7	that	
38. 9	,,	least
38. 14	for	for
39. 23	that	
— of 12. 17 (7 times)		
— that 26. 5	because	
— that 32. 32	,,	because
(2 times)		
— that 39. 23	and that	and
Becher 46. 21		
become, is 3. 22		
(2 times)		
—, is 38. 24	is gotten	is
Bedad 36. 35		
bedd 48. 2 (3 times)		
beddes 47. 31		beds
bedellion 2. 12		bdellium
beestes 45. 17	beastes	beast
See beastes		
beasts		
befor 43. 26	before	to

	C	A
before 2. 5 (27 times)		
2. 4	*omit*	*omit*
13. 9 (3 times)	open before	
23. 12 (4 times)	*omit*	
27. 23 (2 times)	afore	
23. 17 (2 times)	ouer before	
49. 30 (2 times)	over against	
13. 4		at the first
13. 10	for before	
23. 7	*omit*	to
24. 40	with	
24. 45	or euer	
24. 63	aboute	at
25. 18	towarde	
— tyme 28. 19	afore	at the first
30. 39	ouer	
30. 41	,,	among
31. 35	vnto	
37. 10		to
37. 18	afore	euen before
43. 33	ouer agaynst	
47. 15		in
— him 48. 12	vpon their face	with his face to the earth
48. 20	aboue	
began 4. 26 (4 times)	beganne	began
— to trauell 35. 16	traueyled	traueiled
— to hunger 41. 55	beganne to suffre honger	was famished
beganne to breake vp 19. 9	whan they ranne to, and wolde haue broken vp	came neere to breake
begat 5. 25 (3 times)		
4. 26 (42 times)	begat	begate
4. 18		was borne
4. 26		to him also there was borne

	C	A
begat 5. 4		had begotten
5. 10	*omit*	begote
10. 1		vnto them were sonnes borne
10. 21		euen to him were children borne
10. 25		were borne, vnto
37. 3	had begotten	was the sonne of his old age
44. 20	begotten	a childe of his old age
begete, shall 17. 20	shal beget	
begon 11. 6	haue begonne	begin
begonne, haue 18. 3	haue taken vpon me	haue taken vpon mee
begot 10. 8	begat	begat
—, had 5. 7 (14 times)	,,	begate
6. 1	had begot	were borne vnto them
begoten, had 12. 5	begat	had gotten
begotten, had 6. 4	had begotten	bare children to
begyled, went about to 27. 12	begyled	as a deceiuer
—, hast 29. 25		hast beguiled
begynnynge 1. 1 (2 times)		beginning
2. 8	*omit*	*omit*
10. 10	origenall	beginning
41. 21	afore	,,
beheld 13. 10	behelde	behelde
behelde 31. 2		
1. 31		behold
31. 41	hath loked vpon	hath seene
43. 29	sawe	sawe
48. 8	loked vpon	
behind 18. 10	behynde	
behinde, taried 32. 24	taried alone	was left alone

	C	A
behinde 50. 8	*omit*	*omit*
See behynde		
behold 19. 8		
22. 20 (4 times)	beholde	
6. 17	lo	
beholde 24. 43		
(5 times)		
4. 14 (28 times)		behold
8. 11 (2 ,,)		loe
16. 2 (2 ,,)		behold now
22. 13 (3 ,,)	saw	behold
27. 37 (2 ,,)	*omit*	,,
8. 13	saw that	,,
18. 27	O se	,,
24. 51	there is	,,
31. 50	but, lo	see
37. 7	me thought	
37. 19	lo	behold
38. 27	*omit*	
41. 41		see
See boholde		
behynde 19. 17		behind
19. 26		backe from behind
45. 6		*omit*
See behind		
behinde		
Bela 14. 2 (4 times)		
46. 21		Belah
beleved 15. 6 (2 times)		beleeued
beleved, may be	wyll I beleue	† shall be verified
42. 20		
belongeth 40. 8		doe belong
bely 3. 14		belly
Ben Ammi 19. 38	the sonne Ammi	Ben Ammi
bene, had 26. 8		
19. 28 (2 times)		*omit*
—, hath 31. 5		

	C	A
bene, haue 31. 38 31. 42		had bin
—, haue 30. 29	† hast	was
— baren, haue 31. 38		cast their yong
—, haue 32. 4 38. 15		stayed to be
—, haue 47. 9	is	
benethe 35. 8	beneth	beneath
Ben Iamin 35. 18 (13 times)		Beniamin
42. 4	Ben Iamyn	,,
Ben Iamins 43. 34.		Beniamins
44. 12	of Ben Iamin	of Beniamin
45. 14	Ben Iamyns	Beniamins
Ben Oni 35. 18		
Beor 36. 32		
Bera 14. 2		
bere, shall 17. 17 (4 times)	shall beare	shall beare
bere 1. 11	may beare	yeelding
— company, to 3. 12	to beare company	to be with
—, cannot 16. 2	cannot beare	† from bearing
—, shalt 16. 11	shalt bringe forth	shalt beare
—, dyd 22. 23	bare	did beare
— no perell, shalt 24. 41	shalt be discharged	shalt be cleare
—, let 43. 9	I wil beare	
—, will 44. 32		shall beare
bere ruele, doughters come forth to 49. 22	† doughters goe vpon the wall	† branches runne ouer the wall
See bare beare		
Berseba 21. 14 (9 times)		Beer-sheba
26. 33	Bersaba	,, ,,
Bery 26. 34	Beri	Beeri

	C	A
	bearinge	yeelding

berynge 1. 12   bearinge   yeelding
  See bearinge
    bearynge
best 43. 11 (3 times)
— liked 6. 2   *omit*   chose
   20. 15   „   *omit*
— saue one 41. 43   seconde   second
beste 9. 10   beastes   beast
   9. 10   beast   „
  See beast
beste 45. 18   of the goodes   good
besought 42. 21
besyde 16. 7   by
   46. 26   besides
BETHEL 12. 8   Bethel   Beth-el
   (4 times)
Bethel 35. 16
Bethell 28. 19 (7 times)   Bethel   Bethel
Bethlehem 35. 19
   48. 7   Bethleem
Bethuel 22. 22 (5 times)
Bethuell 24. 15   Bethuel   Bethuel
   (2 times)
betokeneth 41. 32   signifieth   is because
better 29. 19
better, fare the 12. 13   be wel
betwene 3. 15   betweene
   (18 times)
   9. 15 (4 times)   betwixte   „
   1. 6   in the midst of
—, from 49. 10   from   from betweene
betwixte 17. 11   betwene   betwixt
betwyxte 23. 15   betwixte   „
   (3 times)
   31. 37 (3 times)   „
   31. 50 (2 times) betwene   „
betymes 29. 8   by tymes   earely

	C	A
be warre of that 24. 6	beware of that	beware thou
bewepte 50. 3	bewayled	mourned for
bewtifull 29. 17	beutyfull	beautifull
bewtyfull 2. 9	pleasant	pleasant
26. 7	beautifull	faire
beynge an husband man, went furth 9. 20	beganne to take hede vnto the tyllinge of the grounde	began to bee an husbandman
12. 8	† had	† hauing
14. 18		was
35. 29	was	being
beyonde 35. 21 (3 times)		beyond
Bezara 36. 33	Bosra	Bozra
Bilha 29. 29 (9 times)		Bilhah
Bilhan 36. 27		
birdes 7. 21	foules ·	fowle
See byrdes		
Birsa 14. 2		Birsha
bisse 41. 42	whyte sylke	fine linnen
bitterly 27. 34	loude	† with a bitter
blacke 30. 32 (3 times)		browne
30. 35	black	,,
blame 43. 9 (2 times)		
blasted 41. 6 (3 ,,)		
blesse 27. 34 (6 ,,)		
—, maye 27. 19 (4 times)		
—, will 12. 2 (5 times)		
—, ,, 17. 20	haue blessed	haue blessed
—, ,, 22. 17	wyll prospere	
—, ,, 26. 3	blesse	
—, let me 48. 9	that I maye blesse	I will blesse
—, shall 48. 20		
—, ,, 49. 25	art blessed	
See blysse		

	C	A
blessed 1. 22 (26 times)		
—, shall be 12. 3		
(7 times)		
—, had 24. 1 (2 times)		
—, hath 27. 28		
(4 times)		
—, haue 27. 33		
9. 2 (4 times)	praysed	
—, hath 24. 35	hath prospered	
47. 7	thanked	
blessing 27. 30	blessynge	
blessinge 12. 2	blessynge	blessing
(3 times)		
See blessynge		
blessinges 49. 25		blessings
(2 times)		
49. 25 (2 times)	blessynges	,,
49. 26	*omit*	,,
49. 26	these	they
blessynge 27. 36		
(5 times)		blessing
27. 35	blessinge	,,
33. 11	present in good worth	,,
39. 5	nothynge but the very blessynge	,,
See blessing blessinge		
bloud 4. 11 (4 times)		
9. 4	bloude	blood
bloude 9. 5 (5 times)		,,
blossoms 40. 10		
blow, to 8. 1	to come	to passe ouer
blyndnesse 19. 11		blindnes
blysse, maye 27. 10	maye blesse	may blesse
See blesse		

	C	A
bode 49. 24		abode
bodies 47. 18	body	bodies
bodye 15. 4		bowels
boholde 26. 9	lo	behold
See behold		
beholde		
boke 5. 1		booke
boldly 34. 25		
bond 21. 17 (3 times)		couenant
9. 9 (3 times)	counaunt	,,
—, be 47. 9		be seruants
— vnto, was 47. 26	was bonde vnto	became
See bonde		
bondage, in 43. 18	for bonde seraunts	for bondmen
bonde 17. 2 (5 times)	couenaunt	couenaut
17. 19	*omit*	,,
bondmayde 21. 10	bond mayden	bond woman
bondman 44. 33	bondeman	
bondmayde 21. 12	hand mayde	,,　　　,,
bondmen 44. 9		
— of, shall make	shall make bonde	† shal serue
15. 13	men of	
bondwoman, of 21. 10	bonde maydens	of bond woman
(2 times)		
bone 2. 23 (2 times)		
boones 2. 23 (2 times)	bones	bones
boothes 33. 17	tents	
borders 23. 17ˉ	*omit*	
49. 14		burdens
bordreth vpon 14. 6		by
borne 14. 14 (2 times)		
—, was 21. 3 (2 times)		
—, shall be 17. 17		
—, were 17. 27		
(8 times)		
—, had 21. 9 (2 times)		
—, hath 22. 20		

	C	A
borne, haue 29. 34		
(3 times)		
—, where he was		
11. 28		of his natiuity
15. 3	of my housholde	
17. 13	*omit*	
17. 23		that were borne
—, shulde haue 21. 7	beare	haue borne
—, where I was 24. 7	of my kyndred	of my kindred
—, where thou wast	of thy kynred	of thy kindred
31. 13		
41. 12		*omit*
bosome, into thy 16. 5	by the	
botell 21. 15		bottle
See bottell		
both 2. 25 (18 times)		
3. 5 (6 times)		*omit*
19. 4 (4 times)	*omit*	
6. 18 (17 times)	,,	*omit*
24. 54	also	,,
34. 12	*omit*	neuer so much
bothe 7. 21		
bottell 21. 14 (2 times)	botell	bottle
See botell		
bought 17. 27		
(3 times)		
—, was 17. 23	were bought	were bought
17. 13	*omit*	
—, haue 30. 16		haue hired
47. 20	toke	
boughte 17. 12	bought	bought
(3 times)		
25. 20	,,	purchased
47. 20	toke	bought
—, haue 47. 23	haue taken	,,
	possesion of	
bounde 39. 20	*omit*	bound

	C	A
bounde, be 42. 19	lye bounde	be bound
See bownd		
bownde		
bowe 9. 13 (6 times)		bow
27. 29	fall downe	,,
bowed 19. 1		
(4 times)		
— him selfe before		
23. 7	thanked	bowed himselfe to
— him selfe to 23. 12	,,	bowed downe him-
		selfe before
—, him selfe vnto		worshipped . . .
24. 52		bowing
43. 28		bowed downe
49. 15	bowed downe	bowed
bowels 25. 23	body	
bownd, was 40. 3	laye presoner	bound
bownde 22. 9	bande	,,
38. 28	bounde	,,
—, were 40. 5	*omit*	were bound
See bounde		
bowshote 21. 6		bow shoot
boye 21. 19	childe	lad
boyes 25. 27	boies	
bracelets 24. 22		
bracelettes 24. 30		bracelets
brande 15. 17		burning lampe
brasse 4. 22	all connynge	
	poyntes of metall	
braunche, vyne 49. 11	noble braunch	choice vine
braunches 40. 10		branches
(2 times)		
bread 28.20 (11 times)	bred	
51. 54	*omit*	
See bred		
brede		
breed		

	C	A
breake vp, beganne	wold haue	came neere to
to 19. 9	broken vp	breake
breaketh 32. 26	breaketh on	
breakynge 32. 24	break	breaking
bred 45. 23		bread
brede 3. 19 (4 times)	bred	,,
35. 16	felde brode	litle way
37. 25	*omit*	,, ,,
48. 7		little ,,
breed 14. 18 (4 times)	bred	bread
31. 54	*omit*	
See bread		
bredth 6. 15 (2 times)		breadth
brente, let be 38. 24	may be brent	let be burnt
brestes 49. 25		breasts
breth 2. 7 (4 times)		breath
brethed 2. 7		breathed
brethern 29. 4	brethren	brethren
(38 times)		
42. 7 (2 times)	them	,,
45. 4	*omit*	,,
brethren 9. 22		
(27 times)		
37. 27	they	,,
bretren 42. 32	brethren	,,
See brothren		
bring 1. 24	brynge	
— to passe 50. 20	is come to passe	
bringe 1. 11		bring
24. 6 (6 times)	brynge	,,
—, to 27. 5		
27. 9	fetch	fetch
—, shalt 27. 9	brynge	,,
—, shall 27. 12	,,	shall bring
– , will 46. 4	wil brynge	will ,,
See brynge		
brode, last 30. 42	later	feebler

	C	A
broght, haue 43. 21	haue brought	haue brought
See brought		
broughte		
broken vp, were 7. 11		
—, hath 17. 11		
brother 4. 2 (74 times)		
—, of 10. 25	brothers	brothers
13. 11 (2 times)		*omit*
24. 53	brethren	
brothers 4. 9 (9 times)		
24. 27		of brethren
— seruaunte, shalt be	shalt serue thy	shalt serue thy
thy 27. 40	brother	brother
27. 44	of thy brother	
27. 45	his	brethren
brothren 16. 12	brethren	,,
(3 times)		
47. 6	them	,,
See brethern		
brethren		
bretren		
brought 1. 12		
(27 times)		
—, had 19. 17		
—, was 39. 1 (2 times)		
—, hath 39. 14		
—, have 43. 21		
(3 times)		
— him	bad him	brought him
out at the doores	go forth	forth abroad
15. 5		
24. 32	gaue	gaue
—, be 29. 8		bee gathered
33. 11		is brought
27. 2	tolde	
—, caused to be		brought
37. 32		

	C	A
brought 39. 1		had brought
—, hast 39. 17	broughtest	hast brought
43. 2	had brought	had brought
— together 47. 14		gathered vp
—, were 48. 1	was tolde	told
broughte 14. 16	brought	brought
(8 times)		
—, had 24. 48	had brought	had led ... in
24. 59	let go	sent away
—, shuldest haue	haddest broughte	
26. 10		
—, myghte haue	might haue	might haue sent
31. 27	brought	
43. 34	there were	tooke and sent
	brought	
See broght		
Brya 46. 17 (2 times)	Bria	Beriah
brycke 11. 3 (2 times)	bryck	bricke
brymstone 19. 24		brimstone
brynge 9.14 (12 times)		bring
—, will 28. 15		
(3 times)		
—, shall 44. 29		
(2 times)		
—, to 18. 16		to bring
—, may 18. 19	maye bringe	may bring
27. 25 (2 times)	bringe	bring
8. 17	let go	shalt bring
—, shuldest 20. 9		hast brought
—, shall 24. 5	shal cary	must needes bring
—, to 29. 3		were gathered
—, helpe to 40. 14	that he maye	bring
	bringe	
42. 19	cary	carry
—, shuld 42. 38	shulde bringe	shall bring
—, 43. 11		carie
—, to 43. 18	to take	take

	C	A
brynge 45. 13	come downe with	bring
47. 16		giue
See bring		
bringe		
brynke 41. 3	water syde	brynke
bucked 31. 10	leapte vpon	leaped vpon
buckinge 30. 41	buckynge	† did conceive
buckynge tyme, in the latter 30. 42	in the latter buck- ynge tyme	when the cattel were feeble
— tyme, in the 31. 10	whan the buck- ynge tyme came	at the time that the cattell con- ceived
budded 40. 10		
bulles 32. 15	bullocks	
bundell 42. 35	boundell	bundle
bundells 42. 35	bundels	bundels
burie 47. 29 (2 times)	burye	bury
—, to 50. 7	to burye	to bury
See bury		
buried 23. 19 (5 times)		
—, was 25. 10		
48. 7	buryed	
See buryed		
burne 11. 3	*omit*	
bury 23. 6 (2 times)		
—, to 23. 4 (3 times)		of a burying place
—, may 23. 4		
—, will 23. 13		
—, shuldest 23. 6		mayest bury
—, shall 23. 8	burye	should bury
—, to 23. 11	to burye	bury
See burie		
burye		
buryall 47. 30		burying place
50. 5 (2 times)		bury
burye 49. 29		burie
—, to 49. 30	to burye	of a burying place

	C	A
burye, se that thou 50. 5	burye	shalt thou bury
— in, to be a place to 50. 13	for a possession to bury in	for a possession of a burying place
—, to 50. 14		to bury
buryed, was 35. 5 (2 times)	was buried	was buried
49. 31		buried
50. 13 (2 times)	buried	„
Bus 22. 21		Buz
bush 21. 15		one of the shrubs
bushels 26. 12	buszshels	fold
busynes, do 34. 10	occupie	trade
39. 11	busynesse	busines
but 27. 22 (3 times)		
— and yf 4. 7 (2 times)		and if
41. 26 (2 times)	*omit*	*omit*
3. 1		now
— and yf 24. 40	and so . . . yf	and if
24. 55	neuerthelesse	and
— even 24. 55	at the leest	at the least
26. 29	but all	
27. 38	*omit*	
— euen 28. 17	but	but
— and yf 34. 17		but if
35. 16	*omit*	but
44. 22		*omit*
butlar 40. 1 (4 times)		butler
buttelar 40. 20 (3 times)	butlar	„
buttelarshipe 40. 21		butlershipe
butter 18. 8		
buylde, let 11. 4		let build
—, to 11. 8		to „
buylded 10.11 (4 times)		builded
13. 18 (2 times)		built
See bylt		

	C	A
buyldinge, was 4. 17	buylded	builded
by 6. 21 (39 times)		
7. 9 (3 times)		*omit*
16. 7 (3 times)	besyde	
19. 6 (2 times)		vpon
31. 40 (3 times)		in
31. 32 (2 „)		with
42. 25 (2 „)		for
— and by 4. 7	*omit*	*omit*
6. 21		to
8. 14	vpon	on
— reason of the 12.13		for thy sake
by, faste 16. 12	ouer agaynst	in the presence of
18. 3		from
19. 20		neere
24. 30	at	at
—, holdynge 25. 26	held with	tooke holde on
26. 10	with	with
— tymes 26. 31	*omit*	betimes
—, laye 29. 30	laye with	went in vnto
30. 40	vnto	
—, lay 38. 18	lay with	came in vnto
38. 18	of	lay by
— daye, daye 39. 10	daylie	
— 39. 11	there by	there within
— reason of 41. 31	because of	
43. 2	bye	buy
— this 43. 10	now	now
45. 10	with	neere vnto
46. 2		of the
— the 47. 13		by
47. 22	for	*omit*
byd, wolde 43. 7	wolde saye	would say
byde, will 19. 2		
22. 5 (2 times)	tary	abide
26. 2	„	dwell
44. 33		abide

	C	A
bye. 43. 4 (2 times)	bye	buy
—, bye, to 41. 57 (7 times)	to bye	to buy
—, and 42. 2		buy
47. 19	take	,,
bylt 33. 17	buylded	built
See buylded		
bynd, shall 49. 11		binding
byrdes 6. 20 (3 times)	foules	fowles
40. 17 (2 times)	,,	birds
7. 8	fethered foules	,,
7. 14	foules	euery foule
byrth daye 40. 20		birthday
byrthrighte 25. 31 (5 times)	byrthright	birthright
byte 49. 17		biteth
Cades 16. 14 (2 times)		Cadesh
14. 7		Kadesh
Cadmonites 15. 19	Kydmonites	Kadmonites
Cain 4. 1 (15 times)		
cakes 18. 6		
19. 3		vnleauened bread
Calah 10. 11		
cald 25. 1	called	and her name was
See called		
calfe 18. 8		
18. 7	calf	
call, wold 2. 19		
—, to 4. 26		
—, shalt 16. 11 (2 times)		
—, will 30. 13		
—, let vs 24. 57		wee will call
—, yf . . . 46. 33		shall call
calle, to 26. 7	to saye	to say
called 1. 5 (60 times)		

	C	A
called, shall be 2. 23 (2 times)		
—, was 11. 29 (4 times)		
—, is 11. 9		
—, shalt be 17. 5		
—, was 4. 22 (3 times)		was
—, is 14. 24 (2 „)		is
—, is 19. 22 (3 „)		was called
22. 24 (2 „)		whose name was
2. 12	*omit*	*omit*
4. 19		the name was
12. 6	of	of
16. 14		was called
—, shall be 17. 15		shalt call
—, is 22. 31		called
23. 2	which is called	the same is
23. 19	that is	the same is
24. 29		and his name was
—, was 25. 30	is called	
31. 4	bad call	
—, shalt be 32. 28		shall be called
35. 6	which is called	that is
35. 10		shall bee called
—, shalt be 35. 10		shall bee called
—, was 35. 10	was called	called
35. 19		is
35. 20	is	
35. 27		which is
41. 38	caused to call	
46. 2	*omit*	said
—, shalbe 48. 6	shalbe named	
—, maye be 48. 16		let be named
—, is 50. 11		was called
See cald		
came 8. 11 (67 times)		
1. 10 (2 times)		*omit*
7. 6 (2 „)		was

	C	A
came 7. 9 (6 times)	wente	went
8. 12 (3 „)		returned
8. 18 (3 „)	wente out	went foorth
13. 12 (3 times)	*omit*	*omit*
— to passe 24. 15 (6 times)		
— to passe 24. 15 (2 times)	*omit*	
26. 23 (7 times)	„	
41. 3 (2 times)	sawe come	
— of hym 4. 21		hee was the father
7. 10		were
16. 2	*omit*	went
16. 2		„
10. 5	are deuided	were diuided
10. 9	commeth	it is saide
10. 32	spred abrode	were diuided
11. 2	wente	iourneyed
12. 10	was	was
12. 14		was come
14. 3		were ioyned
15. 12	fell	fell
19. 8	are come	
24. 32	brought	
24. 45	commeth	
28. 11		lighted vpon
32. 10	wente	passed
35. 9	was come	
— to Israel ears 35. 22		Israel heard it
37. 25	commynge	
37. 35		rose vp
41. 54	beganne to come	beganne to come
43. 18	came agayne	was returned
— home 43. 26	went into the house	
44. 14	wente	came
44. 24	wente vp	
46. 26	proceaded	

	C	A
camel 24. 64	camell	
camels 12. 16		
(23 times)		
24. 32	them	
camest 19.9 (3 times)		
Canaan 9. 18		
(43 times)		
See Chanaan		
Canaanites 15. 21	Cananites	
Canaanyte 38. 2	man of Canaans	Canaanite
Canaanytes 10. 18	Cananites	Canaanites
(4 times)		
12. 6	,,	Canaanite
See Canaanites		
Cananytes		
Cananitish 46. 10		Canaanitish
Cananytes 13. 7	Cananites	Canaanites
(3 times)		
See Canaanites		
Canaanytes		
captayne 21. 22		captaine
(2 times)		
See captyne		
Capththerynes 10. 14	Capthorims	Caphtorim
captyne 31. 26		captines
34. 29		captine
carcases 15. 11	flesh	
care for, will 50. 21		will nourish
carie, to 46. 5	to cary	to cary
—, can 44. 1	maye carye	
45. 27	to fetch	to carie
47. 30	shalt carye	shalt carye
See carye		
caried 31. 18 (3 times)		
—, hast 31. 26	caried	caried
carye 50. 25	cary	shal carie
See carie		

	C	A
case, good 40. 14	thy prosperite	it shall be well with the
Casluhim 10. 14		
cast 37. 20 (4 times)		
cast slomber on 2. 21	caused an herde slepe to fall vpon	caused a deepe sleepe to fall vpon
—, out 3. 23	put out	sent foorth
—, out 3. 24		droue out
21. 15	layed	
castels 25. 16	courtes	
castest 4. 14		hast driuen
catche, to 27. 5	to hunte	to hunt for
catell 1. 24 (27 times)		cattell
31. 9 (2 times)	goodes	„
3. 14		cattel
13. 5		heards
47. 18		heards of cattell
50. 8	oxen	heards
caue 19. 30 (11 times)		
23. 17		*omit*
caught 39. 12		
19. 16		laid hold vpon
22. 13	holden fast	
cause, for this 2. 24		therefore
caused, hath 41. 52		
caused to spede him 19. 15		hastened
20. 13	charged	
37. 32		*omit*
causedest me to take 12. 19	wherfore I toke	I might haue taken
ceased 8. 1	ceassed	asswaged
— to be 18. 11	wente no more	ceased to be
ceasse, shall 8. 22		shall cease
ceasseth not to deal mercyfully 24. 27	hath not withdrawen his mercy	hath not left destitute

	C	A
certanly 41. 32	surely	*omit*
certayne 37. 15		certaine
Cesed 22. 22		Chesed
Chalah 10. 12	Calah	Calah
Chaldea 11. 28		Chaldees
(2 times)		
15. 7		Caldees
Chalne 10. 10		Calneh
chambre 43. 30	chamber	chamber
Chanaan 11. 31	Canaan	Canaan
(3 times)		
See Canaan		
changed, hast 31. 41		
See chaunged		
Charan 36. 26	Charan	Cheran
charett 41. 43		charet
(2 times)		
charettes 45. 9		wagons
(4 times)		
50. 9		charets
charge, 28. 6		
—, gaue a 12. 20		commanded
—, gaue 40. 4	put vnto them	charged
43. 18		*omit*
charged 28. 1		
26. 11 (2 times)	commaunded	
50. 16	,,	did command
Charmi 46. 9		Carmi
chased 14. 15		pursued
chaumbers 6. 14	chambers	roomes
chaunced 21. 22	*omit*	came to passe
35. 22	chaunsed	,, ,, ,,
40. 1	fortuned	,, ,, ,,
See chaunsed		
chaunge 35. 2		change
45. 22 (2 times)		changes

	C	A
chaunge, I haue made a 30. 8	God hath turned it	with great wrast- lings haue I wrastled . . . and I haue pre- uailed
chaunged 31. 7 (2 times)		changed
chaunsed 14. 1		came to passe
22. 20	fortuned	,, ,, ,,
See chaunced		
chefe 21. 22 (12 times)		chiefe
37. 36 (7 times)		*omit*
49. 3 (2 times)		excellencie
chefest 23. 6	best	choise
—, shalt not be 49. 4		shalt not excel
chere, be of 43. 23	be content	peace be to you
cherubin 3. 24	cherubes	cherubims
chest 50. 26		coffin
chestnottrees 30. 37		chestnut tree
Chesyb 38. 5	*omit*	Chezib
cheyne 41. 42		chaine
child, make the oft with 3. 16	increase thy sorrow whan thou art with childe	multiply thy con- ception
—, was with 38. 18		conceiued
childe 11. 30		
16. 11 (5 times)		child
18. 3 (2 ,,)	*omit*	
21. 17 (2 ,,)		lad
—, was with 21. 2		conceiued
21. 17		ladde
—, with 25. 22		thus
49. 22	sonne	bough
49. 22	,,	

	C	A
childern 18. 19	children	children
(42 times)		
21. 23 (2 times)	„	sonne
31. 28 (22 „)	„	sonnes
34. 29 (7 times)	„	little ones
17. 10	manchilde	man-child
— of Heth 23. 10	Hethites	
(4 times)		
—, mothers 27. 37	brethren	brethren
34. 15 (2 times)	males	male
48. 6	those	thy issue
childerne 16. 1	children	children
See children		
chyldren		
childerns 21. 23	childers	sonnes
31. 16	children	childrens
45. 10		„
childlesse 15. 2	childles	
children 6. 4		
(5 times)		
6. 4 (4 times)		sonnes
6. 4 (2 times)		*omit*
17. 23		male
— of Heth 23. 5	Hethites	
(2 times)		
See childern		
childerne		
chyldren		
chilhode 46. 34	youth	youth
chode 31. 36		
chose 13. 11		
Chus 10. 6 (3 times)		Cush
chyde with 49. 23	strove with	shot at
chyldren 10. 20	children	sonnes
See childern		
childerne		
children		

	C	A
circumcised, was 17. 26	was circumcyded	
circumcyse, shall 17. 11	shall circumcyde	shall circumcise
circumcysed, must needes be 17. 13	*omit*	must needs be circumcised
17. 23	circumcyded	circumcised
—, was 17. 25	was circumcyded	was circumcised
—, were 17. 27	were „	were „
21. 4	circumcided	circumcised
—, be 34. 15	be circumcided	be circumcised
—, to be 34. 17	to be circumcided	to be circumcised
—, be 34. 22	circumcyse	are „
—, were 34. 24	circumcided	was „
circumsyse 17. 10	shalbe circum-cyded	shall circumcise
circumsysed 17. 12	circumcyded	shalbe circum-cised
cite 19. 14 *See* citie cyte cytie		citie
Cithim 10. 4		Kittim
citie 24. 13 (3 times) *See* cite cyte cytie		
cities 19. 29 (4 times) 41. 46	*omit*	storehouses
cleane 35. 2	cleanse	
clene 7. 2 (4 times)	cleane	cleane
cleve 2. 24		cleaue
clooke 38. 14	*omit*	vaile
cloothes 37. 29 (2 times)	clothes	clothes
28. 20 *See* clothes	clothinge	raiment

	C	A
closed to, hath 16. 2		hath restrained
—, had 20. 18		
clothe, sacke 37. 34	sack cloth	sackcloth
clothes 44. 13		
See cloothes		
cloudes 9. 13 (4 times)		cloud
clove 22. 3		claue
colde 8. 22		cold
31. 40	frost	frost
colt 49. 11	colte	
coltes 32. 15	foales	colts
coloured 30. 35		*omit*
coloures, of 30. 32	coloured	„
(2 times)		
comaunded 2. 16	commaunded	commanded
(2 times)		
See commaunded		
comaundmentes 26. 5	commaundmentes	commandements
come 19. 32 (16 times)		
—, is 6. 13 (2 „)		
—, shall 6. 20 (4 „)		
—, are 18. 5 (6 „)		
—, will 32. 11 (3 „)		
—, wyll agree to 24. 5	wyl folowe	will be willing to
(2 times)		follow
—, be 19. 22		*omit*
39. 7 (2 times)	*omit*	
— on 11. 3		goe to
—, shalt 6. 18	shalt go	
— out 8. 16	go out	goe forth
10. 19	commest	commest
10. 19	*omit*	„
10. 30	come	goest
—, were 12. 5		came
— to passe 12. 12	*omit*	shall come to passe
—, tyll thou 13. 10	† it rounde aboute	as thou commest
—, shall 15. 14	go forth	

	C	A
come will 18. 10		will returne
— hither 19. 9		stand backe
—, to 19. 31	can come	
— nye, had 20. 4	had touched	had come neere
— nygh, to 20. 6	to touch	to touch
20. 13		shall come
22. 5	wyll come	
24. 11	used to go forth	goe
—, will 24. 13		come
—, was 25. 24	came	were fulfilled
—, will 27. 40	shall come to passe	shall come to passe
—, I 28. 21	brynge me	
—, tyme is 29. 21		days are fulfilled
—, when euen was 29. 23	at euen	*omit*
—, mornynge was 29. 25	on the morow	in the morning
— in to 30. 16	shalt lye with	must come in vnto
—, is 31. 35	it goeth	*omit*
—, will 31. 52	yf I passe	will passe
—, shalt 31. 52	yf I passe	shalt passe
33. 1	commynge	came
—, was 33. 18		came
—, were 34. 5	came	
— to, wyll 37. 20	are	will become of
—, was 37. 23	came	was come
— on 37. 37	come	come
38. 16	*omit*	goe to
—, was 38. 27	came	came to passe
—, wyll 38. 28	shal come	came
— luckely to passe 39. 23	to come prosper-ously to passe	to prosper
—, shall 41. 29		come
— after, shall 41. 31	commeth therafter	following
41. 35	shal come	
—, shall 41. 36		shall bee

	C	A
come, be 42. 15	come	come
—, is 42. 21	commeth	
43. 10	had now bene come	had returned
—, is 44. 31	be with	is with
—, shall 44. 34	shulde happen	
—, was 45. 16	came	was heard
—, were 45. 16	are come	are come
—, be 45. 18	come	*omit*
—, be 45. 18	come	come
49. 1	gather you	gather yourselues
—, art 49. 9		art gone
— forth to bere ruele 49. 22	go vpon the wall	runne ouer the wall
—, shall 49. 24	are come	is
comen saynge 22. 14	comon sayenge yet	it is said to
—, to 34. 6	to comen	to commune
comened 34. 8 (2 times)		communed
42. 24 (2 times)	talked	,,
See comoned		
comenynge 18. 33	talkynge	communing
comest 16. 8	commest	camest
24. 40	,,	commest
29. 6 (3 times)	commeth	commeth
cometh 24. 43	yf there come	,,
24. 65	commeth	walketh
27. 20	*omit*	is
— after 32. 18	commeth behynde	is behinde
— ,, 32. 20	is behynde	,, ,,
cometh it that, how 42. 28	wherfore	what is this
49. 20	commeth	shall yeeld
See commeth		
comforte, shall 5. 29		shall comfort
—, to 18. 5		and comfort
—, to 37. 35		to comfort

C	A
comforted, was 24. 67	
—, would not be 37. 35	refused to be comforted
cominge, ever goinge and 8. 7 came	to and fro
24. 62 comynge	came
24. 63 „	coming
See comynge	
commaunde, will	will command
18. 19	
27. 8	command
commaunded 3. 17 (4 times)	
2. 16 (9 times)	commanded
45. 1	cried
47. 11	had commanded
—, had 49. 33 had ended this commaundment	had made an end of commanding
See comaunded	
commaundment commaundement	commandement
45. 21	
—, dyd a 50. 16 let they saye	sent a messenger
commeth 48. 2	
9. 10 is gone	goe
30. 33	to come
See cometh	
commyted, hath 39. 8 put under	committed
39. 22 committed	„
comoned 23. 8 talked	communed
See comened	
companies 23. 7 droues	bands
company 2. 18	*omit*
—, to bere me 3. 12 to beare me company	to be with me
—, will kepe me 29. 34	will be ioyned vnto me

	C	A
company, in thy 33.12	in thy company	before thee
—, in her 39. 10		with her
companye 37. 25	company	company
(2 times)		
2. 20	,,	*omit*
compasse 6. 16	*omit*	,,
compassed 19. 4	compased	
compasseth 2. 11	runneth aboute	
compassyth 2. 13	,, ,,	compasseth
compelled 19. 3		pressed vpon
33. 11		vrged
comynge 42. 9	are come	are come
(2 times)		
See cominge		
conceaue, shulde		
30. 38		
—, mighte 30. 41	shulde conceaue	
conceaued 4. 1		conceiued
(16 times)		
—, hath 16. 5		had conceiued
38. 5	proceaded	conceiued
See conceyved		
concernynge 5. 29	in	concerning
17. 20		for
19. 21	in their poynte	concerning
41. 32	where as	for that
conceyved 16. 4	conceaued	conceiued
See conceaued		
concubine 22. 24	concubyne	
(3 times)		
concubines 25. 6	concubynes	
confederate 14. 13		
confounded 11. 9		did confound
congregation 49. 6	congregacion	assembly
conscyence 18. 19	conscience	iudgement
consent, will 34. 22		
34. 15	wyll consente	

	C	A
consente 34. 23	consent	consent
consume, shall 41. 30		
consumed 31. 40		
content, were 37. 27	herkened	
—, I am 46. 30		now let me
contente, I am 30. 34	let it be so	I would
continually 6. 5	contynually	
continue, myghte	might let . . .	to preserue
45. 7	remayne	
continued 39. 2	was	was
See contynued		
contre 2. 12 (2 times)	countre	land
12. 1 (3 times)	,,	countrey
13. 10 (2 ,,)	,,	plaine
14. 7 (2 ,,)	,,	country
21. 23 (2 ,,)	londe	land
13. 10	countre	*omit*
See countre		
cuntre		
contrees 10. 31	londes	lands
contreis 26. 3	londe	countreys
contres 10. 5	countrees	lands
See countrees		
contynued 39. 21	laye	was
40. 4	were	continued
See continued		
conynge 25. 27	*omit*	cunning
coole 3. 8		
cooples 7. 9	pares	two and two
7. 15		,, ,, ,,
coorse 23. 3	coarse	dead
coote 37. 3 (5 times)	cote	coat
37. 23	,,	coate
37. 33	coate	coat
corne 27. 28 (13 times)		
42. 3 (2 times)		*omit*
41. 57	*omit*	

C	A
corne 43. 2	vytales	
corrupte 6.11 (2 times)		corrupt
—, had 6. 12		had corrupted
costes 10. 19	coastes	border
13. 11	„	plaine
couche 49. 4	couch	
couched 49. 9		
49. 14	laye	couching
couered 38. 14		
—, were 7.19 (2 times)		
—, had 38. 15		
couerynge 20. 16		couering
councell, toke 37. 18	deuysed	conspired
counted, was 15. 6		
countenaunce 31. 5	countenance	countenance
countre 29. 1 (2 times)		countrey
34. 2 (3 times)	londe	
31. 13	„	land
42. 30	lande	countrey
See contre		
cuntre		
countrees 41. 57		countreys
See contrees		
contreis		
contres		
coupled, be 49. 6	be ioyned	be vnited
covenaunte 15. 18	couenant	couenant
cownteth 31. 15	hath counted	are counted
created 1. 1 (7 times)		
—, were 2. 4 (2 times)		
created 2. 4	made	made
creatures 1. 20		creature
(2 times)		
1. 24	soules	„
crepe 1. 26 (3 times)		creepeth
crepeth 7. 8 (2 „)		„
1. 30	hath life	„

C		A
crepeth 9. 2		moueth
crepte 7. 21	moued	creepeth
crie 18. 20		cry
See crye		
cried 39. 14		
41. 55	cryed	
See cryed		
crossinge 48. 14	did so wyttingly with	guiding
cruel thing 45. 5	eny wrath	bee angry with your selues
cruell 49. 7	rigorous	
cruelly 43. 6	euell	ill
crye 18. 21		cry
19. 13		crie
See crie		
cryed 27. 34 (3 times)	cried	cried
22. 15		called
41. 43	caused it to be proclaimed	cried
See cried		
cryeth 4. 10	crieth	
cubyte 6. 16		cubite
cubytes 6. 15	cubites	cubits
(3 times)		
7. 20		„
cuntre 30. 25	lande	countrey
32. 9	londe	„
See contre		
countre		
cuppe 40. 11 (9 times)		cup
44. 5	it	it
currant 23. 16		
curse, wyll		
8. 21		
12. 3 (3 times)		
12. 3		curseth

	C	A
cursed be 9. 25		
(3 times)		
—, hath 5. 29		
— be 3. 14		art cursed
— 3. 17		cursed is
— be 4. 11	shalt be cursed	art cursed
curseth 27. 29		
curteously 43. 27		*omit*
cutt of 17. 14	*omit*	circumcised
— of 17. 24		was „
cyte 4. 17 (3 times)	cite	city
10. 12 (28 „)	„	citie
10. 11	Niniue	Nineueh
19. 1	cite	Sodome
—, head 23. 2	head cite	Kiriath-arba
See citie		
cytie		
cyteis 19. 25	cities	cities
cytes 13. 12 (2 times)	„	„
See cities		
cyties		
cytie 19. 21 (5 times)	cite	citie
cyties 19. 29 (2 times)	cities	cities
dale 14. 17		
Damasco 15. 2	Damascos	Damascus
Damascos 14. 15		„
damsell 24. 14 (7 times)		
damsells 24. 61		
Dan 14. 14 (6 times)		
danger 19. 29	*omit*	midst
See daunger		
darcke 15. 17		darke
darcknesse 1. 2	darcknes	darkenesse
(3 times)		
1. 5	„	darknesse
See darknesse		

	C	A
dare 49. 9	wil	*omit*
darknesse 15. 12	darcknes	darkenesse
See darcknesse		
dates 43. 11		nuts
daunger, without 24.8	discharged	cleare
See danger		
day 4. 14 (3 times)	daye	
daye 1. 5 (57 times)		day
5. 1	tyme	
7. 10	dayes	dayes
18. 1	daie	day
— of mi deth 27. 2	whan I shal dye	day of my death
—, this 30. 32	to daye	to day
31. 40	daye tyme	day
—, yester 31. 42	yesterdaye	yesternight
35. 3	tyme	
— by day 39. 10	daylie	
40. 19	*omit*	*omit*
dayes 1. 14		
(23 times)		
—, all the 5. 5	whole age	
(9 times)		
26. 1 (6 times)	tyme	
6. 4	,,	daies
21. 4	daye	
24. 1	age	age
25. 7	age	
35. 28	*omit*	
—, full of 35. 29	had lyued enough	
49. 1	times	
dead 23. 6		
—, was 36. 34	dyed	died
(2 times)		
23. 4	coarse	
36. 37	died	died
44. 20	deed	dead
deade 23. 6	dead	,,

	C	A
deade 23. 8	coarse	dead
50. 15	deed	„
See deed		
deede		
deades 15. 1	actes	things
48. 1	this	„
See dedes		
deale, will 19. 9		
—, shalt 21. 23	shalt shewe	wilt deale
— mercyfulle, ceasseth not to 24. 27	hath not withdrawen his mercy	hath not left distitute
—, great 26. 16	farre	much
47. 26	shewe	
See deall		
dealeth 42. 28	hath done	hath done
deall, shuld 34. 31		
—, will 24. 49	shew	
deall well with the, will 32. 9	wyl do the good	
See deale		
dealt, hast 12. 18		hath done
See delt		
Debora 35. 8		Deborah
deceaved 3. 13	desceaued	beguiled
See disceaued		
deceytefully 34. 13	disceatfully	deceitfully
declare it, to 40. 8		interpreter of it
declared 41. 12		interpreted
(2 times)		
decreased 8. 5		
Dedan 10. 7 (3 times)		
dede, in very 20. 12		indeed
44. 15		deed
dedes, hast done 20. 9	hast dealt	hast done deeds
22. 1	actes	things
See deades		

	C	A
deed 20. 3 (2 times)		dead
—, am but 30. 1		die
— man, were 44. 22		would die
deede 23. 11 (2 times)	deed	dead
34. 27	slayne	slaine
See dead		
deade		
deeth 25. 11	death	death
deferde 34. 19		deferred
defyled, had 34. 5		had defiled
—, had 34. 13	was defyled	„ „
—, be 34. 27		„ „
—, be 37. 27		*omit*
defyledest 49. 4		defiledst
deleverd, shalt be	shalt beare	shalt bring forth
3. 16		
See delyuered		
delt 43. 6	have done	dealt
See dealt		
delyuer 20.7 (2 times)		restore
—, shalt 40. 13	mayest geue	shalt deliuer
—, will 42. 34	shal delyuer	will „
42. 37		deliuer
delyuerance 45. 7		deliuerance
delyuered, hath		hath deliuered
14. 20		
20. 14		restored
—, to be 25. 24		to be deliuered
32. 16	put	deliuered
—, and 37. 22		to deliuered
—, that she shulde be		of her trauaile
38. 27		
40. 11	gaue	gaue
—, hath 48. 16		redeemed
See delevered		
denyed 18. 15		denied
39. 8		refused

	C	A
departe 13. 9		depart
—, let me 24. 54		send me away
—, shall 49. 10	shal be remoued	shall depart
departed 14. 12		
(8 times)		
13. 1 (4 times)		went vp
20. 1 (3 „)		iourneyed
28. 10 (2 „)		went out
13. 11 (2 „)		separated
12. 5		went foorth
12. 8		remoued from
12. 9	wente downe	*omit*
18. 22	turned their face	turned their faces from
26. 22	gatt him from	remoued from
26. 23		went vp from
—, are 31. 49		are absent
—, are 37. 17	are gone from	
54. 24	*omit*	
departinge, was a 35. 18	was departynge	was in departing
depe 1. 2 (3 times)		deepe
derth 12. 10 (12 times)		famine
41. 54		dearth
—, of 41. 54	deare yeares	„
descende 11. 7	go downe	go downe
despised, was 16. 4	despysed	was despised
—, am 16. 5	must be despysed	„ „
—, was 29. 31	was nothinge regarded	was hated
—, am 29. 33	am despysed	am „
destroy, wyll 6. 7	wyll destroye	
(6 times)		
—, to 6. 17 (3 times)	to destroye	
—, wylt 18. 23	wilt „	
(2 times)		
—, wyll 8. 21	wil smyte	will smite

	C	A
destroy, must 19. 13	must destroye	will destroy
destroyed 13. 10		
(2 times)		
—, were 7. 23		
—, was 7. 23		
—, shall be 34. 20		
—, shall be 9. 11		shall be cut off
desyre 49. 26		† vtmost bound
deth 26. 18 (2 times)	death	death
20. 7	dyed	*omit*
— of 36. 35 (2 times)	„	died
—, daye of mi 27. 2	whan I shal dye	day of my death
—, his 50. 16	his death	he died
devided it selfe 2. 10	deuyded it selfe	was parted
See deuyded		
deuoure 49. 27		
deuoured 37. 20		
37. 33	rauyshed	
deuowred 41. 24	deuoured	deuoured
deuowerd 41. 7	ate vp	„
deuyde 1. 14 (4 times)		diuide
1. 7		diuided
deuyded 1. 4 (4 times)		„
—, was 10. 25		was diuided
See devided		
dewe 27. 28 (2 times)	dew	dew
did 38. 11	*omit*	did
42. 20	dyd	„
See dyd		
didest 3. 13	hast done	hast done
See dydest		
die 50. 24	dye	
See dye		
digged 26. 18	dygged	
See dygged		
Dikela 10. 27		Diklah
Dina 30. 21 (6 times)		Dinah

	C	A
Dina 34. 3	her	Dinah
Dinas 34. 25		Dinahs
Dinhaba 36. 32		Dinhabah
Disan 36. 21 (3 times)		Dishan
disceaued hath 31. 7		hath deceiued
See deceaued		
disease 31. 35	maner	custome
disgyssed 38. 14	dysgysed	wrapped
dishobedient 26. 35		a griefe of minde
Dison 36. 40 (4 times)		Dishon
displeased 38. 10		
(2 times)		
do 19. 8 (2 times)		
16. 6 (7 „)		doe
—, to 11.6 (4 „)		to doe
—, can 19. 22 (3 times)		can doe
—, wyll 18. 29 (3 „)		will doe
—, shall 25. 32		shall doe
—, shulde 18. 25		should doe
—, aboute to 18. 17	wil do	will doe
(2 times)		
—, to 18. 14	*omit*	*omit*
—, shuldest 18. 25		to do
—, shulde 18. 25		shall doe
— oure lust with,	may knowe	may know
may 19. 5		
—, to 20. 10	hast done	hast done
—, shuldeste 26. 29	shall do	wilt doe
—, can 27. 37	„ „	shall doe
—, wilt 30. 31		wilt doe
—, to 31. 29	hast done	hast now done
—, I am able to 31. 29	so moch might I haue made, that I coude haue done	it is in the power of my hand to doe
—, to 31. 52		for
—, woldest 32. 12	wyll do	will do

	C	A
do busynes 34. 10	occupie	trade
— occupation 34. 21	occupye	,,
—, can 39. 9	shulde do	can doe
— shame, to 39. 14		to mocke
— shame, to 39. 17	for to do shame	to mocke
See doo		
Dodanim 10. 4		
doist 21. 22	doest	doest
domynyon 1. 28	domynion	dominion
done, haste 3. 14		
(5 times)		
—, haue 8.21 (9 times)		
done, had 9. 24		
(2 times)		
—, ought to be 20. 9	† shulde deale	
—, hast 20. 9	hast dealt	
—, ought to be 34. 7	was the vse to do	
—, was 39. 22	were done	did
—, was 42. 25		,,
dongeon 40.15		dungeon
doo 31. 16 (3 times)	do	doe
—, shulde 44. 7		
—, is aboute to 41.28	wyll do	is aboute to doe
See do		
doore 43. 19		
18. 10 (4 times)	dore	
See dore		
doores 19. 6	dore	doore
—, brought out at	bad go forth	brought him forth
15. 5		abroad
dore 4. 7 (6 times)		doore
7. 16		*omit*
See doore		
dost 4. 7	do	doest
4. 7	,,	doe
— me vnrighte 16. 5	must suffre wrong	my wrong be vpon
		thee

	C	A
doth 31. 12		doeth
18. 13		did
Dothan 37. 17		
(2 times)		
double 23.19 (3 times)	dubble	*omit*
See dubill		
duble		
doue 8. 8 (4 times)		
8. 11	she	
—, turtill 15. 9	turtyll doue	turtle doue
doughter 20. 12		daughter
(40 times)		
19. 33		*omit*
— of 24. 15		who was borne to
34. 3	her	daughter
— in lawe 11. 31		,, in lawe
(3 times)		
38. 11	sonnes wyfe	,, ,, ,,
doughters 5. 4		daughters
(46 times)		
5. 10 (9 times)	daughters	,,
49. 22		branches
doune 12. 10	downe	downe
(14 times)		
—, vpp and 21. 14	out of the waye	*omit*
31. 34	downe	,,
down 19. 35	,,	downe
downe 11.5 (11 times)		
13. 18	*omit*	*omit*
—, apon it, went vpp		ascending and des-
and 28. 12		cending on it
38. 14		*omit*
— to 43. 15	in to	
46. 3	*omit*	
dowry 30. 20		
34. 12	dowrye	dowrie
drancke 9. 21	dranke	dranke

	C	A
dranke 24.46 (2 times)		
24. 54	dronke	did drịnke
drawe, to 24. 11		to draw
(3 times)		
—, will 24.19 (2 times)		
dreame 20.3 (19 times)		
— which 37. 6	what	
37. 8		dreames
40. 8	*omit*	
—, in my 40. 9	I dreamed	
—, in my 41. 17	I dreamed that	
dreamed 28. 12		
(5 times)		
— haue 40. 8 (2 times)		
—, hast 37. 10		
37. 9 (2 times)	had	
37. 5	had once	
—, haue 37. 6	dreamed	
dreamer 37. 19		
dreames 37. 20		
(3 times)		
41. 12	dreame	dreame
41. 25		,,
drede 9. 2		dread
dresse, to 2. 15		
dressed 22. 9	layed vpon	layd in order
—, haue 24. 31		haue prepared
drewe 24. 20 (2 times)	drew	drew
18. 23	stepte vnto	,,
47. 29	came	
dreyed vpp, were 8. 7	were dryed vp	were dried vp
See dryed		
drincke 19. 35	drynke	drinke
drinke 19. 34 (3 times)	,,	,,
See drynke		
droncke 9. 21	dronken	drunken
dronke 25. 34 (2 times)		did drinke

	C	A
dronke, haue 24. 19		haue done drinking
43. 34		drunke
43. 34	merry	merry
drooue 32. 16	flock	droue
32. 16	flocke	„
droue 15. 11		
drooues 32. 10	flockes	droues
38. 8	droue	droue
droues 32. 10		bands
drye 1. 9 (2 times)		dry
1. 10 (2 times)		drie
8. 14		was dried
dryed vpp were 8. 13		
See dreyed		
dryncke 19. 32	drynke	drinke
(2 times)		
24. 45	a drynke	
See drincke		
drinke		
drynke		
drynckynge, had left	had dronken	had done drinking
24. 22		
drynke 24. 14		
(7 times)		
19. 33 (2 times)		drinke
—, to 30. 38		
—, to 24. 43	to drinke	
drynkeoffringe 35.14	drynkofferynges	drinke offering
drynketh 44. 5		drinketh
dryue, will 33. 14		will leade
dubbill 23. 17	dubble	*omit*
dubill 23. 9	„	„
duble 25. 9	„	„
See double		
dubled, was 41. 32	† the seconde tyme	was doubled
duke 36.15 (29 times)	prynce	
36. 18 (5 times)	prince	

	C	A
dukedoms, in their 36. 20	which ruled	among their dukes
dukes 36. 15 (7 times)	prynces	
36. 19 (3 times)	princes	
Duma 25. 14		Dumah
durst 35. 5	*omit*	did
dust 13. 16 (4 times)		
dweld 21. 20 (3 times)	dwelt	dwelt
See dwelled		
dwelt		
dwell 24. 3 (5 times)		
20. 15 (3 times)		dwel
—, shall 16. 12		
(2 times)		
—, myght 13. 6		
—, coude 13. 6		
—, will 30. 20		
—, maye 46. 34		
4. 20	dwelt	
14. 7	„	dwelt
34. 10		shall dwell
—, will 34. 16	dwell	
—, will 34. 21		let ... dwel
—, for to 34. 22	to dwell	
—, maye 34. 23		will dwell
—, coude 36. 7		might dwell
—, shall 45. 10	shalt dwel	shalt „
dwelle, may 9. 27	let ... dwell	shal „
dwelled 11. 2 (8 times)	dwelt	dwelt
13. 7 (2 times)	„	
12. 6	„	was
16. 3	had dwelt	had dwelt
19. 25		*omit*
19. 30	remayned	dwelt
25. 27		dwelling
See dweld		
dwelt		

	C	A
dwellinges for, pre-pared 47. 11		placed
dwellynge 10. 30		dwelling
— place 27. 39	dwellinge	„
dwelt 4. 16 (10 times)		
16. 3	was a straunger	dwelt
38. 11	remained	
See dweld		
dwelled		
dyd 6. 22 (11 times)		did
— their obaysaunce	kneled vnto him	bowed themselves
33. 7 (2 times)		
21. 1	dealt	did
21. 26		hath done
— obaysaunce 33. 6		bowed themselves
39. 19	hath done	did
—, he 39. 22	might be done by him	he did
— commaundment 50. 16	let . . . saye	did command
See did		
dydest 20. 6	dyddest	didst
40. 13	*omit*	*omit*
See didest		
dye 3. 3 (8 times)		die
—, shalt 2. 17 (2 times)		
—, shall 3. 4		
—, am at the poynt to 25. 32	must dye neuer-thelesse	
—, let . . . 31. 32		let . . . not liue
—, wolde 33. 13		will die
—, must 35. 18		died
42. 20	shall dye	shall die
—, will 44. 31	„ „	
—, am content to 46. 30		let me die

	C	A
dye, wherfore suffrest ... vs to 47. 15		why should we die
47. 19	to dye	shall die
—, must 47. 29	shulde dye	must die
See die		
dyed 5. 5 (23 times)		died
—, mighte haue 26. 9		die
35. 19	died	died
—, shulde haue 38. 11	might dye	die
49. 33	died	yeelded vp the ghost
dygged 26. 15 (5times)		digged
—, haue 21. 30		haue digged
26. 18	had dygged	had .,
—, had 26. 32	„ digged	„ „
See digged		
dymme 27. 1		dimme
48. 10	heuy	„
dyne, shall 43. 16		shall dine
—, shulde 43. 25		shulde eate bread
dypped 27. 31		dipped
dyuerse 30. 32	partye	*omit*
— coloures, partie and of 30. 35	speckled and partye coloured	ring straked and spotted
eare, came to Israels	came to Israels eares	Israel heard
eares 20. 8 (11 times)		
earende 24. 33	earande	errand
early 19. 27 (4 times)		earely
19. 2 (2 times)	by tymes	„
earynge 24. 22		eare-ring
24. 47	earinge	earering
45. 6	plowinge	earing
earynges 24. 30		eare-ring
35. 4		eare-rings
east 4. 16 (8 times)		

	C	A
easte 2. 14 (2 times)	east	east
eastward 13. 14	eastwarde	
eat, let 27. 4	may eate	may eate
eate 3. 22 (3 times)		
—, shall 3. 1 (2 times)		
—, shuldest 3. 11		
—, shalt 3. 14 (3 times)		
—, will 24. 33		
—, may 27. 7		
—, to 28. 20 (2 times)		
—, for to 1. 30	to eate	for food
—, to 2. 9		„ „
—, se . . . 2. 16	shalt eate	mayest eate
—, se . . . 2. 17	„ „	shalt „
—, may 3. 2	eate	shal „
—, se . . . 3. 3	„	„
—, shulde 3. 5	„	
— of, to 3. 6		for food
—, se . . . 3. 17	shalt eate	shalt eate
—, se . . . 9. 4	eate	shall „
—, to 24. 33	*omit*	to eate
—, dyd 25. 28	ate	did eate
—, shal 27. 10	maye eate	may eate
—, let 27. 25	to eate	will eate
27. 31		eat
—, to 37. 25		to eat
—, may 43. 32	darre eate	might eate
—, shulde 47. 22		did eate
—, to 47. 24	*omit*	for food
eaten, hast 3. 11		
(2 times)		
—, haue 27. 33		
(2 times)		
—, had 41. 21		
(2 times)		
—, may be 6. 21		is eaten
—, haue 14. 24	haue spent	

	C	A
eaten vp, hath euen 31. 15	spent vp	hath quite deuoured
—, had 43. 2	† were spent	
eatest 2. 17		
Ebal 36. 23		
Eber 10. 21 (5 times)		
11. 15	*omit*	
Ebron 13. 18		Hebron
23. 19	Hebron	„
ech 40. 5	euery	each
eche 40. 5 (2 times)	„	each
edder 49. 14		adder
Eden 2. 8 (6 times)		
Eder 35. 21		Edar
edge 34. 26		
Edom 25. 30 (5 times)		
36. 16	*omit*	
36. 17	Edomites	
36. 21	Idumea	
36. 31	Edumea	
Edomea 36. 32	„	Edom
Edomytes 36. 9 (2 times)	Edomites	Edomites
Egipte 12. 10 (65 times)		Egypt
40. 5 (4 times)	*omit*	Egypt
41. 55	the Egipcians	the Egyptians
—, of 47. 26	Egipcians	of Egypt
See Egypte		
Egiptian 16. 1 (5 times)	Egipcian	Egyptian
—, of 39. 2	Egipcians	of Egyptian
Egiptians 12. 12 (11 times)	Egipcians	Egyptians
See Egyptians		
Egypte 15.18 (7 times)	Egipte	Egypt
See Egipte		

	C	A
Egyptians 43. 32	Egipcians	Egyptians
See Egiptians		
Ehi Ros Mupim 46. 21	Ehi, Ros, Mupim	Ehi and Rosh, Muppim
Ela 36. 41		Elah
Elam 10. 32 (3 times)		
Elbethel 35. 7	Bethel	El-Bethel
Elda 25. 4	Eldaa	Eldaah
elder 19. 31 (4 times)		first borne
elder 48. 14	firstborne	first borne
elders 50. 7 (2 times)		
49. 26	fore elders	progenitors
eldest 24. 2		
10. 15 (4 times)		first borne
10. 21 (2 times)	elder	elder
27. 19 (3 times)	firstborne	first borne
25. 3	greater	elder
27. 1	greater	
27. 15	elder	
29. 16		elder
38. 7	*omit*	
44. 12	greatest	
48. 18	firstborne	
49. 3	first	first borne
Eleasar 15. 2		Eliezer
Eliphas 36. 4 (5 times)		Eliphaz
36. 12 (2 times)	Elyphas	,,
Elisa 10. 4		Elishah
Ellasar 14. 1 (2 times)		
ells 30. 1		
See els		
Elou 26. 34 (3 times)		
els 42. 16		
See ells		
embawme, to 50. 2		to imbalme
embawmed 50. 2		imbalmed
(2 times)		

	C	A
embawminge 50. 3	embawming	are imbalmed
embraced 29. 13		
48. 10		imbraced
Emori 10. 46		Emorite
emptie 31. 42 (2 times)	emptye	emptie
1. 2		without forme
41. 27	thynne	emptie
emptied 42. 35	opened	
Emyms 14. 5	Emim	Emims
Enaim 38. 14 (2 times)	*omit*	*omit*
Enanum 10. 13	Enamim	Anamim
encrease, will 3. 16	will increase	will multiply
9. 7	increase	be fruitfull
—, will 16. 10		will multiply
17. 20	will increase	make fruitfull
47. 24	corne	increase
See increase		
encreased, was 6. 5	was increased	was great
—, are 26. 22	letten vs growe	shall be fruitfull
—, may be 30. 3	may be increased	may haue children
—, is 30. 30	is growne	is increased
See increased		
end 6. 13 (3 times)		
41. 1	*omit*	
ende 8. 3 (2 times)	„	end
—, an 28. 18	„	*omit*
(2 times)		
— of speakynge, had	had spoken	had done speaking
made an 24. 45		
—, vp an 28. 22	*omit*	*omit*
ended 2. 2		
—, were 41. 53		
—, was 47. 18		
—, were 50. 4		were past
endewed 30. 20		endued
endure, be able to	can go	
33. 14		

	C	A
endureth 8. 22		remaineth
enhabiters 50. 11	people	inhabitants
enheritaunce 31. 14	inheritaunce	inheritance
enheritaunces 48. 6	,,	,,
enimies 14. 20	enemies	enemies
(2 times)		
24. 60	enemies	those which hate them
Enos 4. 26 (3 times)		
5. 7 (3 times)	*omit*	
ensample of these, at the 48. 20	in ye	in thee
enteringe of, at the 3. 24	before	at the East of
See entrynge		
entre, for to 12. 11		to enter
entreate evell 15. 13	intreate euell	afflict
entreated 12. 16	was intreated	entreated
entred 31. 3 (2 times)	wente in to	
19. 3	turned in	
19. 23	came in to	
39. 11	wente in to	went in to
entrynge 38. 14	*omit*	*omit*
See enteringe		
Ephraim 41. 52 (7 times)		
—, of 48. 17	Ephraims	
Ephraims 48. 14	of Ephraim	
48. 17	Ephraims	
50. 23	Ephrayms	
Ephrat 48. 7	Ephrath	Ephrath
48. 7	Eprath	Ephrath
Ephrath 35. 16 (2 times)		
Ephron 23. 8 (9 times)		
—, of 23. 17		

	C	A
Er 38. 3 (4 times)	he	
38. 7		
Erech 10. 10		
Eri 46. 16	earth	
erth 1. 1 (93 times)	earth	earth
2. 7 (12 times)	earth	ground
3. 19 (2 times)	londes	dust
11. 4 (3 times)	londe	earth
4. 14	*omit*	,,
9. 3	worlde	*omit*
10. 25	*omit*	earth
26. 4	londe	,,
26. 22	earth	land
erthe 2. 4	,,	earth
5. 29		ground
Esau 25. 25 (52 times)	Esaus	
—, of 27. 15 (3 times)	him	
— 25. 34	*omit*	
27. 5	he	
27. 38	his elder sonne	
27. 42	he	
36. 19		who
Esaus 28. 5 (7 times)	of Esau	
27. 23 (3 times)		
escaped, had 14. 13	Escol	
Eschol 14. 3	,,	Eshcol
Escholl 14. 24		,,
Eseck 26. 20.	Ezer	Esek
Eser 36. 21	both	Ezer
ether 2. 25 (2 times)	euery man	both
34. 25 (2 times)	nether	each man
24. 50	*omit*	*omit*
41. 44	either	,,
44. 8		,,
evelfauored 41. 3		ill fauored
euell 2. 9 (11 times)		euill
41. 20 (3 times)		ill

ERRATA   1. 1 and 11. 4 to 34 C. *drop one space.*

	C	A
euell 4. 7		not well
8. 21		euil
—, entreate 15. 13		afflict
—, to do 31. 29		hurt
— fauordnesse 41. 19	*omit*	badnes
See evill		
evyll		
even 9. 3 (3 times)		
1. 30 (27 times)	*omit*	*omit*
2. 7 (10 times)		,,
13. 3 (3 times)	*omit*	
19. 1 (2 times)	euenynge	
29. 23 (2 times)		euening
euen so 18. 5 (2 times)		*omit*
— as 40. 22 (2 times)	like as	,,
2. 17	† loke	in
10. 19	and	
17. 23		in
18. 32	yet	this
23. 16	namely	
42. 28	lo	
47. 18	onely	
49. 26	*omit*	aboue
eventyde 8. 11		euening
24. 63		euentide
evenynge 1. 5 (6 times)		evening
ever 3. 22	for euer	for euer
8. 7	*omit*	*omit*
everlastinge 17. 13		euerlasting
(3 times)		
everlastynge 9. 16		euerlasting
17. 7 (3 times)	euerlastinge	,,
euery 1. 20 (15 times)		
1. 11 (3 times)		*omit*
7. 2 (2 times)	*omit*	
— thynge, of 6. 19	even	of every sort
7. 16	*omit*	all

	C	A
euery pece 15. 10	the one part	each peece
— drooue, betwyxte	betwixte one	betwixte droue
32. 16	flocke after the	and droue
	other	
Euila 25. 18	Heuila	Hauilah
evill 41. 4	euell	ill
evyll 37. 2	,,	euill
41. 21	,,	ill
See euell		
Euphrates 2. 13		
(2 times)		
exceading 41. 31	very	very
exceadinge 26. 13		,,
17. 13	very	,,
50. 10	*omit*	,,
exceadingly 4. 5	exceadinge	,,
7. 18	sore	greatly
47. 27		exceedingly
exceadynge 1. 31	exceedinge	very
15. 1	exceadinge	exceeding
50. 9	,,	very
exceadyngly 13. 13	exceadingly	exceedingly
excedingly 7. 19	*omit*	,,
excedynge 18. 20	exceadinge	very
30. 43	,,	exceedingly
excedyngly 17. 2	exceadyngly	,,
17. 6	exceadingly	exceeding
17. 20	,,	exceedingly
19. 3	sore	greatly
excepte 32. 26		except
(5 times)		
31. 42	yf	except
43. 10 (2 times)	yf not	,,
excuse, and an 20. 16	and a sure excuse	thus shee was
		reproued
44. 16	excuse	*omit*
exercyse on 4. 21	occupied	handle

	C	A
eye, to the 26. 7	to loke vnto	to looke vpon
eye, vn to the 49. 22	to loke vpon	*omit*
eyed 29. 17		
eyes 3. 5 (27 times)		
—, in youre 34. 11	with you	
43. 9		*omit*
— apon him, maye	will se him	
sett myne 44. 21		
—, cruel things in	eny wrath	*omit*
youre 45. 5		
47. 19	*omit*	
50. 4	sight	
eyght hundred 5. 4	eight hundreth	eight hundred
Ezbon 46. 27		
Ezer 36. 27 (2 times)		
face 3. 19 (20 times)		
2. 6 (3 times)	*omit*	
2. 7		nostrils
3. 8	presence	presence
4. 16		,,
24. 51	*omit*	thee
—, sett his 31. 21	went straight	
faces 9. 23		
30. 40	*omit*	
facion 6. 15	fashion	fashion
faintie 25. 29	weery	faint
See fayntie		
fall 45. 24		
19. 19	might fall	take
37. 10		to bow down our-selves
— vpon me 42. 36	goeth all ouer me	are against me
—, shall 49. 17	maye fall	
49. 26	shal light	shall bee
fallen, were 8. 8		were abated
fameshment 47. 4	derth	famine

	C	A
fameshyd, were 47. 13	were fameshed	fainted
fare, maye 12. 13		it may be wel
fared 16. 6	dealt	dealt
farr, not 18. 2	ouer agaynst	by
farre 18. 25 (2 times)		
See ferre		
farthermore 9. 8		and
faste by 16. 12	ouer agaynst	in the presence of
fast 49. 24		in strength
father 2.24 (132 times)		
—, of 20. 12 (2 times)	fathers	
—, which is the 19. 37 (2 times)	of whom come	the same is the father
27. 19 (2 times)	*omit*	
44. 22 (2 times)	him	
4. 22	worker	instructor
— of 22. 21	of whom came	
31. 16	fathers	
— of 36. 9	of whom are come	
47. 6	them	
48. 16	fathers	fathers
— in lawe 38. 13 (2 times)		father in law
fathers 9.23 (32 times)		
9. 22 (2 times)		of . . . father
31. 53 (2 times)		father
27. 41	father	
28. 21	,,	,,
—, lande of 31. 3	fatherlande	of . . . fathers
31. 9		
fatnesse 27. 28		
fatt 4. 4 (2 times)		fat
4. 3 (4 times)	fat	,,
fauoure 18.3 (3 times)		fauour
50. 4		grace
fauored 29. 17 (7 times)	fauoured	fauoured

	C	A
fauored, well 41. 18	goodly	fauoured
fouordnesse, euell 41. 19	*omit*	badnes
fawte 41. 9		faults
fayle to, will not 50. 25	*omit*	will surely
fayled 42. 28 (2 times)		failed
fayntie 25. 30		faint
See faintie		
fayre 12. 11 (2 times)		faire
12. 14	faire	,,
33. 14		*omit*
feade shepe, that 46. 34	kepers of catell	shepheard
feaders of shepe 47. 8	kepers of catell	shepheards
feare 9. 2 (9 times)		
15. 12		horrour
— of, for 27. 46	because of	because of
35. 5		terrour
— not 46. 3	be not afrayed	
— not 50. 21	be not ye now afrayed	
feared 19. 30 (2 times)	was afrayed	
31. 53	by the feare of	by the feare of
— lest 38. 11	thought	said
fearest 22. 12		
feareth 31. 42	the feare of	the feare of
fearfull 38. 17		dreadful
fearsnes 27. 44	furiousnes	furie
fearsness 49. 7	indignacion	wrath
feast 21. 8 (4 times)		
29. 22	mariage	
fed 47. 17		
36. 17	kepte	
fedd 41. 2 (2 times)	wente fedinge	fed
—, are 47. 12	*omit*	*omit*
—, hath 48. 15		fedde
fede 29. 7		feed

	C	A
fede 30. 31	wyll fede	feed
See feade		
federed 1. 21	feth'ered	winged
feders 7. 14	fethers	*omit*
feld 3. 14 (7 times)	felde	field
— brede 35. 16	felde brode	litle way
47. 30	londe	field
felde 2. 5 (21 times)		,,
2. 20 (3 times)		fielde
2. 5	earth	field
32. 3		country
49. 30	*omit*	field
50. 10	playne	threshing floore
50. 11	,,	floore
feldes 4. 8 (6 times)	felde	field
34. 28	londe	
— brede 48. 7		little way
fele, shal 27. 12	might fele	will feele
—, let 27. 21	may ,,	may ,,
fell 13. 7 (9 times)		
26. 1 (2 ,,)	came	was
18. 2 (2 ,,)	bowed him selfe	bowed himselfe
--- seke 25. 8 (2 times)	fell sicke	gaue vp the ghost
— vppon 4. 8	rose agaynst	rose vp against
13. 7		was
14. 15		*omit*
— on 15. 11	fell vpon	came downe vpon
26. 1	was	was
42. 8		bowed downe themselues
43. 28		made obeisance
48. 12		bowed himselfe with his face to the earth
felle seke 35. 29	fell sicke	gaue vp the ghost
felowe 24. 21 (2 times)	man	man
felt 27. 22		

	C	A
female 1. 27 (7 times)		
ferre 44. 4	farre	farre
See farr		
farre		
fetch 27. 13 (2 times)		
See fett		
fette		
fete 18. 4 (3 times)		feete
24. 32		feet
24. 32	*omit*	,,
29. 1		*omit*
fett, let . . . be 18. 4	shalbe brought	let . . . be fetched
18. 5	fet	fetch
18. 7	,,	fetcht
—, to 24. 20	to drawe	to draw
27. 14	fetched	fetched
—, went and 27. 15	toke	toke
— 27. 45	cause the be fetched	fetch
—, to 28. 6	that he might take	to take
fette, lette . . . 42. 16	to fetch	let . . . fetch
See fetch		
finde 33. 15 (2 times)	fynde	finde
—, may 32. 5	might fynde	may find
—, to 33. 8	,, ,,	,, ,,
—, cannot 38. 22	haue not founde	cannot finde
—, coudest 38. 23	hast ,, ,,	hast not found
—, shall 41. 38	myght fynde	can find
47. 25	fynde	find
fingre 41. 42	hande	hand
See fyngre		
finysh 6. 16	*omit*	finish
firmament 1. 14		
See fyrmament		
first 25. 25 (7 times)		
26. 1	other	
30. 41		stronger

	C	A
first 30. 42	firstlinges	stronger
See fyrst		
flat 43. 26	*omit*	*omit*
flatt 24. 52	flat	,,
42. 6	*omit*	,,
fled 14. 10 (6 times)		
—, was 31.22 (2 times)	fled	
14. 10	were put to flight	
fleddest 35. 1		
flee, for to 1. 20	for to flye	that may flie
16. 8	fle	
—, to 19. 20	maye flee	
27. 43	flye	
flesh 8. 21 (28 times)		
fleshed 41. 2 (4 times)		
flocke 27. 9 (4 ,,)		
flockes 29. 2 (2 ,,)		
29. 2 (3 times)		flocks
30. 40	flocke	flocke
30. 40	,,	cattell
florishing 49. 22	florishinge	fruitfull
florishynge 49. 22	fruteful	,,
floud 6. 17 (8 times)	floude	flood
floude 9. 28 (4 ,,)	,,	,,
flyght, shall turne	shall hurte them	shall ouercome at
them to 49. 19	in the hele	the last
fode 41. 48	foode	foode
44. 25	,,	food
See food		
foode		
folde, vii. 4. 15	seuenfolde	seuen fold
fole, was a 31. 28	hast done foolishly	hast done foolishly
fole 49. 11	foale	foale
foles 32. 15	foales	foales
folie 34. 7	foly	folly
folke 33. 15	people	folke
47. 28	,,	people

	C	A
folowe, will 24. 39		will followe
—, durst not 35. 5	folowed not	did not pursue
44. 4		follow
folowed 14. 14		pursued
(3 times)		
foloweddest 31. 36	are so whote vpon	,,
food 43. 4 (2 times)	foode	food
43. 2	,,	foode
foode 42. 33		
41. 35 (4 times)		food
41. 35	sustenaunce	,,
41. 54		bread
42. 19		corne
foorde 32. 22		foord
for 1. 29 (189 times)		
1. 20 (6 ,,)		*omit*
1. 30	to	to
1. 30 (19 times)	*omit*	
2. 3	because that	because that
3. 6 (14 times)	,,	*omit*
6. 17 (7 ,,)		and
10. 25 (4 ,,)	because	
18. 28	,, of	
— feare of 27. 46	,, ,,	because of
— indede 28. 19	but afore	but
—, make provysion	loke to	shall prouide for
30. 30		
30. 30		since
30. 33	with	
31. 10		and it came to
		passe
— to goo 31. 18	that he might	
	come	
31. 32	but	
37. 22	*omit*	that
38. 23		behold
33. 11 (2 times)		because

	C	A
for to 38. 16	that thou mayest	that thou mayest
43. 30 (2 times)		where
43. 32 (2 „)	vnto	
44. 33	in steade of	in stead of
— this cause 2. 24	*omit*	therefore
4. 24	„	if
4. 25		in stead of
6. 4		and also
— perauenture 11. 4	afore	lest
19. 19	*omit*	and
— the which 19. 21	wherof	
21. 6		so that
21. 25		because of
— as soone as 24. 30	by the reason that	*omit*
40. 13	and	yet
40. 15		for indeed
40. 19	and after	yet
41. 21	and	but
— as moch as 41. 39	for so moch as	forasmuch as
42. 4		but
43. 32	to	
47. 18	vnto	*omit*
49. 1	*omit*	vnto
50. 17	that	
forbidden, was 8. 2	was forbydden	was restrained
forbyd, shall 23. 6		shall withhold
forbydd, 44. 7 (2 times)	forbyd	forbid
forced 34. 2		defiled
foreskynne 17. 11		foreskinne
(4 times)		
17. 14	foreskinne	„
for euer 9. 12	for euermore	for perpetuall generations
for ever 13. 15		
43. 9	my life longe	
forgeten, shalbe 41. 30	shalbe forgotten	shall be forgotten
forgett 27. 45 (2 times)	forget	forget

	C	A
forgeue 50. 17		forgive
(2 times)		
forgeven, may be 4. 14		can beare
formed, had 2. 8	had made	
formest 32. 17	first	formost
fornace 19. 28		furnace
See furnesse		
forth 8. 7 (7 times)		
8. 8 (5 times)		foorth
8. 12 (3 „)	*omit*	*omit*
3. 22	„	foorth
—, and proceded 4. 2		againe
19. 10	out	forth
forth 22. 10	„	foorth
—, sent 28. 5	let departe	sent away
33. 6		neere
40. 10	*omit*	
49. 22	† vpon	† ouer
forties 18. 29	fourtyes	fourties
fortune, myght 50. 15	might happly	will peraduenture
fortuned 4. 3 (4 times)		came to passe
41. 11	*omit*	„ „ „
foryner 23. 4	indweller	soiouner
fote 8. 9	fete	foote
41. 44		„
foule 8. 17 (2 times)		fowle
6. 7		foules
16. 6	hardly	hardly
foules 1. 20 (9 times)		foule
8. 19 (3 times)		fowle
15. 11		fowles
found 6. 8	founde	
—, is 2. 12	is founde	is
—, is 44. 10	shall be founde	is found
founde 11. 2 (10 times)		found
—, haue 18. 3 (5 „)		
—, hast 31. 27		hast found

	C	A
foundé, was 44. 12		was found
(2 times)		
—, is 44. 16 (2 times)		is ,,
— out, hath 44. 16		hath ,, out
—, is 2. 20	was founde	was ,,
—, be 18. 29	might be founde	shall be found
4. 15		finding
26. 12		receiued
37. 29		*omit*
—, be 44. 9	shall be founde	be found
See fownde		
fourth 15. 16		
fownde, hath 19. 19	hath founde	hath found
—, hast 29. 20		
31. 33 (3 times)	founde	found
—, haue 30. 27	can fynde	haue found
See found		
founde		
frely 33. 11	*omit*	graciously
34. 12	hardely	neuer so much
frende 26. 26		friends
38. 12	shepherde	friend
from 1. 4 (95 times)		
2. 8 (2 times)	towarde	*omit*
6. 17 (4 ,,)	*omit*	
13. 9 (7 times)	fro	
22. 11 (3 ,,)		out of
7. 7	for	because of
7. 17	ouer	aboue
8. 12	*omit*	*omit*
8. 21		,,
— whence 10. 14		out of whome
—, out 19. 39	out of	,, ,,
—, kepte 22. 12	spared	
33. 18	agayne out of	
35. 16		to come to
—, put 38. 19	layed of	

	C	A
from 45. 25.	out of	̦out of
48. 7	,, ,,	
from of 4. 14	from out of	from
6. 7	from	,,
7. 4	,, of	,, off
7. 17	ouer	aboue
8. 3	awaye from	from off
8. 8	vpon	,, ,,
24. 46	from	,,
27. 40	,,	,, ,,
frute 1. 11 (5 times)		fruit
3. 2 (2 times)		fruite
— in them, that haue	frutefull	in the which is the
1. 29		fruit of a tree
— can lyne, as soon	yf I lyne	accórding to the
as the 18. 10		time of life
— can haue lyfe	,, ., ,,	according to the
18. 14		time of life
frutefull 1. 11		yeelding fruit
—, made her 29. 31		opened her wombe
(2 times)		
frutes 43. 11		fruits
full 15. 16 (3 times)		
— 6. 11 (2 ,,)		filled
— of, was 14. 10	had many	
— of dayes, was	had lyued ynough	
35. 29		
43. 21		ful
—, shall be 48. 19		shall become a
		multitude
furnesse 15. 17	fornace	furnace
See fornace		
further 16. 11		*omit*
fyfte 41. 34 (3 times)	fifth	fift
fyfth 1. 23	,,	,,
fyftye 7. 24	fiftie	fifty
fygge 3. 7		figge

	C	A
fyghte, sette to 14. 8	prepared to fight	ioyned battell
fyll 1. 22 (2 times)		fill
1. 28 (2 „)		replenish
—, to 42. 25		to fill
fylled 21. 19 (3 times)		filled
2. 21		closed
fynde, coude 8. 9		found
fyndest 31. 32		findest
fyndeth 4. 14		findeth
fyne 18. 6		fine
fyngre 41. 42	hande	hand
See fingre		
fynished 2. 1		finished
fyre 19. 24 (3 times)		fire
—, with		thorowly
— brande 15. 17		burning lampe
fyrmament 1. 6	firmament	firmament
See firmament		
fyrst 1. 5 (4 times)	first	first
— tyme 13. 3	„	beginning
27. 36	*omit*	*omit*
See first		
fyrstlynges 4. 4	firstlings	firstlings
fysh 1. 26		fish
1. 28	fish	„
fyshes 9. 2		fishes
fyue 43. 34 (3 times)		fiue
Gad 30. 11 (4 times)		
Gaetham 36. 11		Gatam
36. 16	Gaethan	„
Gaham 22. 24	Sahan	
garden 2. 8 (14 times)		
garment 39. 12		
(5 times)		
49. 11		garments
garmentes 3. 21		coates

	C	A
garmentes 35. 2	clothes	garments
38. 14		,,
gate 19. 1 (4 times)		
gates 23. 10 (2 times)		
22. 17 (2 times)		gate
34. 24	gate	,,
gather 31. 46 (2 times)		
—, shall 34. 30	gather	
— ... together 49. 2	come together	
gathered 41. 48		
—, shulde be 29. 7	to dryue in	
gatheringe 1. 10		gathering
gatt 38. 1	gat	turned in to
38. 19	,,	arose
48. 22	,,	tooke
gaue 2. 20 (30 times)		
— names 26. 18	called	called
— wyne 19. 33		made ... drinke
(2 times)		
— charge 12. 20		commanded
— ... drynke 24. 46		made ... drinke
26. 18	had named	called
— charge 28. 6	charged	
38. 6		tooke
40. 4	put vnto	*omit*
45. 21	*omit*	
gavest 8. 12		
gay 37. 23	partye coloured	of many colours
37. 32	partie ,,	,, ,, ,,
gedder, all to 18. 21	all together	altogether
See gether		
generacion 5. 1		generations
7. 1	tyme	generation
generation 15. 16	generacion	,,
(2 times)		
generations 2. 4	generacions	generations
(3 times)		

	C	A
generations 6. 9	generacion	generations
(7 times)		
11. 27	generations	,,
12. 3	generacions	families
17. 12	posterities	generations
gentylls 10. 5	Heithen	Gentiles
Gera 46. 21		
Gerar 20. 2 (6 times)		
Gerara 10. 19	Gerar	Gerar
Gergesites 15. 21		Girgashites
Gerson 46. 11		Gershon
get 19. 14 (2 times)		
22. 2 (2 times)	go	get
42. 33	,,	be gone
gete 42. 2	,,	get
See gett		
getest 48. 6	begettest	begettest
gether 1. 9	gather	be gathered
Gether 10. 23		
gether, to 22. 19	together	together
See gedder		
gett 12. 1	get	get
27. 3 (5 times)	,,	goe
27. 9	go	,,
42. 2 (2 times)	,,	get
26. 16	departe	goe
— the mastrye 27. 40	put of his yock	haue dominion
See get		
gete		
geue 23. 4 (20 times)		giue
—, wyll 12. 7		will giue
(19 times)		
—, wilt 15. 2		
—, to 15. 7		
—, shall 28. 31		
(4 times)		
—, shalt 30. 31		

	C	A
geue, shall 4. 12		shall yeeld
(2 times)		
9. 3 (2 times)	haue geuen	haue giuen
— ... wyne 19. 32		make ... drinke
(2 times)		
—, wyll		*omit*
—, „ 15. 18		haue giuen
— to lust, shall 18. 12		shall haue pleasure
—, will 23. 13	geue	will giue
— dryncke 24. 45		let drinke
—, shalt 28. 22	geuest	
30. 24		shall adde
--, shulde 34. 14	to geue	to giue
34. 21	wyl geue	wil giue
—, wold 38. 9	shulde geue	should giue
38. 17		will giue
—, must 47. 26	to geue	should giue
See gyue		
geuen, haue 1. 29		haue giuen
(2 times)		
—, hast 15. 3		hast „
—, hath 24. 35		hath „
(5 times)		
—, hath 4. 25	hath apoynted	hath appointed
—, are 9. 2	be geuen	are deliuered
—, haue 16. 5	layde	haue giuen
—, shulde haue 24. 19	had geuen	had done giuing
—, shall be 29. 27	will geue	will giue
—, hath 30. 18	gaue	haue giuen
—, „ 33. 11		hath dealt with
go 19. 2 (2 times)		
—, will 18. 21		
(3 times)		
—, to 11. 31		to goe
—, shall 42. 38		
— in vnto 30. 3	lye with	goe in vnto

	C	A
go, for to 37. 14	to go	he came
44. 26	can go	will goe
See goo		
God 1. 1 (180 times)		
7. 9 (2 times)	LORDE	
12. 17 (3 times)	„	LORD
—, LORde the ever-		
lastynge 21. 33		
23. 6 (2 times)		*omit*
—, LORde thy 27. 20		
—, LORde 28. 13		
—, walked with 5. 22	led a godly con-	
	uersacion	
—, walked wyth 6. 9	led a godly life	
— most hygh, LORDE	LORDE the most	LORDE, the most
14. 22	high God	high God
—, LORde the 24. 42	LORDE thou	LORD God
— whom Isaac feareth	the feare of Isaac	the feare of Isaac
31. 42		
— of Israel, myghtie		El-Elohe-Israel
33. 20		
— of Jacob, myghtye	the mightie in	
49. 24	Jacob	
goddes 31. 30 (4 times)		gods
19. 7	*omit*	*omit*
godes 30. 12 (2 times)	Gods	Gods
28. 22	of God	„
godly lyfe, lyved a		walked with God
5. 24		
goeth 32. 20		
goinge and cominge	came agayne	went foorth to and
agayne 8. 7		fro
gold 2. 11 (5 times)	golde	
golde 24. 53		gold
44. 8		
golden 24. 22		
41. 42	of golde	golden

	C	A
Gomorra 10. 19		Gomorah
(2 times)		
14. 2 (7 times)		Gomorrah
Gomyr 10. 2 (2 times)	Gomer	Gomer
gone, was 27. 30		
(2 times)		
—, was 24. 63 (2 times)		went
— in vnto, had 6. 4	had lyen with	came in vnto
27. 5	wente	went
goo, shalt 3. 14	shalt go	shalt goe
—, to 12. 5 (3 times)	to go	
16. 2 (2 times)	go	go
—, wylt 16. 8		
—, „ 24. 58		
(4 times)		
—, will 22. 5		will goe
24. 51 (19 times)	go	goe
24. 56	maye departe	may goe
—, may 30. 26		
—, shall 37. 30	shal go	shall goe
—, to 47. 19 (2 times)	*omit*	*omit*
7. 1	go	come
—, shalt 15. 15	shalt departe	shalt goe
— by 18. 3	go by	passe away
18. 5	shall go	passe on
19. 34	mayest go	goe
—, shalt 24. 4	go	shalt go
24. 38	„	„ goe
24. 55	shall go	shall „
—, shulde 25. 22		be
—, to 18. 5	might go	*omit*
—, 31. 18	„ come	to goe
32. 16	go	passe
32. 17	thou dryuest	*omit*
33. 12	go on	
33. 14	„ „	passe
—, will 34. 17		will be gone

	C	A
goo, shall 42. 15	shall get	shall goe
—, let 44. 3		sent away
44. 17		get you vp
— from, coude 44. 22	can come from	can leaue
—, coude 44. 26	can go	can goe
—, can 44. 34	„ „	shall „
- - shuld 45. 1	to „	to „
47. 19	become	be
—, to 48. 7	*omit*	to come
—, let me 50. 5	wyl go	let me goe
See go		
good 1. 4 (28 times)		
— health, in 29. 6		well
(3 times)		
14. 12		goods
—, seemeth 19. 8	liketh you	is good in your eyes
28. 15		*omit*
— lucke 30. 11		a troupe commeth
—, made 31. 29	was fayne to paie	bare the losse
— case, in 40. 14	in prosperite	well
41. 35	plenteous	
— chere, be of 43. 23	be content	Peace be to you
45. 22	goodes	
goode 31. 29	good	good
46. 29	*omit*	
goodes 14. 11		goods
(5 times)		
12. 5	goodes	substance
31. 1	good	that which was of
34. 23		cattell
36. 6		beasts
45. 20		good
goodly 49. 20		
41. 5	good	good
27. 15	costly	
— person 39. 6	fayre of bewtye	

	C	A
goodly 41. 2		well fauoured
49. 22	*omit*	*omit*
goost 28. 15 (3 times)	goest	goest
goote 37. 31	goate	goats
See gotte		
gootes 30.35 (2 times)	goates	goates
32. 14 (2 times)	„	goats
30. 33	kyddes	goates
30. 35	*omit*	goats
Gosan 45.10 (9 times)	Gosen	Goshen
got 19. 27	gat	gate
39. 15	ranne	
See gott		
gotte		
goten, had 12. 5		
—, hath 31. 1		
—, haue 32. 10	am become	am become
goth 38. 13	goeth	goeth
33. 14	can go	„
gott 21. 21	toke	tooke
22. 3	gat	went
—, had 36. 6	had gotten	had got
39. 12	gat	got
39. 21	caused to fynde	gaue
gotte, haue 4. 23	haue gotten	*omit*
See got		
gotte 15. 9	goate	goat
See goote		
gotten, had 31. 18		
(2 times)		
4. 1	haue opteyned	
—, haue 32. 5	haue	
gouerner 42. 6	gouernoure	gouernour
45. 26	a lorde	„
goynge 37. 25	goinge	going
49. 4		*omit*
grace 6. 8 (8 times)		

	C	A
grace 32. 5 (2 times)	fauoure	
—, receaue me to 33. 10	be at one with me	thou wast pleased with me
grapes 40.10 (3 times)		
grasse 1. 11 (2 „)		
1. 30	*omit*	*omit*
graue 35. 20 (6 times)		
35. 20	grauestone	
grave, all that 4. 22	*omit*	artificer
gray 44. 29 (2 times)		
42. 38	graye	
great 1. 16 (18 times)	greate	
—, make 19. 19	make greate	hast magnified
21. 16	*omit*	good
— whyle to nyghte 29. 7	yet hye day	yet high day
great 38. 24	*omit*	*omit*
41. 31		grieuous
— nombre 48. 4	multitude	multitude
greate 1.21 (11 times)		great
— deale, a 26. 16	farre	*omit*
50. 11		grieuous
See grete		
greater 1. 16 (3 times)		
See greatter		
greatly 27. 33	exceadingly	very exceedingly
— and bitterly 27. 34	loude	exceeding bitter
greatlye 32. 7	sore	greatly
greatter 39. 9	so greate	
See greater		
greavous 21. 11	sore	grieuous
— vnto, be 21. 12	displease	be grieuous in
See grevous		
grene 9. 3 (2 times)		greene
grete 7. 11 (4 times)	greate	great
greued 34. 7		grieued
—, be 45. 5	vexe	be grieued

	C	A
grevous 18. 20		grieuous
grewe 19.25 (5 times)	grew	grew
2. 10	*omit*	became
25. 27	wer growne	grew
41. 5		came vp
41. 48		was
ground 44. 14	grounde	
2. 6	earth	
33. 19	londe	a field
grounde 4.12 (4 times)		ground
37. 10 (4 times)		earth
38. 10	earth	ground
43. 28	*omit*	*omit*
See grownde		
growe 1. 22 (3 times)		be fruitfull
23. 17	*omit*	were
growe into 24. 60		be the mother of
35. 11	be frutefull	be fruitfull
—, to 41. 52		to be fruitfull
48. 4		fruitfull
—, maye 48. 16	maye growe	let . . . grow
groweth 33. 3	is founde	is
grownde 33. 3	grounde	ground
See ground		
grounde		
growne, be 38. 11		be growen
--, was 38. 14		was ,,
Guni 46. 24		
gutters 30. 41	drynkinge troughes	
39. 38	*omit*	
gyftes 34. 12	gift	gift
Gylead 31.47 (2 times)	Gilead	Gileed
gyue, wyll 13. 15	wyll geue	will giue
14. 21	geue	giue
—, wylt 38. 16	wylt geue	wilt giue
See geue		

	C	A
habitations 36. 43	*omit*	
had 11. 30 (22 times)		
7. 22 (4 times)		was
24. 2 (3 „)	*omit*	
7. 14		*omit*
7. 15	was	is
— rule 24. 2		ruled
— with him 24. 10		were in his hand
— envy 26. 14		enuied
27. 15		were
31. 21	was his	
— a dreame, haue	had another	haue dreamed
37. 9	dreame	
39. 4	his goodes	
40. 16	bare	
Hadad 36. 35		
(2 times)		
36. 39		Hadar
Hadar 25. 15		
haddest 30. 30		hadst
Hadoram 10. 27		
Hagar 16. 1 (11 times)	Agar	
21. 14	Agars	
Haggi 46. 16		
halfe 24. 22	half	
halted 32. 31		
Ham 5. 32 (10 times)		
hamati 10. 18		Hamathite
Hamul 46. 12		
hand 3. 20 (5 times)	hande	
hande 9. 5 (41 „)		hand
14. 22 (2 „)	honde	„
39. 22 (2 „)	handes	„
16. 6	auctorite	„
—, at 19. 15		here
27. 20		*omit*
—, at 27. 41	shortly	at hand

	C	A
hande, haue goten the vpper 30. 8		haue preuailed
—, vnder myne 33. 18	by me	with mee
38. 20	*omit*	hand
—, apon my 48. 7	by me	by me
handes 24. 22		
20. 5 (13 times)		hands
9. 2 (7 „)		hand
19. 16 (3 „)	hande	„
43. 12 (2 „)	*omit*	„
5. 29	hondes	hands
16. 9	hande	„
19. 10	hondes	hand
31. 42	*omit*	hands
43. 22	„	handes
See hondes		
handmayde 29. 29	mayden	hand mayd
(2 times)		
16. 1		handmaide
25. 12	mayde	hand mayd
hange, shall 40. 19		
40. 22		
hanged, was 41. 13		hanged
hangeth 44. 30		is bound vp
Hanoch 25. 4 (2 times)		
happen, myght 42. 4	might happen	befall
—, myght 42. 38	shulde „	„
44. 29		„
—, shall 49. 1		shall befall
happened 26. 8	*omit*	came to passe
—, had 42. 29		befell
happy 30. 13	well	
Haran 11. 26 (11 times)		
Harans 11. 31		of Haran
hard 3. 10 (3 times)	herde	heard
18. 14	harde	
See heard		

	C	A
harken 23. 15	heare	hearken
—, will 34. 17	wyll herken	will hearken
See herken		
harkened 33. 16	herkened	hearkened
(3 times)		
26. 5	was obedient	obeyed
harme 31. 52		
harmlesse 44. 10		blamelesse
harnessed 14. 14		armed
harpe 4. 21	harpes	
harpes 31. 27	„	harpe
harte 17. 17 (2 times)	hert	heart
27. 41	herte	„
34. 3	hert	soule
See hert		
herte		
hartes 42. 28	hertes	heart
harts 18. 5	„	hearts
harvest 8. 22		
See hervest		
hasell 30. 37		hasel
Haso 22. 22		Hazo
hast 19. 12 (4 times)		
43. 30 (3 „)	haist	haste
—, thou 20. 7	is thine	are thine
—, „ 33. 5	are with the	are with thee
—, „ 45. 11	is thyne	thou hast
haste 19. 22	haist	
—, made 24. 46	immediately	
41. 14	*omit*	hastily
hasted 24. 18	haistely	
hastely 24. 20	made haist	hasted
hatches 8. 13		couering
hate 26. 27		
—, to 50. 15	haue indignacion	hate
hated 37. 5 (3 times)		

	C	A
hated 27. 41	bare euell wyll vnto	
37. 4	had euell wyll at	
37. 11	had envie at	enuied
hath 23. 9 (3 times)		
17. 14	*omit*	*omit*
39. 8 (2 times)	is	is
hath 15. 2		*omit*
hatred 3. 15	enemyte	enmitie
haue 1. 28 (12 times)		
17. 14 (2 „)	*omit*	*omit*
—, shall 18. 10 (2 times)		
31. 14 (3 times)		is
—, shalt 35. 17		
1. 20		hath
—, may 1. 26		haue
1. 29	beare	is
—, may 1. 30	*omit*	haue giuen
—, shall 9. 6	shall be	shall be
— lyfe, as soon as the frute can 18. 14	this tyme	at the tyme appointed
19. 12	hast	hast
—, shalt 27. 39		shall be
— to lyue, what lust shuld I 27. 46	what shal life profit me	what good shall my life doe me
33. 13		*omit*
34. 10		get
47. 18	† is spent	† is spent
hauen 49. 13		
havock, made 34. 29	spoyled	spoiled
havynge 1. 11		is
1. 12		was
— lyfe 9. 3	hath life	liueth
Hazezon Thamar 14. 7	Hazezon Thamar	Hazezon-tamar
head 47. 31 (7 times)	heade	
40. 20	*omit*	

	C	A
head 42. 38	hayre	haires
heade 40. 16 (3 times)		head
28. 11 (2 times)		† pillowes
40. 13 (2 „)	*omit*	head
— cyte 23. 2	head cite	Kiriath-arba
healed 20. 17		
health 43. 28		
—, in good 29. 6		well
(2 times)		
heape 31. 46 (6 times)		
31. 52	*omit*	
hearde, haue 42. 2	heare	
See herd		
herde		
heare 4. 23 (6 times)		
21. 1	here	here
—, wold 42. 21		
(2 times)		
27. 8 (2 times)		obey
21. 6	heareth	
21. 12	folowe	hearken
23. 13	might heare	
27. 13	folowe	obey
hearest 41. 15		*omit*
heate 18. 1		heat
See hete		
heaven 1. 1 (29 times)		
2. 1 (3 times)		heauens
Heber 46. 17		
Hebrewe 39. 14	Hebrue	Hebrew
See Hebrue		
Hebron 23. 2 (3 times)		
Hebrue 41. 12	Hebrue	Hebrew
14. 13	Aleaunt	„
See Hebrewe		
Hebrues 40. 15		Hebrewes
39. 17	Hebrue	Hebrew

	C	A
Hebrues 43. 32	Ebrues	Hebrewes
hede, take 31. 24	bewarre	
(2 times)		
helde 24. 21 (2 times)		
hele 3. 15 (2 „)		heele
heles 49. 17		heeles
helpe 2. 20		helpe meete
40. 14	*omit*	*omit*
—, shall 49. 25	art helped	
helper 2. 18	helpe	helpe meet
helpeth it, what 25. 22	why	why
Heman 36. 22		
Hemdan 36. 26		
Hemov 39. 2 (9 times)		
hence 37. 17 (3 „)		
7. 4	yet after	yet
—, get 45. 17	go youre way	*omit*
henceforth 4. 12	henszforth	
8. 21 (2 times)		againe
9. 11 (3 „)		*omit*
Henoch 4. 17 (5 times)		Enoch
5. 19 (2 times)	*omit*	„
5. 23	his	„
5. 24	he	„
Hephron 23. 10	Ephron	Ephron
See Ephron		
herbe 1. 11 (2 times)		
herbes 1. 29 (3 „)		herbe
2. 5 (2 times)	herbe	„
herd 3. 8 (2 „)	herde	heard
herde 14. 14 (14 times)		„
—, haue 17. 20		haue heard
—, hath 21. 17		
(3 times)		
—, haue 21. 26		haue heard
(2 times)		
20. 17 (2 times)		hearkened

	C	A
herde 16. 2	herkened	hearkened
34. 5	vnderstode	heard
35. 3		answered
See hearde		
herdman 49. 24	herdmen	sheapherd
herdmen 13. 7	hirdmen	heardmen
(2 times)		
13. 8 (3 times)	hyrdmen	„
here 16. 13 (11 times)		
22. 1		heere
22. 7 (3 times)		*omit*
31. 51 (2 „)	*omit*	„
38. 21 (2 „)		in this place
30. 3	there	behold
31. 50	„	*omit*
— by 42. 15		hereby
herin 34. 22	*omit*	herein
herken 4. 23 (2 times)		hearken
—, shall 49. 10	shal fall	shall the gathering be
hert 6. 5 (7 times)		heart
43. 30		bowels
hervest 45. 6		
See harvest		
hete 8. 22	heate	heat
31. 40	„	drought
See heate		
Heth 10. 15 (3 times)		
—, of 23. 3 (10 „)	Hethites	
Hethite 23.10(7 „)		Hittite
See Hethyte		
Hethites 15. 20		Hittites
Hethyte 49. 29	Hethite	Hittite
See Hethite		
Heva 3. 20 (2 times)		Eve
Heuila 10. 7 (2 times)		Hauilah
2. 11	Heuyla	„

	C	A
Heuite 34. 2		Hiuite
Heuyte 36. 2	Hethite	„
heyfer 15. 9	cow	heifer
hinder 24. 56	holde	
hindermost 33. 2	hynder most	
Hira 38. 1 (2 times)	Hyra	Hirah
hither 42. 15 (4 times)		
—, come 19. 9		stand backe
43. 20	downe	downe
Hiui 10. 17		Hiuite
Hoba 14. 15		
holdynge 25. 26	helde	tooke holde on
hole 13. 9 (2 times)	whole	whole
13. 13	„	all
home 17. 12 (3 times)		house
43. 16	in	„
—, goo 44. 33	go vp	goe vp
honde 8. 9 (3 times)	hande	hand
See hand		
hande		
hondes 24. 47	handes	hands
See handes		
honoure 31. 1	riches	glory
45. 13	worshipe	„
49. 6	„	honour
hony 43. 11		honie
hoore 38. 15	whoore	harlot
hoost 32. 2		hoste
Hori 36. 22		
36. 29	Horites	Horites
See Hory		
Horite 36. 20		
Horites 36. 21		
hornes 22. 13		
horse 49. 17		
horsemen 50. 9	horses	
horses 47. 17		

	C	A
Hory 36. 30	Horites	Hori
See Hori		
Horyms 14. 6	Horites	Horites
houghed an oxe 49. 6		† digged down a wall
housbond 30. 18 (2 times)	huszbande	husband
housbonde 30. 15	„	„
See husband husbond husbonde		
house 12. 1 (61 times)		
39. 22 (2 times)	*omit*	*omit*
45. 2 (3 „)	housholde	
—, in to thy 19. 5	vnto the	in to the
28. 21	home	
44. 4		*omit*
50. 7	courte	
50. 8	lande	
See housse		
households 42. 19	home	houses
See housholdes		
houses 34. 29		house
houshold 39. 11	folkes of the house	men of the house
housholde 18. 19 (2 times)	householde	household
45. 11 (2 times)	house	houshold
26. 14	householde	seruants
31. 17	„	houshold
See houssold husholde		
housholdes 42. 33	houses	housholds
45. 18	housholdes	„
47. 24	houses	households
See households		
housse 15. 2 (6 times)	house	house
—, in 17. 13 (2 times)	at home	„

	C	A
housse in 15. 3	housholde	house
houssold 7. 1	house	„
See houshold		
housholde		
how 27. 20 (6 times)		
— that 3.7 (3 „)	that	that
— „ 20. 13 (2 „)	„	*omit*
31. 12 (2 „)	*omit*	„
42. 28	wherfore	what
Hul 10. 23		
hundred *see* Intro-		
duction p. xxvii		
hunger 41. 27	derth	famine
(7 times)		
—, of 41. 36	deare	famine
41. 36	honger	„
—, began to 41.55	beganne to suffre	was famished
	honger also	
hunted, he that hath	the hunter that	he that hath taken
27. 33	brought	
hunter 10. 9 (3 times)		
huntynge 27. 30	huntinge	hunting
Hupim 46. 21		Huppim
hurt, wylt 21. 23		wilt deale falsly
hurte 26. 29 (2 times)	harme	hurt
—, meane no 42. 19	be vnfayned	be true men
Hus 22. 21		Huz
Husam 36.34 (2 times)		Husham
husband 3. 6	husbande	
See housbond		
housbonde		
husbond		
husbonde		
husband man 9. 20	*omit*	husbandman
husbond 3. 16	huszbande	husband
husbonde 16. 3	„	„
(3 times)		

	C	A
See housbond		
housbonde		
husband		
husholde 41.51	house	house
See houshold		
housholde		
houssold		
Husim 46.23		Hushim
hyd 3.8 (2 times)		hid
35.4	buried	„
hyde, will 47.18		
—, must 4.14		shall be hid
—, can 18.17		„ hide
25.25		hairy garment
hye 7.19		high
7.20		vpward
49.9	vp hye	vp
See hygh		
hye-wayes 38.14	waye	way
hygh 14.22	hye	high
See hye		
hyghest, most 14.18	most hye	most high
(2 times)		
14.20	Hyest	„ „
hyll 31.54	mount	mount
hylles 7.19	mountaynes	hils
7.20	„	mountaines
hynde 49.21		hinde
hyther 15.16	hither	hither
See hither		
Hyzarmoneth 10.26	Hazarmaphet	Hazarmaueth
Iabal 4.20		
Iabok 32.22	Iacob	Iabbok
Iachim 46.10		Iachin
Iacksan 25.2 (2 times)		Iakshan
Iacob 25.26 (128 „)		

	C	A
Iacob 25. 28 (2 times)		Jacob
27. 14 (2 „)	he	hee
27. 30 (4 „)	*omit*	
29. 15 (3 „)	him	
31. 1	he	he
31. 32 (4 times)	„	
32. 32	Iacobs	Iacobs
—, of 34. 7 (3 times)	„	of Iacob
27. 17	„	
30. 2		Iacobs
47. 28	Israel	
Iacobs 27.22 (7 times)		
45. 26 (3 times)	his	
46. 8	of Iacob	
Iacob's 31. 33	Iacobs	Iacobs
Iaelam 36. 5 (3 times)		
Iaheleel 46. 14	Iahleel	Iahleel
Iahezeel 46. 24	Iahzeel	Iahzeel
Iaketan 10.25 (2 times)	Iaketan	Joktan
10. 29	„	Ioktan
Iamin 46. 10		
Iaphet 5. 32		Japheth
Iapheth 6.10 (2 times)	Iaphet	„
9. 18 (6 times)	„	Iaphet
Iarah 10.26		Ierah
Iared 5. 15 (2 times)		
5. 16 (2 times)	*omit*	
5. 20	his	
Iauan 10. 2 (2 times)		
Iealam 36. 14		Iaalam
Iebusi 10. 16		Jebusite
Iebusites 15. 21		
Iedlaph 22. 22		Iidlaph
Iemna 46. 17		Iimnah
Iemuel 46. 10		
Iesua 46. 17		Ishuah
Iesui 46. 17		Isui

	C	A
Ietheth 36. 40		Jetheth
Iethran 36. 26		Ithran
Ietur 25. 15	Iethur	Jetur
Ieus 36. 5 (3 times)		Ieush
iewells 24. 53	iewels	iewels
iewelles 24. 53	*omit*	,,
Iezer 46. 24		
if 23. 8 (3 times)	yf	
30. 27	*omit*	
See yf		
Iisca 11. 29		Iscah
Iles 10. 5		
imagynacion 8. 21	ymaginacion	imagination
See ymagynacion		
in 1. 11 (349 times)		
1. 11 (15 ,,)	after	after
1. 29 (40 ,,)	*omit*	
2. 2 (2 ,,)		on
2. 5 (17 ,,)	vpon	
2. 15 (7 ,,)		into
3. 1 (5 ,,)		of
4. 3 (3 ,,)	after	in
4. 22 (7 ,,)		*omit*
4. 22 (14 ,,)	*omit*	*omit*
6. 4	at	at
10. 9	before	before
13. 17	thorow	through
16. 6 (2 times)	vnder	
17. 12 (2 ,,)	thorow out	
18. 12	with in	within
20. 6 (4 ,,)	with	
20. 13 (2 ,,)	*omit*	at
—, possessim to bury		burying place
23. 4 (4 times)		
25. 16 (2 ,,)		by
30. 35 (2 ,,)	vnder	into
— good health 29. 6		well
(3 times)		

in

	C	A
in tymes past 31. 2 (2 times)	yesterdaye and yeryesterdaye	before
36. 40 (2 times)		according to
38. 7 (2 „)	before	in
— and out 3. 24	*omit*	euery way
—, open 4. 7	open in	at
— that tyme 4. 26	at the same tyme	then
6. 16		to
— stoore, laye vp 6.21	laye it vp in stoare	gather
7. 11	of	*omit*
9. 14		a
9. 21		within
15. 3	of	in
15. 7	„	of
18. 14	aboute	at
19. 9	herin	
19. 17	vpon	to
— very dede 20. 12	*omit*	indeed
— that 22. 12	*omit*	seeing that
25. 13	of	according to
26. 31	on	in
27. 8	*omit*	according to
27. 18		vnto
— what takynge 30. 29	in what maner	how
— the tyme 30. 41		whensoeuer
31. 34	vnder	in
36. 30		among
—, begat 37. 3		sonne of
39. 10	in	with
39. 11	thereby	there within
— good case 40. 14	in thy prosperite	well
41. 36	*omit*	for
41. 36	for	to
41. 45	*omit*	ouer
42. 6	in	„
43. 18	for	in

	C	A
in mornynge 44. 3	on the morow	as soone as morning was light
—, begat 44. 20		childe of
45. 7	vpon	in
45. 8		throughout
49. 13		for
in as moch as 19. 19		*omit*
increase 9. 1		bee fruitful
9. 27		shall enlarge
28. 3	make the frutefull	make thee fruitfull
See encrease		
increased 7. 17		
7. 18		encreased
See encreased		
Inde 2. 13	Morians	Ethiopia
indede 28. 19	*omit*	*omit*
inhabitoure 36. 20	that dwelt in the lande	who inhabited
inhabitoures 34. 40	inhabiters	inhabitants
inne 42. 27 (2 times)		
innocent 20. 5		innocencie of
in so moch 46. 30	for so moch as	since
„ „ much 26. 15		*omit*
in stede 2. 21	in steade	in stead
instrumentes 49. 5		instruments
intercession, made 25. 21	besought	intreated
interpretate, had well 40. 16	interpretacion was good	interpretation was good
—, coude 41. 8	coude tell the interpretacion	could interprete
—, can 41. 15	can interprete	can interpret
—, dost 41. 15	declarest	canst vnderstand
interpretation 40. 5 (4 times)	interpretacion	to interpret
interpreter 42. 23		
interpretynge 40. 8	interpretinge	interpretations

	C	A
into 2. 7 (55 times)		vnto
11. 31 (2 „)		
29. 13 (2 „)		to
31. 3 (3 „)	to	
46. 4 (3 „)	*omit*	
7. 9	in vnto him to	
12. 6		through
16. 5	by	
19. 5	vnto	
19. 26		*omit*
—, growe 24. 60		bee thou the mother of
34. 25		vpon
41. 48		in
in that 22. 12	and	seeing
intreated, was 25. 21		
invade, shall 49. 19	shal fall violently vpon	shall ouercome
Iob 46. 13		Job
Iobab 10. 29 (3 times)		
Iordane 13.10 (2 times)	Iordan	
32. 10 (2 times)	„	Iordan
50. 10		„
Ioseph 30. 24 (107 times)		
39. 20	him	him
41. 46 (6 times)	he	
—, of 46. 27 (3 times)	Iosephs	
47. 2	he	hee
50. 16 (2 times)	him	
41. 41	*omit*	
50. 16	him	
50. 25	he	
Iosephes 45. 16	Iosephs	Iosephs
Iosephs 37. 31 (12 times)		
39. 22 (2 times)	his	

	C	A
Iosephs 41. 45	him	
iourney 24.21 (5 times)		
13. 11 (2 times)		iourneyed
28. 20 (5 „)		way
12. 9	iourneye	iourneyed
—, on his 13. 3	forth	on his iourneyes
Irad 4. 18 (2 times)		
Iram 36. 43		
is 2. 8 (100 times)		
—, name 2. 11	is called	
(3 times)		
2. 11 (9 times)	*omit*	
10. 9 (3 „)		*omit*
14. 9 (4 „)	*omit*	„
18. 20 (2 „)	are	
19. 15	„	are
— the father of 19. 37	of whom came	
(2 times)		
—, here 22. 7		behold
(2 times)		
24. 14 (2 times)	be	let be
41. 7	was	was
— your comynge	ye are come	you are come
42. 12 (2 times)		
1. 30	hath	
— full 6. 13		is filled
—, there 12. 19		behold
17. 4	haue	
17. 17	am	
18. 14	shulde be	
19. 13		is waxen
— a saynge, it 22. 14		it is said
— worth 23. 9	† reasonable	
23. 17	*omit*	was
— not the maner, it		it must not be so
29. 26		done
30. 15	hast thou	

	C	A
is, name 35. 10	art called	
— to say, that 37. 1	namely	*omit*
38. 18	thou hast	
38. 26		hath bin
45. 6	are	*omit*
— so sore 47. 4	doth oppresse	is sore
49. 14	shal be	
49. 27	*omit*	shall rauine as
49. 3	lyeth	
Isaac 17. 19 (70 times)		
21. 4 (2 times)	him	
18. 26	he	
Isaacs 26. 19 (3 times)		
26. 25	his	
Isachar 30. 18 (4 times)		Issachar
Ismael 16. 11 (10 „)		Ishmael
See Ismaell		
Ismaelites 37. 25		Ishmeelites
(4 times)		
Ismaell 16. 15 (6 times)	Ismael	Ishmael
See Ismael		
Ismaels 36. 3		Ishmaels
Israel 32. 28 (26 times)		
45. 28 (2 „)	he	
46. 2	him	
See Israell		
Israelites 48. 20	Israel	Israel
Israell 32. 28 (10 times)	„	„
33. 20		El-Elohe-Israel
—, of 48. 10	Israels	of Israel
See Israel		
Israels 48. 13 (2 times)		
35. 22		† Israel
Iubal 4. 21	Iuball	Jubal
Iuda 29. 35 (18 times)		Iudah
Iudas 38. 12		„
38. 11 (3 times)		Iudahs

	C	A
Iudas 38. 7	*omit*	Iudahs
38. 20 (3 times)	Iuda	Iudah
iudge 15. 14 (4 times)		
—, let 31. 37	maye iudge	may iudge
—, be 31. 53		iudge
—, shall 49. 16	shal be iudge in	
Iudith 26. 34		
iugmente, well of 14. 7		En-mishpat
Joseph 33. 7 (2 times)	Ioseph	Ioseph
Kahath 46. 11	Cahath	Kohath
Karnaim, Astarath 14. 5	Astaroth Karnaim	Ashteroth Karnaim
Kariathaim, Sabe 14. 5	Kiriathaim	Shueh Kariathaim
Kedar 25. 13	Cedar	
Kedma 25. 15		Kedemah
Kedorlaomer 14. 1 (5 times)		Chedorlaomer
Kemuell 22. 21	Kemuel	Kemuel
Kenan 5. 9 (2 times)		Cainan
5. 10 (3 times)	*omit*	,,
Kenas 36. 11 (3 times)		Kenaz
Kenizites 15. 19		
Kenytes 15. 19		Kenites
kepe 30. 31 (3 times)		keepe
—, to 2. 15 (2 ,,)		to keepe
— them alyve, to 6. 19 (2 times)	that they may lyue	
—, do 37. 13		
—, see thou 17. 9	kepe	thou shalt keepe
—, shall 17. 10		shall keepe
—, will 29. 34		† will be ioyned
— secrett 37. 26	hyde	conceale
keper 4. 9		
39. 21 (2 times)	officer	keeper
—, wylbe 28. 15	wyll kepe	will keepe

	C	A
kepeth 30. 2		hath withheld
kepinge 30. 35	hande	hand
kepte 26. 5 (2 times)		kept
—, hath 39. 9		
20. 6		withheld
—, haste 22. 12	spared	withhelde
27. 36		reserued
30. 36		fed
37. 2	became a keper	was feeding
—, let them 41. 35	maye kepe	let them keepe
Kethura 25. 4	Ketura	Keturah
Ketura 25. 1		,,
kiddes 27. 9	kyddes	kids
See kyddes		
kinde 6. 20 (5 times)	kynde	
See kynde		
kindes 1. 21		
See kyndes		
kindly 34. 3	louyngly	
See kyndly		
kinge 14. 18 (3 times)	kynge	king
14. 4		*omit*
See kynge		
kinreddes 25. 13	kynredes	generations
See kynreddes		
kynredds		
kynreds		
kissed 27. 27	kyssed	
See kyssed		
kneade 18. 6	knede	knead
knees 50. 23	lappe	
knewe 37. 33 (6 times)		knew
27. 23	knew	discerned
knowe 29. 5		
12. 11 (11 times)		know
—, shall 15. 8		shal know
—, cowd 43. 7		

	C	A
knowe doth 3. 5		doth know
—, shulde 3. 5	shal knowe	knowing
—, may 18. 21	maye „	will know
—, shall 24. 14	„ „	shall know
—, 42. 33	wyl marke	„ „
47. 6	knowest	knowest
knowest 30. 26		
(2 times)		
knoweth 33. 13	knowest	
knowledge 2. 9		
(2 times)		
3. 22	knoweth	to know
knowne, haue 19. 8		haue knowen
knyfe 22. 6 (2 times)		knife
Korah 36. 5 (4 „)		
kydd 38. 20 (2 „)		kidde
38. 17		kid
kyddes 30. 32		goates
See kiddes		
kyll, shulde 4. 15		
4. 14	slaye	slay
—, to 27. 42	wil slaye	to kill
37. 21	sley	kill
kylled, to haue 22. 10	to haue slayne	to slay
—, shulde haue 26. 7	might slaye	should kill
37. 31	slewe	killed
kynde 1. 11 (7 times)		kinde
7. 2 (3 times)	*omit*	*omit*
8. 19	like	kinds
— worde 37. 4	frendly worde	peaceably
See kinde		
kyndes 1. 2 (5 times)	kynde	kinde
See kindes		
kyndnesse 21. 23		kindnesse
20. 13	kyndnes	„
kyne 32. 15 (11 times)		
33. 13	greate catell	heards

	C	A
kyngdome 10. 10		kingdome
kynge 14. 1 (18 times)		king
40. 5 (2 times)	*omit*	,,
14. 22	kinge	,,
37. 8	kinge	*omit*
—, geue pleasures for a 49. 20	geue delicates vnto kynges	yeeld royall dainties
See kinge		
kynges 14. 5 (7 times)		kings
14. 17 (2 times)	kinges	,,
41. 40	,,	*omit*
kynred 12. 1 (4 times)		kinred
10. 5		families
31. 3		kindred
43. 7	kynrede	,,
See kynrede		
kynreddes 10. 20 (2 times)	kynreds	families
10. 31	generacions	,,
10. 32	kynredes	,,
kynreddds 36. 40	kynreds	,,
See kinreddes kynreds		
kynrede 32. 9	kynred	kinred
kynreds 10. 18		families
See kinreddes kynreddes kynreddds		
kysse 27. 26 (2 times)		kisse
kyssed 29. 11 (7 ,,)		kissed
See kissed		
Laban 24. 29 (44 times)		
24. 31	he	he
—, of 29. 10	*omit*	*omit*
—, of 30. 40	Labans	Labans
—, of 30. 40 (2 times)	Labans	of Laban
39. 15	he	,,

	C	A
Labans 30.36 (3 times)		
laboure 31. 42		labour
35. 17	travelynge	,,
41. 51		toile
lacke 18. 28	lesse	
18. 28	*omit*	
lad 37. 2 (9 times)		
21. 18 (3 ,,)	childe	
21. 14 (3 ,,)	,,	child
37. 30 (3 ,,)		childe
15. 3	sonne	one
40. 20	*omit*	*omit*
ladd 21. 12	childe	lad
ladder 28. 12	,,	
laddes 48. 16		
44. 30	of this	lads
lade 45. 17		
laded 42. 26		
44. 13	lade the burthen vpon	
laden 45. 23		
37. 25	which bare	bearing
45. 23	*omit*	
lambes 21. 28 (3 times)		
21. 30		lambs
30. 33 (2 times)		sheepe
30. 32	shepe	,,
33. 19	pens	pieces of money
Lamech 4.18 (7 times)		
5. 26	*omit*	
5. 30	he	
5. 31	his	
lamentation 50. 10	lamentacion	
—, ooke of 35. 8	Oke of lamentacion	Allon-Bachuth
land 26. 2 (13 times)	lande	
24. 5 (2 times)	londe	
36. 6	lande	lande

	C	A
lande 28. 4 (3 times)		
4. 16 (74 „)		land
1. 10 (45 „)	londe	„
10. 30 (2 „)	*omit*	*omit*
41. 53 (2 „)	*omit*	land
23. 15	felde	„
— of thy fathers 31.3	fatherland	
36. 21	londe	
See land		
lond		
londe		
landes 41. 54 (2 times)		lands
47. 19 (2 times)	lande	land
10. 20	londes	countries
See londes		
language 11. 1		
languages 10. 31	tunges	tongues
lappe 30. 3 (2 times)		knees
Lasa 10. 19		Lasha
last 49. 1		
30. 40	later	feebler
— of all 33. 7	afterwarde	after
—, doth 50. 3	endured	*omit*
late 24. 18	let	let
latest dye 47. 19	suffrest to dye	shall die
latter 30. 42		*omit*
laugh at 21. 6	reioyse with	laugh with
laughe, doth 18. 13	doth laugh	did laugh
laughed 18. 12		
(2 times)		
See laughte		
laughing stocke, made me 21. 6	hath prepared a ioye for me	made me to laugh
laughte 17. 17	laughed	laughed
See laughed		
laughtest 18. 15	dyddest laughe	diddest laugh
lawe 47. 26		law

	C	A
lawes 26. 5		
lay 19. 34	laye	
41. 35		
— wyth 4. 1 (2 times)	,,	knew
— by 38. 18	laye with	came in vnto
See laye		
layd 48. 17	layed	
layde 15. 10		layd
22. 6 (3 times)	layed	,,
—, was 25. 17	was gathered	was gathered
— him down 28. 11	layed him down	lay down
—, had 28. 18		had put
— vp 41. 49	layed vp	gathered
47. 14	layed	brought
— him 49. 9	kneled	stouped
See layed		
laye 19. 33 (8 times)		lay
9. 21 (2 times)		was
— vp in stoore 6. 21		shalt gather
29. 2	*omit*	were lying
— by 29. 30	laye with	went in vnto
— vnto, his harte 34. 3	his herte hanged vpon	hee loued
— with 38. 26		knew
39. 20	laie	were
— some thinge to our charge, to 43. 18		fall vpon vs
See lay		
layed 39. 16		laid
See layd		
layde		
Lea 29. 16 (26 times)		Leah
30. 15	she	shee
30. 18	*omit*	Leah
Leabim 10. 13		Lehabim
leade, to 12. 20	to conveye	sent
leane 41. 3		

		C	A
leane 41. 19		leen	
41. 20		leene	
See lenefleshed			
leape 31. 12			
Leas 30. 10 (5 times)			Leahs
leaste 32. 10		*omit*	least
leaue 18. 15 (3 times)			
— of from, wyll 11.6			will be restrained from
44. 22		come from	
See leve			
led 43. 24			brought
leeft, had 24. 15		had left of	had done
lefe 8. 11		leaf	leafe
left 13. 9 (13 times)			
—, had 39. 13			
—, is 42. 38 (2 times)			
— mornynge, had 38. 12			was comforted
44. 12		*omit*	
lefte 13. 9 (4 times)			
left of 11. 8 (2 „)		left of	left off
legges 49. 10		fete	feete
lenefleshed 41. 4		leene	leane
See leane			
length 13. 17			
lenth 8. 15		length	length
lest 3. 3 (4 times)			
19. 17 (2 „)		that not	
38. 11		peraduenture	peraduenture
19. 19		there might	
26. 7		thinkinge thus	
44. 34		then	peraduenture
let 1. 3 (37 times)			
20. 7 (4 „)			shal
24.57 (2 „)			will
23. 9 (4 „)		maye	may

	C	A
let 44.2 (4 times)	maye	
33.15 (3 „)	will	
47.25 (2 „)	„	will
— it devyde 1.17		diuided
4.7	shal	*omit*
— departe 24.54	let departe	send away
— syppe 25.30	let proue	feed
— eate 27.25	to eate	will eate
— vs consente 34.23	yf we consent	
37.27	that	
— them 41.34	se that he	
41.35	*omit*	
— seme 45.5	think	*omit*
47.30		
— me 48.9	that I may	
Letusim 25.3		Letushim
leve 2.24	leaue	leaue
See leaue		
leves 3.7	leaues	leaues
Leui 29.34 (6 times)		
Leumim 25.3		Leummim
lieth 49.25	lyeth	lyeth
See lyeth		
life 3.18 (3 times)		
9.4	bloude	
—, dayes of 25.7	age	dayes of the yeres of life
— long 44.32	lyfe longe	for euer
— longe 48.15	„ „	life long
liffe 7.22	life	life
See lyfe		
lifte vp 33.5	lift vp	lift up
— up, was 7.17	„ „	was lift vp
— vp, shall 41.44	moue	shall lift vp
See lyft		
lyfte		
lifted 31.10	lift	
See lyfted		

	C	A
lighte 44. 3	daye	light
See lyghte		
lightely 26. 10	lightly	lightly
liked 6. 2		chose
lion 49. 9	lyon	lyon
lionesse 49. 9	lionesse	old lyon
lions 49. 9	lyon	lyons
litle 19. 20 (2 times)		
18. 4 (4 „)		little
—, not a 34. 7	very	very
See lytle		
litter 24. 25 (2 times)		straw
livynge 2. 19	liuinge	liuing
See lyvinge		
lyvynge		
lo 15. 3	beholde	behold
18. 2	„	loe
24. 13		behold
29. 7	*omit*	loe
See loo		
lodge 24. 23 (2 times)		
loftes 6. 16		stories
loke 12. 11 (5 times)		looke
48. 3	*omit*	*omit*
—, wyll 9. 16	maye loke	will looke
— upon, to 24. 18	of face	to looke vpon
38. 25	knowest	discerne
loked 6. 12 (5 times)		looked
8. 13 (4 times)	sawe	„
—, hath 29. 32		
— vnto 4. 4		had respect vnto
18. 16	turned them	looked
19. 28	turned his face	„
19. 28	*omit*	*omit*
24. 63	sawe	saw
— vpon nothinge 39. 6	medled with noth- inge	left all
See looked		

	C	A
lokest 16. 13	seist	seest
lond 7. 22	londe	land
47. 6	lande	,,
londe 1. 9 (11 times)		,,
23. 2 (15 ,,)	lande	,,
See land		
lande		
londes 47. 18	lande	lands
47. 19	,,	land
47. 22		lands
See landes		
longe 26. 8 (2 times)		long
— 21. 34 (2 ,,)		many
50. 3 (2 ,,)		*omit*
— as, as 8. 22	so longe as	while
50. 3	*omit*	*omit*
longer 45. 1	*omit*	,,
longest 31. 30	longedest	longedst
longeth 34. 8		
looked 18. 2	loked	
4. 5	,,	had respect
See loked		
loo 15. 12	lo	loe
1. 31 (5 times)	,,	behold
17. 20 (2 ,,)	beholde	,,
30. 34	,,	beholde
12. 19	lo	therefore behold
18. 10	*omit*	loo
37. 7	,,	loe
50. 5	beholde	,,
LORd 6. 3	LORDE	LORD
lord 40. 1 (2 times)	lorde	lord
44. 20	*omit*	,,
LORde 4. 1 (113 times)	LORDE	LORD
21. 2 (2 ,,)	God	God
6. 5	LORDE	,,
11. 9	*omit*	LORD

	C	A
LORde will see, the	the LORDE shall	Iehovah-ijreh
22. 14	prouyde	
27. 37	lorde	lord
30. 27	God	LORD
lorde 18. 12 (27 times)		lord
7. 5 (7 „)	LORDE	LORD
23. 6		„
30. 24	God	„
34. 2		prince
37. 36		officer
39. 1	chefe marshall	„
39. 16	master	lord
42. 33	he	„
44. 21	thou	thou
44. 24	lordes	lord
LORDE 8. 20 (7 times)	LORDE	LORD
LORde God 2. 4		LORD God
(19 times)		
24. 7 (3 times)	LORDE the God	„ „
2. 19	God the LORDE	
15. 8	LORDE LORDE	„ „
24. 12	„ thin God	„ „
24. 48	„	„
— Iehouah 15. 2	„ LORDE	„ „
lordes 19. 2 (3 times)		lordes
12. 15	prynces	princes
LORdes 16. 11	of the LORDE	of the LORD
lordes 44. 18	lorde	lords
44. 33		to my lord
lose 27. 45	be robbed of	depriued
Lot 11. 27 (2 times)		
19. 1	*omit*	
Lothan 36. 20 (2 times)		Lotan
Lothans 36. 22		Lotans
lots 19. 26	his	his
loue 27. 4		
—, will 29. 32		

C A

	C	A
loue 29. 20	loued	
loued 25. 28 (6 times)		
See loved		
louest 22. 2		
loueth 27. 9 (2 times)		
loured 4. 5	his countenance changed	his countenance fell
loureste 4. 6	doth thy countenance change	is thy countenance fallen
loved 25. 28 (3 times)	loued	loued
See loued		
lowde 39. 14	loude	loud
lowse 27. 40	pluck	breake
loynes 35. 11		
37. 34		loines
loyns 46. 26	loynes	,,
lucke 30. 11		a troupe commeth
luckely to passe, come 39. 23	come prosperously to passe	to prosper
luckie 39. 2	luckye	prosperous
Lud 10. 32		
Ludim 10. 13		
Lus 28. 19 (3 times)		Luz
lust 18. 12		pleasure
—, do 19. 5	knowe	know
— to live, what 27. 46	what shall life profit me	what good shall my life doe me
lustes 3. 16	lust	desire
lustie 3. 6	lustye	pleasant to the eyes
25. 8	good	good old
lycknesse 1. 26	licknesse	likenesse
1. 27 (3 times)	,,	image
5. 3	ymage	likenesse
lye 19. 32 (2 times)		
47. 30		lie
—, to 38. 16		come in vnto

	C	A
lye, to 38. 16	lie	come in vnto
—, to 24. 11	lye	to kneele
—, maye 29. 21	shulde lye	may goe in vnto
39. 7	slepe	lie
lyen, had 34. 7	lyen	lying
See lyne		
lyeth 4. 7		lieth
14. 15	lieth	is
21. 17 (3 times)		,,
12. 8	laye	*omit*
20. 15	stondeth open	is
lyfe 1. 20 (10 times)	life	life
7. 11 (2 times)	age	,,
32. 30 (3 ,,)	soule	,,
—, lyved a godly 5. 24		walked with God
9. 3		liueth
—, can have 18. 14	lyue	life
19. 17	souls	,,
19. 19	soule alyue	,,
45. 5	lyues sake	,,
See life		
liffe		
lyft 13. 10 (2 times)	lift	lifted
— vp my voyce 39. 18	made a noyse	lift vp my voice
— vp 40. 13	take	lift vp
48. 14	left	left
lyfte 21. 16	lifte	lift
13. 14 (7 times)	lift	,,
21. 18	take	,,
29. 1	gat him vp vpon	*omit*
29. 11 (2 times)	lift	lifted
— vp 31. 12	,,	lift
39. 15	*omit*	lifted
See lifte		
lyfted 22. 13	lift	lifted
27. 38	,,	lift
40. 20	toke	lifted
See lifted		

	C	A
lyghte 1. 3 (10 times)	light	light
See lighte		
lyghtes 1. 14 (3 times)	lightes	lights
lyghted 24. 64	lighted	lighted
lyke 41. 19	*omit*	*omit*
— vnto the 41. 39	as thou	as thou art
41. 49	as	as
lykewyse 7. 3	like wyse	*omit*
32. 19	*omit*	„
41. 27	and	and
lyne, myght haue	might haue lyen	might lightly haue
26. 10		lien
See lyen		
lyue 3. 22 (3 times)		liue
—, myghte 17. 18	might lyue	might liue
—, maye 42. 2		may „
1. 21		liuing
—, maye 12. 13		shall liue
—, can 18. 20	yf I lyue	† time of life
—, may 19. 20		shall liue
—, mayst 20. 7	shalt lyue	shalt liue
—, shalt 27. 40	shalt get thy lyu-	shalt liue
	inge	
—, what lust to 27. 46	what shall life	what good shall
	profit me	life doe me
—, maye 43. 8	lyue	may liue
—, doth 45. 3	is alyue	doeth liue
lyued 5. 7 (20 times)		liued
5. 6 (8 times)	was	„
5. 5	*omit*	„
— a godly lyfe 5. 24		walked with God
—, had 11. 20	was	liued
lyued, so longe 23. 1		were the yeeres of
		the life of
lyues 45. 7		liues
9. 5	soule	„
—, saued oure 47. 25	let vs lyue	„

	C	A
made 22. 9	buylded	built
24. 11	let	
— prosperous, had 24. 21	had prospered	
24. 31	haue made	haue prepared
24. 37	hath taken	
— an ende of speakynge, had 24. 45	had spoken	had done speaking
— haste 24. 46	immediately	
— intercession 25. 21	besought	intreated
—, had 27. 17		had prepared
—, had 27. 31	made	
—, haue 27. 37		haue giuen
— good, haue 28. 15		haue done
— a chaunge, haue 30. 8	hath turned it	haue wrastled
30. 10	mayde	mayde
30. 27	*omit*	
30. 40		put
— redy 31. 21	gat vp	*omit*
— it good 31. 39	was fayne to paie it	bare the losse
33. 17	buylded	
33. 20	set vp	erected
— havock 34. 29	spoyled	spoiled
34. 30	brought is so to passe	to make
— ... haste 41. 40	let	brought
41. 47	*omit*	brought forth
—, hath 41. 51	hath caused	
42. 7	helde	
— tarieng, had 43. 10		had lingred
46. 29	bended	
— prouysion for 47. 12		nourished
—, was an ordinaunce 47. 22	it was ordered	had a portion assigned
Madianites 37. 28		Midianites

	C	A
Madianytes 36. 35	Madianites	Midian
37. 36	„	Madianites
Maddiel 36. 43		
Magog 10. 2		
Mahala 28. 9	Mahaloth	Mahalath
Mahalaliel 5. 12		Mahalaleel
(2 times)		
5. 13 (2 times)	*omit*	„
Mahalalyell 5. 17	his	„
Mahanaim 32. 2		
make 1. 26 (14 times)		
—, will 2. 18 (8 times)		
—, to 3. 6		
—, shalt 6.16 (2 times)		
—, will 6. 18 (4 „)		will establish
9. 9		establish
—, maye 24.3 (2 „)		will make
—, had 2. 19	had made	formed
— the oft with child	† art with childe	multiply thy con-
3. 16		ception
—, shalt 6. 15	make	
9. 12	haue made	
—, to 9. 15	*omit*	become
—, wyll 12. 2		make
—, shall 15. 13		shall serue
18. 6	bake	
19. 19		hast magnified
—, wolde 26. 28		let us make
—, will 27. 9	maye make	
— the redie 27. 43	get the vp	arise
— provysion, shall	shall loke to	shall prouide
30. 30		
—, woldest 32. 12	make	make
— mencion of 40. 14	mayest certifie	
41. 34	ordene	appoint
— excuse, can 44. 16	shal make excuse	shall cleare our
		selues

	C	A
make prouision, to 45. 7	might let remayne	to preserve
— prouision, will 45. 11		will nourish
— hast 45. 13	haist you	shall haste
46. 15		were
47. 6	let	
—, will 48. 4	wil cause	
48. 20	set	
50. 11		*omit*
makest prosperous 24. 42	hast prospered	prosper
makynge, were 37. 7	made	made
Malchiel 46. 17		
male 1. 27 (8 times)		
34. 25	males	males
Mamre 13. 18 (9 times)		
man 1. 26 (63 „)		
5. 1 (2 times)		Adam
9. 5 (2 „)	*omit*	
10. 5 (2 „)	one	one
41. 21 (2 „)		*omit*
4. 15		any
38. 1		Adullamite
38. 2		Canaanite
— to declare 40. 8		interpreter
41. 15		none
41. 24	they	„
41. 39	none	„
42. 13	*omit*	*omit*
43. 14	one	*omit*
— that was the ruelar 43. 19		steward
Manahath 26. 23	Manahat	
Manasse 41. 51	Manasses	Manasseh
Manasses 46. 20 (8 times)	„	„
48. 14 (2 times)	„	Manassehs

	C	A
manchilde 17. 12		man child
(2 times)		
mandragoras 30. 14		mandrakes
(5 times)		
maner 18. 11 (3 times)		
18. 25	*omit*	
24. 10		*omit*
—, all 1. 25 (10 times)	all maner of	euery
6. 21	,, ,, ,,	*omit*
9. 10	*omit*	euery
— of, all 1. 21 (8 times)	all maner of	,,
7. 14	,, ,, ,,	all the
— off, all 7. 14	,, ,, ,,	euery
See manner		
man-kynde 6. 7	man kynde	man
manner, all 8. 7	all maner	euery
See maner		
mannes 8. 21 (5 times)	mans	mans
40. 5 (2 times)	*omit*	man
44. 26	man	mans
mans 16. 12 (4 times)		
44. 1	mens	
mantell 9. 23		garment
49. 11		clothes
24. 65 (2 times)	cloke	vaile
many 17. 4 (3 times)		
30. 43		much
marchauntes 23. 16		merchant
marchaunt men 37. 28		merchantmen
marcke 4. 15	marck	marke
See marke		
mariages 34. 9	frendshipe	mariages
marie, to 29. 26	to marry	to giue
38. 8	marye	marrie
maried, shulde have		married
19. 14		
marke 31. 51	marckstone	*omit*

	C	A
marke 31. 52	marckstone	pillar
31. 52	„	heape
35. 14	piler	pillar
marshall 37. 36 (3 times)		captaine of the guard
41. 12	marshals	captaine of the guard
marshals 40. 3	„	of the captaine of the guard
41. 10	„	captaine of the guards
marveled 43. 33		marueiled
Mas 10. 23		Mash
Masa 25. 14		Massa
Masreka 36. 36	Masreck	Masrekah
master 24.10 (20 times)		
39. 4	he	hee
masters 24.27 (6 times)		
39. 4		his
mastresse 16. 4 (3 times)		mistresse
mastrye, gett the 27. 40	put of his yock	haue the dominion
Mathusael 4. 18 (2 times)		
Mathusala 5. 21 (2 times)	Mathusalah	Mathuselah
5. 22 (2 times)	*omit*	„
Matred 36. 39		
matryces 20. 18	matrices	wombes
matter 24. 9	the same	
24. 57	therto	*omit*
29. 13		these things
may 29. 8	can	can
mayde 29.24 (2 times)		
16. 2 (5 times)		maid
30. 7		mayd

	C	A
mayde 12. 16	maydens	maid
16. 1	handmayde	maide
24. 16	virgin	virgine
30. 3	mayden	
30. 18	„	mayden
35. 25		handmaid
mayden 34. 4		damsell
maydens 20. 17		maid seruants
(2 times)		
32. 22		women „
33. 1		handmaids
33. 2		handmaides
33. 6		handmaidens
maydeseruantes 24.35	maidens	mayd seruants
maydeseruauntes	maydens	„ „
30. 43		
meale 18. 6	meele	
meane 21. 29		
— truely 42. 11	are vnfayned	are true men
(4 times)		
42. 16	*omit*	*omit*
— no hurte 42. 19	be vnfayned	be true men
meanes 16. 2	*omit*	*omit*
meaneth 37. 10	maner of . . . is	is
—, tell what it 41. 24	tellnothingetherof	declare it to me
meanyst 33. 8	meanest	meanest
measure, out of 24.35	richely	greatly
See mesure		
meate 1. 30 (9 times)		meat
6. 21 (2 times)		food
45. 23	vytayles	meat
Medan 25. 2		
meditations 24. 63	meditacions	to meditate
medowe 41.2(2 times)		medow
Mehetabel 36. 39	Mehet Abeel	
Melcha 24. 15	Milca	Milcah
Melchisedech 14. 18		Melchizedek

	C	A
melt, dyd 43. 30	was kyndled	
men 4. 26 (37 times)		did yerne
17. 10 (2 „)	man	man
12. 16 (3 „)	*omit*	
26. 7 (2 „)	they	
34. 15 (2 „)	males	male
12. 20	officers	
— in aray to fyghte, sette 14. 8	prepared themselues to fight	ioyned battell
17. 23		male
20. 16	*omit*	other
—, of 24. 13	mens	
25. 18		thou
29. 22	people	
39. 14	folkes	
47. 6		man
47. 26	*omit*	*omit*
— of warre 49. 19	wapened hoost of men	troupe
mencion of, make 40. 14	certifie of	make mention of
mens 44. 1		
menservauntes 20. 14 (4 times)		
Merari 46. 11		
mercie 39. 21 (2 times)	mercy	
40. 14	kyndnesse	kindnesse
See mercy		
mercifully 47. 29	mercy	kindly
See mercyfully		
mercy 19. 19		
24. 12 (2 times)		kindnesse
See mercie		
mercyes 32. 10	mercies	mercies
mercyfull 19. 16 (2 times)	mercifull	mercifull

	C	A
mercyfulle, ceasseth not to deale 24. 27	hath not with-drawen his mercy	hath not left desti-tute of his mercy
mercyfully 24. 49 *See* mercifully	mercy	kindly
Mesa 10. 30		Mesha
Mesaab 36. 39	Mesahab	Mezahab
Mesech 10. 2		Meshech
Mesopotamia 24. 10		
25. 20 (6 times)		Padan Aram
28. 5 (4 „)		Padan-Aram
48. 7		Padan
messengers 32. 3 (2 times)	messaungers	
mesure 27. 33	measure	*omit*
—, above 7. 19	so sore	„
mesure, . . . bitterly aboue 27. 34	and was excead-ynge sory	„
metall 4. 22	in all connynge poyntes of me-tall	brasse and iron
mete, to 30. 16		to meet
32. 19		find
meteth 32. 17		meeteth
Methusala 5. 27	his	Methuselah
mett 32. 1 (2 times)		
meyny 22. 3	yonge men	yong men
Mibsan 25. 13		Mibsam
Mibzar 36. 42		
Midian 25. 4		
Midian Iesback 25. 2	Midian, Ieszbak	Midian, and Ishbak
middes 2. 9 *See* myddes myddest	myddest	midst
mightie 46. 3 *See* mightye myghtie myghtye		*omit*

	C	A
mightiest 6. 4	mightie	mightie
mightye 26. 13	greate	great
See mightie		
myghtie		
myghtye		
Milca 11. 29 (2 times)		Milcah
Milcha 22. 20 (2 „)	Milca	„
24. 24	Mylca	„
See Melcha		
Mylca		
Misa 36. 13 (2 times)		Mizzah
mischefe 6. 11	myschefe	violence
See myschefe		
misfortune 19. 19	mysfortune	euill
See mysfortune		
Misraim 10. 6		
(2 times)		Mizraim
Misma 25. 14		Mishma
mo 8. 10		other
See moare		
moo		
more		
Moab 19. 37		
Moabytes 19. 37		Moabites
36. 35	Moabites	Moab
moare 44. 23	more	more
47. 18	„	ought
See mo		
moo		
more		
moch 50. 20		much
moch as, so 14. 23		from . . . euen to
moch . . . as it is worth,	a reasonable	as much . . . as it
as 23. 9		is worth
moch that, in so 26. 15		for
—, so 36. 7	so greate	more than
— as, as 41. 39	so moch as	as much as

	C	A
moch more, as 43. 12	other	double
See much		
mocked, had 19. 14	toke it for sport	mocked
mockynge 21. 9	a mocker	mocking
moneth 7. 11 (7 times)		
7. 11	*omit*	
—, twelue 17. 21		the next yeere
monethes 38. 24		moneths
money 23.9 (22 times)		
17. 13 (3 „)	*omit*	
mony 43. 22	money	money
moo 19. 31	more	not a
45. 6	yet	yet
See mo		
moare		
more		
moone 37. 9		
moornynge 50. 11	mournynge	mourning
50. 11	lamentacion	„
more 8. 12 (9 times)		
29. 27 (2 „)		other
43. 12 (2 „)	other	*omit*
—, no 5. 24		not
18. 32		*omit*
27. 9	yet another	
See mo		
moare		
moo		
More 12. 6		Moreh
moreover 24. 25		
(2 times)		
31. 51 (2 times)		*omit*
47. 6 (2 „)	and	and
27. 37	*omit*	„
31. 16	therfore	for
31. 40	*omit*	thus
32. 20	also	

	C	A
moreover 37. 5	also	and
42. 38	yf	if
45. 15	and	
48. 22	*omit*	
See morover		
Moria 22. 2		Moriah
morne 23. 2	mourne	mourne
morned 50. 10	mourned	mourned
morninge 1. 8	mornynge	morning
mornynge 1. 5	,,	,,
(14 times)		
26. 31 (4 times)	morow	,,
37. 35	with sorowe	mourning
—, had left 38. 12	had left mourn-ynge	was comforted
41. 8	daye	morning
morover 3. 15	and	and
4. 14	and thus it shall go with me that	and it shall come to passe that
20. 10		*omit*
31. 16	therfore	for
See moreover		
morowe 19. 34	morow	morrow
morter 11. 3		
morsell 18. 5		
most 14. 18 (3 times)		
14. 20	*omit*	
mother 27.13 (8 times)		
mothers 24.28 (8 ,,)		
— children 27. 37	brethren	brethren
moulde 2. 7		dust
mountayne 12. 8		mountaine
(2 times)		
10. 30		mount
mountaynes 14. 10		mountaine
mountayns 8. 4	mountaynes	mountaines
(2 times)		

	C	A
mountayns 19. 19 (2 times) *See* mounteyns	mountayne	mountaines
mounte 14. 6 (8 times)		mount
22. 14	mountayne	,,
mounteyns 8. 5 *See* mountaynes mountayns	,,	,,
mouth 4. 11 (7 times)		
8. 11	nebb	
42. 28	*omit*	*omit*
move 8. 17	be ye occupied vpon the earth	breed abundantly
moved 1. 2 (2 times)		
8. 19	crepte	creepeth
20. 10	*omit*	*omit*
moveth 9. 3		mouing
movinge 3. 24	*omit*	which turned
much more, twise so 43. 15 *See* moch	other	double
mules 36. 24		
multiplie 28. 3	multiplye	multiply
48. 16	,,	grow into a multi- tude
multiplye 1. 22 (3 times)	multiplie	multiply
8. 17 (6 times)	multiplye	,,
17. 20	,,	multiplie
—, wyll 17. 2		
—, will 17. 6		will make the ex- ceeding fruitfull
—, will 26. 4		will make thy seed to multiply
—, will 48. 4	will make a multi- tude of people of thee	

	C	A
multiplyed 47. 27	multiplied	multiplied
—, shall be 16. 2	shalbe multiplied	may obtaine children
multitude 16. 10		
(3 times)		
35. 11		company of nations
41. 49	*omit*	very much
myddes 3. 3 (2 times)		midst
myddest, in the 9. 21	in	within
See middes		
mydwife 38. 28		midwife
mydwyfe 35. 17	mydwife	,,
myghte 31. 6	power	power
49. 3	,,	might
myghtie 10.9 (2times)	mightie	mighty
10. 9	,,	mightie
12. 2	,,	great
26. 14	greate	,,
— God of Israel 33.20	mightie God of Israel	El-Elohe-Israel
See mightie mightye myghtye		
myghtier 25. 33	greater	stronger
26. 16	farre mightier	much mightier
myghtye 10. 8	mightie	mighty
(2 times)		
See mightie mightye myghtie		
Mylca 11. 29	Milca	Milcah
See Milca Milcha		
mylch 32. 15	mylck	milch
mylcke 18. 8	mylke	milke
mylke 49. 12	mylck	,,
myndes 23. 8	wyll	mind
myngell 11. 7	confounde	confound

	C	A
myrre 37. 25 (2 times)		myrrhe
myrth 31. 27		mirth
myschefe 6. 13		violence
See mischefe		
mysfortune 42. 4		mischiefe
(3 times)		
See misfortune		
myste 2. 6	myst	mist
na 17. 19	yee	*omit*
See no		
Nabaioth 28. 9	Nebaioth	Nebaioth
See Nebaioth		
Nachor 22.20 (2 times)	Nahor	Nahor
Naema 4. 22		Naamah
Naeman 46. 21	Naaman	Naaman
Nahath 36.13 (2 times)		
Nahor 11.22 (11 times)		
Nahors 11. 29		
24. 47	of Nahor	
naked 2. 25 (4 times)		
3. 24	naked fyrie	flaming
nakydnes 9. 23	secretes	nakednesse
nam, his 30. 8	him	.his name
name 2. 13 (34 times)		
4. 17 (14 times)	*omit*	
— of 4. 25 (12 times)	called him	
29. 32 (2 ,,)	whom	
2. 11	is called	
—, his 25. 30	he	
— is 35. 10	art called	
names 2. 20 (6 times)		
2. 19 (3 times)		name
—, their 25. 13	are named	
36. 40	*omit*	
Naphis 25. 15		Naphish
Naphtuhim 10. 13		

	C	A
nat 27. 1	*omit*	not
See not		
nott		
nation 17. 20	nacion	
15. 14 (2 times)	people	nation
10. 5	,,	nations
25. 23	nacion	people
nations 17.5 (4 times)	nacions	
10. 20 (7 times)	people	
14. 1	Heithen	
—, princes of 25. 16	londeprynces	
nay 33. 10		
42. 10 (2 times)	no	
19. 2	se	
19. 7	O	*omit*
19. 18	no	,,
neadeth 33. 15	nede is	needeth
Nebaioth 36. 3		
See Nabaioth		
necessarie 42. 19	necessary	*omit*
necessary 42. 33		,,
necke 27. 16 (9 times)	neck	
— lace 38. 18	bracelet	bracelets
necklace 38. 25	,,	,,
nedes, must 43. 11		must
needes, must 17. 13	shalbe	,, needs
negligent, why are ye	why gape ye	why do ye looke
42. 1		one vpon an other
Nemrod 10.8 (2 times)		Nimrod
Nephthali 30. 8		Naphtali
Nepthali 35. 25		,,
(3 times)		
nere 27. 21	neare	neere
27. 26 (3 times)	nye	,,
18. 23	vnto	,,
39. 10	by	,,

	C	A
nether 21. 26		neither
8. 22 (5 times)		not
2. 5		and not
19. 33 (2 times)	ner	nor
— any thinge 22. 12	nothinge	neither
28. 15	not	not
29. 7	„	neither
31. 50	or	if
45. 5	not	nor
45. 6	no	neither
47. 18	not	*omit*
Neuaioth 25. 13	Nebaioth	Nebaioth
neuer 41. 19		
27. 36	not one	not a
nevertheles 6. 3	yet	and
neverthelesse 24. 8	but	„
— if 44. 26	excepte	*omit*
nexte 47. 18	next	second
neybure 38. 20	shepherde	friend
Ninyue 10. 12		Nineueh
10. 11	Niniue	„
no 8. 9 (21 times)		
2. 5 (4 „)		not
8. 12 (2 „)		not any
42. 31 (2 „)	neuer	
4. 15		lest eny
19. 31 ·	not a	not a
— perell 24. 41	discharged	cleare
31. 14		any
— man 41. 15		none
— „ 41. 24	they . . . nothinge	„
— „ 41. 39	none	„
42. 13	*omit*	*omit*
— hurte, meane 42. 19	be unfayned	„
45. 1	not	not
47. 18	nothinge	„
Nod 4. 16		

	C	A
Noe 5. 9 (28 times)		Noah
5. 30 (2 „)	*omit*	„
7. 6 (3 „)	he	„
7. 9 (2 „)	him	„
—, of 9. 19	Noes	of Noah
Noes 7. 11		Noahs
7. 13 (2 times)	his	„
nombre 34. 30		number
—, can 13. 16		
28. 3 (2 times)	multitude	multitude
—, to 15. 5	canst nombre	to number
35. 22	*omit*	*omit*
—, was without 41. 49	coude not be nombred	was without number
—, in 46. 18	*omit*	euen
nombred, can be		can be numbred
32. 12		
—, shall be 13. 16	shall nombre	shall be numbred
See numbred		
nombrynge 41. 49		numbring
nomore 32. 28		
17. 5		neither any more
17. 15		not
none 23. 6 (3 times)		
43. 16 (2 „)	no one	noone
28. 7	no thinge	
nor 21. 23 (4 „)	ner	
—, no 31. 14	„	any or
41. 39	and	and
47. 18	not onely but	but and
norse 24. 59 (2 times)		nurse
north 28. 14		
northward 13. 14	northwarde	
nostrels 7. 22	*omit*	nosetrils
not 2. 17 (185 times)		
3. 2 (3 „)		neither
18. 29 (6 „)	nothinge	
19. 9 (4 „)		*omit*

	C	A
not 20. 11 (2 times)	no	
31. 52 (2 „)	yf	
4. 15 (4 „)	*omit*	*omit*
8. 21	nomore	
9. 11	no	neither
11. 16		nothing
17. 14	† vncircumcided	
— farre from 18. 2	ouer agaynst	by
— fynde, coude 19. 11		wearied them-selues to finde
23. 6		but that
— so 23. 11	no	nay
—, regarded 25. 34		despised
31. 50	yf	if
— worthy of 32. 10	to litle	
— a litle 34. 7	very	very
36. 7		† then that
37. 22	no	no
38. 9		least
39. 9		none
43. 7	„	omit
	yet	
—, wold 48. 19		refused
— fayle but, will 50. 25	whan	surely
See not nott		
noted 37. 11	marcked	obserued
nothinge 26. 29 (2 times)		nothing
30. 31		not any thing
39. 6		not ought
39. 9		neither any thing
39. 23	*omit*	not any thing
nothynge 19. 8	nothinge	nothing
19. 22	„	not any thing
nott 19. 21	not	not
See nat not		

	C	A
not withstondynge		
4. 7	*omit*	and
35. 10	neuertheles	*omit*
nought 29. 15		
noughte 47. 19	*omit*	,,
now 3. 22 (32 times)		,,
14. 3 (3 ,,)		,,
14. 8 (2 ,,)	,,	:,
24. 49 (5 ,,)	,,	
16. 15		when
18. 12		after
18. 13	and yet	*omit*
24. 14	now yf	let it come to passe that
26. 29	as for the	
— though 31. 30	for as moch then as	
42. 22		therefore
numbred, shall be	shall be nombred	shall be numbred
16. 10		
See nombred		
nye 12. 11		neere
—, come 20. 4	touched	come neere
—, drewe 47. 29	came	drew nigh
nygh, to come 20. 6	to touch	to touch
nyght 14. 15 (2 times)	night	night
nyghte 1. 5 (24 ,,)	,,	,,
—, great whyle to	yet hye daye	yet high day
29. 7		
—, this 30. 15		to night
—, at 49. 27	in the euenynge	at night
nyghtes 7. 4 (2 times)	nightes	nights
7. 17	*omit*	*omit*
O 18. 30	Oh	Oh
18. 30		behold now
See oh		
Obal 10. 28		
obaysaunce 33. 6	obeysaunce	bowed themselues

	C	A
obaysaunce 33. 7 (2 times) *See* obeysaunce	kneled vnto him	bowed themselues
obey, shall 41. 40	shall obeye	shall be ruled
obeyed, hast 22. 18	hast herkened vnto	
—, hast 3. 17	„ „ „	hast hearkened vnto
—, had 28. 7	obeyed	obeyed
obeysaunce 37. 7 *See* obaysaunce	obeysaunce	obeisance
occupation 46. 33 (2 times)	occupacion	
—, do 34. 21	occupye	trade
occupy 42. 34	maye occupie	shall traffique
occupyde, be 9. 7	be occupied	bring foorth abundantly
—, haue bene 46. 34	haue dealt with	*omit*
Odollam, of 38. 1 (2 times)		Adullamite
38. 20	Odulla	„
of 1. 23 (758 times)		
1. 5 (36 „)		*omit*
1. 14 (3 „)		of the
1. 26 (7 „)	vnder	
2. 4 (32 „)	*omit*	*omit*
2. 5 (4 „)	vpon	
2. 6 (123 „)	*omit*	
2. 19 (2 „)		out of
3. 14 (2 „)	aboue	aboue
4. 1 (5 „)		from
4. 4 (3 „)		therof
6. 4 (10 „)	in	
—, in the syghte 6. 11 (4 times)		before
—, full 6. 11 (2 times)		filled with
—, all maner 7. 14 (3 times)		euery
— him 8. 21 (2 times)		his

C		A
of him 11. 6 (5 times)		off
—, because 12. 17 (3 times)		
— father 20. 12 (2 times)	fathers	
— bondwoman 21. 10 (2 times)	bonde maydens	
24. 3 (3 times)	amonge	
— Abraham 24. 9 (2 times)	Abrahams	
24. 17 (3 times)	out of	
— sonne 27. 15 (2 times)	sonnes	
— Laban 30. 40 (2 times)	Labans	
31. 13 (3 times)	at	
— Iacob 34. 7 (3 times)	Iacobs	
—, in syghte 38. 7 (2 times)	before	
— Pharo 41. 35 (4 times)	Pharaos	
— Ioseph 46. 27 (3 times)	Iosephs	
47. 9 (3 times)		of the yeeres of
— every kynde, vii 7. 2 (2 times)	seuen and seuen	by seuens
— them 10. 30 (2 times)	their	their
1. 25		that creepeth vpon
2. 17	therof	therof
— it 3. 5		,,
—, to eate 3. 6		for food
— both of them 3. 7	*omit*	of them both
— which 3. 11	wherof	whereof
3. 17	,,	
—, in processe 4. 3	after	

	C	A
of, in processe 4. 4		thereof
— Adam 5. 5	his	*omit*
— Seth 5. 8	,,	
— Enos 5. 11	,,	
— Kenan 5. 14	,,	
— Iared 5. 20	,,	
— Henoch 5. 23	,,	
— Methusala 5. 27	,,	
— Lamech 5. 31	,,	
—, all maner 7. 14		all the
— man 9. 5	mans	
—, in the myddest 9. 21	in	within
—, in the syghte 10. 9	before	before
— brother 10. 25	brothers	
— Chanaan 12. 5	same londe	
—, because 12. 17		
13. 4	where he had made	
14. 15	of the cite of	
— L., lacke .v. 18. 28	fyue lesse then fiftie	
— mother 20. 12	mothers	
— Abimelech 20. 18	Abimelechs	
21. 13	beside	
22. 6	to	off
—, in presence 23. 9	amonge	
— Ephron 23. 17	Ephrons	
— the men 24. 13	the mens	
24. 17	out of	
25. 16	*omit*	according to
25. 30		with
— Abraham his father	his father Abra-	
26. 18	hams	
36. 32		concerning
—, the smooth 27. 16	smooth aboute	
— it 28. 12	whose	
28. 17	vnto	

	C	A
of, on the top 28. 18	vpon	
— Laban his mothers brother, shepe 29. 10	his mothers brothers shepe	
29. 26	in	*omit*
30. 33	before	before
— Laban 30. 40	Labans	Labans
— thy fathers, lande 31. 3	thy fatherlande	
— the least of, not worthy 32. 10	to litle for all	
— this maner 32. 19	like as I haue tolde you	on this maner
— all, last 33. 7	afterwarde	after
33. 10		at
— my sonne Sichem 34. 8	my sonne Sichems	
34. 19	aboue	
— Esaus sonnes 36.10	of the children of Esau	
— Esau 36. 10	Esaus	
36. 20	in	*omit*
— Pharaos, a lord 37. 36	Pharaos	
— a man called a Canaanyte, doughter 38. 2	a man of Canaans doughter	
— from 38. 12		off from
— Pharaos 39. 1	Pharaos	of Pharaoh
— his master the Egiptian 39. 2	his master the Egipcians	
39. 4		ouer
— the kynge of Egipte 40. 1	kynge of Egiptes	
—, by reason 41. 31	because of	
— hungers, yeres 41. 36	deare yeares	
—, in rayment 41. 42	clothed with	

	C	A
of, in rayment 41.48	grewe in	
— plenteousnes 41.53	plenteous	
44. 5	out of	in
—, brother 44. 20	his brother	his brother
— syluer, peces 45.22	syluer peces	
— catell 46. 32		† to feed cattell
— Egipte 47. 26	Egipcians	
— Iacob 47. 28	his	
— Israell 48. 10	Israels	
— Ephraim 48. 17	Ephraims	
— thyne enimies 49.8	enemies	
49. 26	promised vnto	
— him 49. 26	his	
off 21. 16 (2 times)	of	
9. 5 (2 „)	„	of
—, all maner 7. 14	all maner of	euery
21. 18	of	*omit*
49. 20	„	out of
offended, haue 20. 9		
—, what haue 31. 36		what is my sinne
—, had 40. 1	offended	
offerynge 4. 3	offrynge	offering
See offrynge		
office 41. 13		
40. 13		place
officers 41. 34		
offred 8. 20		
22. 13 (2 times)		offered
offrynge 4.4		offering
4. 5	offerynge	offring
See offerynge		
offrynges 46. 1	offerynges	sacrifices
oft 3. 16	*omit*	*omit*
oh 19. 18 (2 times)		
18. 32	O	
44. 18	*omit*	
See O		

	C	A
Ohad 46. 10		
Oke 12. 6	okegroue	plaine
See ooke		
okegrove 13. 18		
(2 times)		
18. 1		plaines
old 17. 1 (6 times)	olde	
5. 3 (3 ,,)	,,	*omit*
40. 13	,,	former
olde 17. 12 (3 times)		
12. 4 (28 ,,)		old
21. 4	*omit*	,,
olyve 8. 11		oliue
Omar 36. 11 (2 times)		
on 12. 8 (16 times)		
1. 27 (2 ,,)	opon	vpon
4. 16 (8 ,,)	vpon	
1. 28 (15 ,,)	,,	vpon
3. 15 (4 ,,)		*omit*
—, come 11.3 (3 times)		goe to
33. 4 (2 times)	aboute	
on 4. 21 (4 times)	*omit*	*omit*
37. 10 (3 ,,)	vpon	,,
42. 6 (2 ,,)	to	,,
2. 14	towarde	toward
3. 15	downe	*omit*
7. 22	vpon	in
19. 2	*omit*	
24. 14	vpon	vnto
33. 3	to	*omit*
—, only 39. 6	saue only	saue
44. 34	vnto	
45. 14	aboute	vpon
On 41. 45 (3 times)		
Onan 38. 4 (5 ,,)		
Onam 36. 23		
once 18. 32		

	C	A
once 2. 23		now
—, att 18. 6	at once	quickly
—, this 29. 34	*omit*	this time
41. 31	,,	*omit*
one 10. 25 (38 times)		
8. 19		,,
11. 1 (3 times)	*omit*	
22. 2	a	
22. 20 (5 times)	*omit*	*omit*
24. 41	her	
26. 10	some	
34. 14	man	
37. 4	a	*omit*
—, best saue 41. 43	seconde	second
onix 2. 12		
only 41. 40	onely	
6. 5 (8 times)	,,	onely
47. 22 (2 times)	excepte	,,
9. 4	onely	but
18. 32	*omit*	*omit*
27. 13	,,	onely
34. 15	neuertheles	but
34. 22	but	onely
34. 23	yf	,,
39. 6	onely	*omit*
39. 9	excepte	,,
ooke 35. 4 (2 times)	oke	oke
— of lamentation 35.8		Allon Bachuth
See oke		
ooth 24. 8 (2 times)		othe
oothe 26.3 (2 times)	ooth	,,
24. 41		oath
open 4. 7 (2 times)		*omit*
opened 8. 6 (6 times)		
—, were 3.7 (2 times)		
—, shulde be 3. 5	shalbe opened	shalbee opened
4. 11	hath ,,	hath ,,

	C	A
Ophir 10. 29		
or 13. 9 (5 times)		
ordered, hast 24. 14	hast prouyded	hast appointed
ordinaunce was made 47. 22	it was ordered	had a portion assigned
ordinaunces 26. 5		charge
or els 30. 1		
organs 4. 21	pypes	
other 4. 19 (11 times)		
41. 23 (2 „)	*omit*	*omit*
—, none 28. 17	nothinge els	
41. 3	*omit*	
42. 5		those
otherwise called 23.19	that is	the same is
„ „ 35.8	which is called	that is
„ „ 35.27	„ „ „	which is
oughte saue 31. 24 (2 times)	nothinge but	either
out 3. 24 (22 times)		
2. 21 (2 „)		*omit*
8. 7 (4 „)		foorth
15. 14 (10 „)	forth	
24. 29 (2 „)	*omit*	
15. 5 (2 „)	forth	forth abroad
24. 30 (3 „)	*omit*	*omit*
—, in and 3. 24	*omit*	euery way
out 8. 18		foorth out
—, gaue charge	gaue charge to	
to leade 12. 20	conveye out	sent away
19. 29	out of	out of
27. 34	loude	*omit*
—, passe 29. 27	holde out	fulfill
39. 13		forth
41. 27	vp	vp
— of 2. 9 (44 times)		
4. 10 (5 times)		from
25. 23 (2 „)		*omit*

	C	A
out of 28. 16 (2 times)	from	
21. 16 (2 „)	ouer on	ouer on
2. 6	from	from
3. 23		foorth from
8. 16		foorth
9. 18		forth of
10. 11		forth out of
24. 5		whence
— measure 24. 35	richely	greatly
24. 50	of	from
— measure 27. 33	aboue measure	very exceedingly
36. 33	of	of
41. 22	vpon	in
41. 49	abone	*omit*
45. 23		of
49. 24	of	from thence
oute of 23. 4 (2 times)	by	
ouer 1. 26 (22 „)		
24. 2 (2 times)	of	
25. 25 (2 „)	*omit*	
41. 34 (3 „)	in	
1. 20	aboue	aboue
11. 4	in	vpon
12. 20		concerning
15. 10		*omit*
24. 67		after
32. 22	vnto	
—, ruelar 39. 5	ruler of	ouerseer
43. 19	of	of
45. 8		„
ouerdryue, shulde		
33. 13	shulde be dryuen	
overspred, was 9. 19	were ouerspred	was ouerspread
ouersyghte 43. 12	ouersight	ouersight
ouertake 44. 4	ouertakest	
overthrewe 19. 25		
(2 times)		

	C	A
overthrowe, will 19. 21		will overthrow
overthrowenge 19. 29	ouerthrew	ouerthrow
ouer toke 31. 23		ouertooke
31. 25	drew nye vnto	,,
46. 6	had ouertaken	,,
owne 14. 14 (2 times)		
oxe, houghed an 49. 6		† digged downe a wall
oxen 12. 16 (5 times)		
26. 14 (2 times)	greate catell	heards
32. 7		herdes
47. 17		catell of the heards
oxsen 24. 35		heards
oyle 28. 18 (2 times)		oile
pace, went a 18. 6		hastened
Pagu 36. 39		Pau
Pallu 46. 9		Phallu
parcell 33. 19	pete	
47. 26	parte	part
part 31. 14	porcion	portion
parte 41. 34 (2 times)		part
32. 8	droue	company
43. 34		measse
47. 2	fyue	some
parted 1. 7		diuided
30. 40		did separate
partes 47. 24		parts
7. 19	whole	whole
14. 24	*omit*	portion
14. 24	parte	,,
partie 30. 32 (3 times)	partye	speckled
30. 33	,,	spotted
30. 35		ring-straked
31. 10	,,	grisled
31. 12	partie	,,
parties, sene the backe	sene the back	looked after
16. 13	partes	

C A

passe, came to 27. 1
(3 times)
—, came to 1. 9 (2 times)   was so
—, „ „ 8. 13 (2 „) *omit*
—, „ „ 6. 1   so
—, to 41. 32 (2 times)
25. 22   *omit*   *omit*
— out 29. 27   holde out   fulfill
—, to 39. 23   to prosper
passed 31. 21
29. 28   helde out   fulfilled
37. 28   wente by
See past
passinge 26. 1   passynge   besides
past, tymes 31. 2   yesterdaye and   before
(2 times)   yeryesterdaye
See passed
pasture 47. 4
path 49. 17
Pathrusim 10. 14
payne 3. 16   sorow
paynefull 34. 25   panefull   sore
paynes 35. 17   payne   labour
payre 6. 19 (3 times)   **two**
peace 15. 15 (4 „)
24. 21 (2 times)   tonge
41. 16   prosperous
See pece
peaces 44. 28   peces   pieces
See peces
peeces
peasable 34. 21   peaceable   peaceable
pease, will 32. 20   reconcyle   will appease
pece 15. 10   parte   peece
See peace
peces 37. 28 (2 times)   pieces
15. 17   partes   „

	C	A
peces 37. 33	*omit*	pieces
See peaces		
peeces		
peckes 18. 6		measures
peeces 20. 16	pens	pieces
See peaces		
peces		
Peleg 10.25 (4 times)		
Peniel 32. 30		
32. 31		Penuel
people 11.6 (31 times)		
10. 32 (3 ,,)		nations
12. 2 (6 ,,)		nation
peradventure 27. 12		
(3 times)		
16. 2		it may bee that
20. 11		surely
26. 9		lest
perauenture 11. 4	afore	,,
perceaue, cowde		could be knowen
41. 21		
perceaued 19. 33		perceived
(2 times)		
8. 11		knew
38. 9	knewe	,,
perell, bere no 24. 41	be discharged	be cleare
—, was in 35. 16	the byrth came harde vpon hir	had hard labour
performe, will 26. 3	wyll perfourme	
perish, shall 6. 17		shall die
17. 14	shalbe roted out	shall be cut off
19. 15	perishe	be consumed
45. 11	,,	come to pouertie
perishe 41. 36	be destroyed	perish
See perisshe		
perished 7. 21		died

	C	A
perisshe 19. 17	perish	be consumed
See perish		
perishe		
persone, a goodly 39.6	fayre of bewtye	a goodly person
pertayne, shall 3. 16		shall be
—, vnto whom these	that oweth these	whose these are
38. 25		
pertanyng to, as 4. 11	vpon	from
perteyneth to them	theirs	theirs
15. 13		
Pharan 21. 21		Paran
—, playne of 14. 6		El-Paran
Pharez 38.29 (3 times)	Phares	
Pharao 40. 13		Pharaoh
(56 times)		
12. 15 (3 times)	him	„
12. 20 (2 „)	he	„
—, of 41.35 (5 „)	Pharaos	
41. 39 (3 „)	*omit*	
41. 43		*omit*
Pharaos 12. 15		Pharaohs
(7 times)		
12. 15 (3 times)		of Pharaoh
40. 11 (3 „)	the	Pharaohs
40. 11 (2 „)	his	„
Phelistinlande 21. 32	londe of the Phili-stynes	land of the Phili-stines
Pherezites 15. 20		Perizzites
34. 30	Pheresites	„
Pherysites 13. 7	„	„
Phicol 26. 26		Phichol
Phicoll 21.22 (2 times)	Phicol	„
Philestians 26. 14	Philistynes	Philistines
(2 times)		
Philistians 26. 1	„	„
26. 8	Phylistynes	„
Philistines 21. 32	„	„

	C	A
Philystyns 10. 14	Phylistynes	Philistiim
Phisicions 50. 2	Phisicians	Physicians
(2 times)		
Phison 2. 11		Pison
Phut 10. 6		
Phuva 46. 13	Phua	Phuuah
pigeon 15. 9		
Pildas 22. 22		Pildash
pilgremage 47. 9		pilgrimage
pilgremages 47. 9		,,
pillar 35. 10		
35. 10	stone	
pillare 19. 26	pillar	pillar
See pilloure		
pilled 30. 37	pylled	
—, had 30. 38	had pylled	
pilloure 35. 14	piler	pillar
See pillar		
pillare		
Pinon 36. 41	Pynon	
pitched 26. 17		
(3 times)		
31. 25 (2 times)	pytched	
33. 19 (2 ,,)		spread
28. 18	set	set
See pytched		
pitcher 24.20 (4 times)		
pither 24. 17	pitcher	pitcher
See pytcher		
place 1. 9 (36 times)		
26. 7 (2 ,,)	*omit*	
27. 39 (2 ,,)	,,	*omit*
2. 21		† flesh
—, restinge 8. 9		rest
— of the contre, any	all this countre	all the plaine
19. 17		
29. 26	countre	country

	C	A
place 47. 6		*omit*
50. 11		it
50. 13	possession	
places 36. 40		
— where, all 20. 13	where so euer	euery place
—, all 28. 15	„ „ „	
plaged 12. 17		plagued
plages 12. 17		plagues
planted 2. 8 (3 times)		
played, hath 38. 24	hath plaied	
— with, hast 29. 25	hast begyled	hast beguiled
playne 11. 2		plaine
13. 12	same coastes	„
— of Pharan 14. 6		El-Paran
playnge 38. 24	hath plaied	† by
pleasant 2. 9 (3 times)	pleasaunt	
pleased 34. 18		
(2 times)		
28. 8	loked gladly vpon	
41. 37		was good
pleaseth 16. 6		
20. 15	liketh	
pleasure, at your	open vnto you	before you
34. 10		
pleasures 49. 20	delicates	dainties
pledge 33.17 (3 times)		
plenteous 41. 34		
(2 times)		
— contre of water		well watered
13. 10		
plenteousnes 41. 29		plentie
(3 times)		
41. 53	plenteous yeares	plenteousnesse
plentie 27. 28	plenteousnes	plenty
ploweman 4. 2	huszbande man	tiller of the ground
plucked, had 8. 11	broken of	pluckt
38. 29	pluckte	drewe

	C	A
plucked, had 49. 33	pluckte	gathered
poore 41. 19	thynne	
popular 30. 37	wyllies	poplar
porcyon 48. 22	pece	portion
porte 49. 13		hauen
possesse, shall 15. 8		
(2 times)		
24. 60		
—, mayst 28. 4		
4. 20	had	haue
—, to 15. 7		to inherit
possession 17. 8		
(4 times)		
23. 18	owne good	
26. 14	moch good	
possessions 34. 10		
36. 43		possession
47. 11	a possession	,,
47. 27	,,	
possessor 14. 19		possessour
(2 times)		
potage 25.29 (3 times)	meace of meate	pottage
Potiphar 39. 1		
See Putiphar		
Potiphara 41. 45	Potiphar	Poti-phera
(3 times)		
poured 28. 18		powred
— out 24. 20		emptied
See powred		
power 49. 3		
4. 12		strength
41. 35		hand
powred 35. 14	poured	
(2 times)		
See poured		
poynte to dye, at the	must dye	
25. 32		

	C	A
prauender 42. 27 (2 times)	prouender	prouender
prauonder 24. 25 (2 times)	,,	,,
praye 13. 9 (6 times)		pray
12. 13 (3 ,,)	pray	,,
13. 8 (3 ,,)	*omit*	,,
prayde 20. 17	prayed	prayed
prayse, shall 49. 8		shall praise
—, will 29. 35	wyll geue thankes	wil ,,
praysed 12. 15		commended
preased 19. 9	pressed	pressed
preasence 27. 30 *See* presence	*omit*	presence
preasent 32. 13 (2 times) *See* present	present	present
preason 42. 16 (2 times) *See* preson	preson	prison
preast 41. 45 (3 times) *See* prest	prest	priest
preastes 47. 22 (2 times) *See* prestes	prestes	priests
precious 2. 12		**good**
prepared, had 18. 8		had dressed
—, hath 24. 44	hath prouyded	hath appointed out
—, is 41. 32		is established
43. 32	brought	set on
47. 11		placed
presence 25. 18		
45. 3 *See* preasence	face	
present 32.18 (7 times) *See* preasent		
presented 47. 2		

	C	A
presented 43. 15	stode before	stood before
46. 29	sawe	
preson 39. 20 (6 times)		prison
41. 14	dongeon	dungeon
See preason		
presoners 39. 22		prisoners
See prisoners		
prest 14. 18		priest
See preast		
prestes 47. 22		priests
See preastes		
prevayle, coude 32. 25	might ouercome	preuailed
prevayled 7. 18		,,
(3 times)		
7. 20		did preuaile
—, hast 32. 28		hast preuailed
prevytees 9. 22	preuities	nakednesse
price of vs 31. 15	oure wages	our money
princes of nations	londeprynces	princes
25. 16		
See prynces		
principall waters 2. 10	heade waters	heads
35. 27	head	*omit*
prisoners 39. 20	presoners	
See presoners		
proceded 4. 2	proceaded	againe
—, is 24. 50	is come	proceedeth
processe of tyme 4. 3	certaine daies	
— of tyme 38. 12	whan many dayes	
	were past	
profit 25. 32	good	
prolonged the tyme		lingred
19. 16		
promysed, hath 18. 19	hath promised	hath spoken of
—, haue 28. 15		have spoken of
prophesie, doth 44. 5	prophecieth	divineth
—, can 44. 15	can prophecy	can diuine

	C	A
prophete 20. 7	prophet	prophet
prosper 24. 40	prospere	prosper
39. 3	to prospere	to prosper
prospered, hath 24. 56		
prosperous 24. 21	had prospered	
—, makest 24. 42	hast „	doe prosper
proue, dyd 22. 1	tempted	did tempt
proued, shall be 42. 15	wyll proue	
—, shall be 42. 16	„ try out	may be proued
proverbe 10. 9		† it is saide
prouision, to make 45. 7	let remayne	to preserve
—, will make 45. 11	wyll make pro- uysion	wil nourish
provysion, shall make 30. 30	shall loke to	shall prouide
—, made 47. 12		nourished
prouyde, wyll 22. 8	shall prouyde	will prouide
41. 33		looke out
prynces 17. 20		princes
See princes		
pulled 19. 10		
8. 9	toke	
punyshed, shall be 4. 15	shalbe auenged	vengeance shall be taken
pure 20. 5		in integritie of
purenesse 20. 6	pure	integritie
purposed, haue 11. 6		haue imagined
put 19. 10 (18 times)		
—, will 3. 15		
— of 38. 14		
— on 38. 19		
24. 2 (3 times)	laye	
24. 9 (5 „)	layed	
—, was 25. 8 (3 times)	was gathered	was gathered
30. 38 (2 times)	layed	set
31. 37 (2 „)	laye	„

	C	A
put 1. 17	set	set
2. 15	„	
— on 3. 21		cloathed
4. 15		set
— awaye 21. 10	cast out	cast out
—, haue 26. 27		haue sent
27. 17		gaue
— from 38. 19	layed of	laid by
—, shulde haue 40. 15		should put
41. 42	gaue	
41. 42	honge	
41. 48	layed	laid vp
—, to 42. 25		to restore
—, hath 43. 23	hath geuen	hath giuen
—, shall 46. 4	shal laye	
—, shall be 49. 29	shal be gathered	am to be gathered
Putiphar 37. 36	Potiphar	Potiphar
See Potiphar		
pyke a quarell with,		that hee may seeke
to 43. 18		occasion against
pyne tree 6. 14	pyne	gopher-wood
pytch 6. 14 (2 times)	pitch	pitch
pytched 12. 8	pitched	pitched
See pitched		
pytcher 24. 24		pitcher
(2 times)		
24. 16 (2 times)	pitcher	„
See pitcher		
pither		
pytt 37. 20 (6 times)		pit
pyttes 14. 10		pits
quarell with, to pyke		that hee may seeke
a 43. 18		· occasion against
quarters 19. 4		quarter
quicly 27. 20	soone	quickly
quiver 27. 3	quyuer	quiuer

	C	A
Raemses 47. 11	Raemses	Rameses
Rahel 29. 6 (36 times)	Rachel	Rachel
29. 12	she	
Rahels 30. 7 (4 times)	Rachels	Rachels
ram 15. 9　(3　„　)	ramme	ramme
rammes 31. 10 (4 „)		
ran 18. 2　(2　„　)	ranne	ranne
See ranne		
rancke 41. 5	full	ranke
41. 7	greate	ranke
ranne 24. 17 (6 times)		
33. 4		ran
See ran		
Raphaims 15. 20	Giauntes	Rephaims
Raphayms 14. 5	„	„
raven 8. 7		
raueshynge 49. 27	rauyshinge	shall rauine as
Rayma 10. 7 (2 times)	Reyma	Raamah
rayment 24. 53		raiment
(3 times)		
27. 27 (2 times)	clothes	„
38. 19	garmentes	garments
41. 42	*omit*	vestures
rayne 7. 12 (2 times)		raine
2. 5		to raine
7. 4	raine	raine
rayned 19. 24	caused to rayne	rained
reach, may 11. 4		
—, shall 49. 13	shal border vpon	shall be
reached 28. 12		
See reched		
reade 38. 20	reed	skarlet
See redde		
reed		
reason of, by 12. 13		because of
41. 31	because of	
47. 13	by the reason of	

	C	A
Rebecca 22. 23		Rebekah
(25 times)		
Rebeccas 35. 8		Rebekahs
29. 12	of Rebecca	
rebelled 14. 4	fell from him	
rebuke 30. 23		reproch
rebuked 31. 42		
21. 25		reproued
37. 10	reproued	
receaue 33. 10		receiue
—, shalt 4. 7		shalt be accepted
—, to 4. 11	receaued	to receiue
—, 13. 6		to beare
—, shall 30. 33	*omit*	*omit*
—, will 32. 20	shall receaue	will accept of
— me to grace 33. 11	be at one with me	*omit*
—, coude 36. 7	might holde	coude beare
receaved, haue 19. 21	loked vpon the	have accepted
receauynge 49. 3	gouernaunce	dignitie
reched 40. 21	reached	gaue
See reached		
redde 25. 25 (2 times)	reed	red
25. 34	*omit*	*omit*
See reade		
reed		
redie 43. 16	ready	ready
43. 25	readye	„
—, make 27. 43	get the vp	arise
—, made 46. 29	bended fast	made ready
redy att once 18. 6	haist	ready quickly
—, made 31. 21	gat vp	rose vp
reed 38. 28		skarlet
See reade		
redde		
refrayne 45. 1		refraine
refrayned 43. 31		refrained
regarde 45. 20		regard

C   A

	C	A
regarded not 25. 34		despised
region 19. 25 (2 times)		plaine
Regu 11. 18 (2 times)		Reu
11. 19	*omit*	,,
Reguel 36. 4 (5 times)		Reuel
Rehoboth 26. 22		
(2 times)		
10. 11	*omit*	
reign, shalt 37. 8	have domynion	
reigned 36. 3		
36. 3	ruled	
36. 32 (8 times)	was kinge	
remayne 39. 11		remaine
45. 11	are	are
remembre, to 9. 16	and remembre	that I may re-member
—, do 41. 9		doe remember
remembred 8. 1		
30. 22 (2 times)	thought vpon	
removed, to haue	to remoue	to remoue
48. 17		
rennagate 4. 12	rennegate	fugitive
rent 37. 29 (2 times)		
44. 13	rente	
37. 33	*omit*	
— a rent, hast 38. 29	is a rent made	hast broken foorth
renowne 6. 4		
repented 6. 6		
repenteth 6. 7		
request, thy 17. 20		thee
19. 21	the	,,
require, wyll 9. 5	wyll requyre	
requyre, wyll 9. 5		will require
43. 9	shalt requyre	shalt ,,
—, wyll 9. 5	*omit*	will ,,
requyred 42. 22		is required
reserved, was 7. 23	remayned	remained

	C	A
reserved, is 32. 30	is recouered	is preserved
Ressen 10. 12		Resen
rest 18. 4 (2 times)		
19. 4		*omit*
30. 36	residue	
rested 2. 2 (3 times)		
restinge 8. 9	restynge	rest
restore 40. 13	putt	
restored 40. 21		
—, was 41. 13		restored
—, is 42. 28		
resydue 14. 10	residue	they thatremained
retourned 14. 17	came	returne
See returned		
returne 19. 6		
3. 19	be turned agayne	
—, will 18. 14	will come „	
31. 13	go agayne	
32. 9	departe agayne	
returned 18. 33		
8. 3	ranne styll awaye	
8. 9	came agayne	
50. 14	toke his iourney	
See retourned		
rever 2. 10	ryuer	riuer
See river		
ryver		
reviued 45. 27	reuyued	reuiued
rewarde 15. 1		reward
30. 28 (2 times)		wages
30. 32		hire
30. 18	rewarded	„
50. 15	recompense	requite
rewarded, haue 44. 4		
50. 17	dyd vnto	dyd vnto
rewardes 43. 34	sundrye meates	measses
rich 13. 2		
See ryche		

	C	A
riches 13. 6		*omit*
right 13. 9 (5 times)		
righte 18. 25 (2 „)	right	right
18. 19		iustice
See ryghte		
righteous 7. 1		
6. 9		iust
rightewes 20. 4	righteous	righteous
rightwes 18. 23		
(8 times)		
rightwesnes 15. 6	righteousnes	righteousnesse
(2 times)		
Riphat 10. 3		Riphath
river 2. 14 (2 times)	water	
See rever		
ryver		
Rheuma 22. 24	Rehuma	Reumah
robbed, haue 42. 36		haue bereaued
43. 14	that is robbed	bereaued
roddes 30. 37	staues	rods
rofe 19. 8		roofe
rose vp 19. 1 (5 times)		
19. 33 (2 times)		arose
22. 3 (2 „)	stode vp	
22. 19 (2 „)	gat vp	
24. 54 (2 „)	arose	
— vpon 32. 31		
— vp 19. 27		gate vp
20. 8		rose
21. 32	rose	
43. 15	gat them vp	
46. 5	„ him „	
roudier 49. 12		red
rough 25. 25		*omit*
27. 23		hairie
See rugh		
roull, to 29. 3	to roule	rolled

	C	A
roulled be, 29. 8	roule	rolle
See rowled		
rounde 23. 17		round
— aboute 35. 5		„ about
(3 times)		
See rownde		
rowled 29. 10	rouled	rolled
See roulled		
rowme 24. 23 (4 times)		roome
— ynough 34. 21	brode of both the	large enough
	sydes	
rownde 19. 4	rounde aboute	round
See rounde		
Ruben 29. 32		
(13 times)		
ruelar 43. 16		
39. 4 (2 times)	ruler	ouerseer
43. 19 (2 „)		steward
—, made 41. 43	set ouer	made ruler
49. 10	master	law-giuer
See rueler		
ruelars 47. 6	rulers	rulers
ruele, come forth to	† go vpon the wall	† runne ouer the
bere 49. 22		wall
See rule		
rueler 44. 1	ruler	steward
45. 8	prynce	ruler
See ruelar		
rugh 27. 11	rough	hairy
See rough		
rughly 42. 7 (2 times)	roughly	roughly
rule, to 1. 16 (3 „)		
—, shall 3. 16		
1. 26		dominion
4. 7	wilt rule	shalt rule
—, had the 24. 2		ruled
See ruele		

	C	A
runneth 2. 14		goeth
rybbe 2. 22		rib
rybbes 2. 21		ribs
ryche 14. 23		rich
30. 43	riche	*omit*
See rich		
ryches 36. 7	substaunce	riches
See riches		
ryd, went aboute to 37. 21	wolde haue dely-uered	deliuered
rydd, wolde haue 37. 22	wolde haue delyu-ered	might rid
ryder 49. 17		rider
ryghte 48. 13 (2 times)	right	right
See right		
righte		
rynge 41. 42	ringe	ring
rype 40. 10		ripe
ryse vp 19. 2	ryse	rise vp
—, redde 25. 34		lentiles
— vp, can 31. 35		can rise vp
— vp, wyll 43. 8	maye get vs vp	will arise
ryver 2. 13 (8 times)	water	riuer
32. 23	„	brooke
See rever		
river		
ryvers 31. 21 (3 times)	water	riuer
Sabe Kiriathaim 14. 5	the felde of Kiria-thaim	Shueh Kiriathaim
Sabta 10. 7	Sabtha	Sabtah
Sabtema 10. 7	Sabtheca	Sabtheca
sacke 42. 25 (4 times)		
43. 21 (3 „)	sack	
— clothe 37. 34	sack cloth	sackcloth
sackes 42. 25 (7 times)		
42. 35		sacks

	C	A
sackes 42. 28	sack	sacke
43. 12	sacke	
44. 2	„	
sacks 42. 27	sack	sackes
sacrifice 8. 20	brent sacrifices	burnt offring
22. 3 (3 times)	brentofferynge	„ offering
22. 6	„ „	„ offring
22. 2	offre	offer
22. 2	burntofferynge	burnt offring
sacrifyce 22. 13	brent sacrifice	„ offering
—, dyd 31. 54	offred an offerynge	offred sacrifice
sadd, were 40. 6	loked sadly	were sad
sadled 22. 3		
sadly 40. 7		
saftie 28. 21	peaceably	in peace
saide 50. 11	sayde	
26. 9 (2 times)	„	said
—, hath 21. 12	hath sayde	hath said
See sayde		
sayed		
sainge 27. 6	sayenge	saying
32. 6 (5 times)	and sayde	„
32. 29	„ „	and saide
43. 27	„ „	„ said
26. 22	„ „	he „
See sayenge		
saying		
sayinge		
sayng		
saynge		
sake 3. 17 (11 times)		
20. 3 (2 times)		*omit*
— of, for the 18. 24	sake	„
—, for goddes 19. 7	*omit*	I pray you
26. 9	*omit*	*omit*
—, for my 30. 30		since my comming
sakes 18. 26		

	C	A
Sala 10. 24 (2 times)		Salah
11. 12 (2 times)	Sahah	„
11. 13	*omit*	„
Salem 14. 18		
33. 18	„	Shalem
Saleph 10. 26		Sheleph
salt 14. 3		
salte 19. 26	salt	salt
same 5. 29 (10 times)		
19. 33 (4 „)		*omit*
21. 8 (2 „)	*omit*	
28. 11 (2 „)		that
39. 11 (2 „)	*omit*	this
2. 17	what so euer	*omit*
21. 2	appoynted	set
32. 22	*omit*	that
—, the 41. 48	therin	
Samla 36. 36 (2 times)		Samlah
Samma 36. 13 (2 „)		Shammah
sanctyfyed 2. 3	sanctified	sanctified
sande 41. 49	sonde	sand
Sara 17. 15 (29 times)		Sarah
18. 12	she	„
23. 2	*omit*	
Sarai 11. 29 (15 times)		
Sarais 16. 8		
Saras 24. 67 (2 times)		Sarahs
sat 18. 1 (2 „)		sate
sate 31. 34	sat	
satt 24. 61		rode
19. 1 (7 times)	sat	sate
38. 21	„	was
43. 33	were set	sate
50. 23	*omit*	were brought vp
Saue, vale of 14. 17	playne felde	valley of Saueh
Saul 36. 37 (2 times)		
46. 10		Shaul

	C	A
saue 14. 24 (2 times)		
19. 17 (3 „)		escape
— good, oughte 31. 24	nothinge but good	either good or bad
(2 times)		
7. 23		*omit*
—, shall 12. 12		will saue
—, can 19. 19		can escape
—, may 32. 8	shal escape	shall „
— one, best 41. 43	seconde	second
— lyfe, to 45. 5	youre lyues sake	to preserue
—, to 45. 5		„ „
—, 50. 20	for the sauynge of	to saue
saued, hast 47. 25	*omit*	
sauynge 49. 18	saluacion	saluation
savinge 19. 19	sauest	sauing
savoure 8. 21		sauour
27. 27		smell
sawe 28. 6 (6 times)		
1. 4 (39 times)		saw
49. 15	saw	„
44. 28 (2 times)	*omit*	
9. 23	shulde se	„
12. 14		beheld
19. 1		seeing
26. 28	se	
33. 1		looked and behold
43. 16	behelde	
sawest 20. 10		
say 37. 17	saye	
—, shalt 32. 18	shalt saye	
—, wyll 12. 12	wil „	shall say
—, to 14. 9	*omit*	*omit*
50. 17	shal saye	shall say
See saye		
sayd 4. 23	sayde	
3. 4		said
11. 3	saide	

	C	A
sayd 1. 3 (56 times)	sayde	said
7. 1 (4 times)	,,	saide
11. 6 (2 ,,)	saide	said
—, hath 3. 1	hath sayde	hath said
3. 3	,, ,,	,, ,,
sayde 15.5 (225 times)		said
17. 9 (29 ,,)	saide	,,
18. 32 (31 ,,)		saide
—, had 17. 23 (2 ,,)		had said
—, woulde haue 21.7	wolde haue saide	would haue said
—, hath 31. 16		hath said
—, hast 47. 30		hast ,,
—, hast 18. 5	hast spoken	,, ,,
18. 9 (19 times)	answered	said ·
29. 4	,,	saide
29. 5	,,	
—, had 23. 16		had named
24. 30 (5 times)		spake
—, hath 24. 51		hath spoken
24. 65 (2 times)		had said
26. 28	deuysed	said
—, hast 30. 34		to thy word
—, had 44. 2		had spoken
44. 20	*omit*	said
41. 32 (3 times)		saying
41. 52		*omit*
—, the 15. 17	*omit*	those
—, haue 24. 33	haue tolde	haue tolde
—, had 44. 24	of lordes words	*omit*
See saide		
sayed		
saydest 26. 9 (3 times)		saidst
12. 19		saidest
saye 12. 13 (6 times)		say
44. 4	saie	,,
—, shuldest 14. 23		shouldest say
—, shall 44. 16		shall say

	C	A
saye 24. 14 (2 times)		shall say
— on 24. 33	tell on	speake on
—, can 24. 50		can speake
26. 2	shall saye	tell of
34. 12	wyll axe	shall say
—, that is to 37. 1	*omit*	*omit*
—, let us 37. 20	saye	will say
—, haue herde 41. 15	haue herd tell	haue heard say
43. 25	*omit*	*omit*
46. 34	shal saye	shall say
48. 20	it shal be sayde	saying
See say		
sayed 13. 14	saide	and said
24. 42	sayde	said
See saide		
sayd		
sayde		
sayenge 15. 4	saide	saying
17. 1	sayde	and said
See sainge		
saying		
sayinge		
sayng		
saynge		
sayeth, what a nother	what another	one anothers
11. 7	saieth	speech
45. 9	sendeth the this worde	saith
See sayth		
saying 1. 22	sayenge	saying
sayinge 2. 16	,,	,,
sayng 5. 29	and sayde	,,
saynge 3. 17 (3 times)	sayenge	,,
8. 15 (37 times)	and sayde	,,
9. 8 (10 ,,)	*omit*	,,
18. 13	and saye	,,

	C	A
saynge, it is a comen	it is a comon	it is said
22. 14	sayenge	
24. 37 (5 times)	and saide	saying
41. 37	sayenge	thing
14. 18	and sayde	and saide
22. 11 (9 times)	,, ,,	,, said
29. 35	,, ,,	,, she said
30. 2	,, ,,	,, he ,,
37. 2	reporte	report
37. 9 (3 times)	and saide	and said
42. 7	,, ,, vnto them	and he said

    See sainge
           sayenge
           saying
           sayinge

sayth 22. 16 (2 times)	sayeth	saith
44. 7	saieth	,,
32. 4	sendeth thee this worde	,,

    See sayeth

scace 27. 30		scarce
scater 49. 7		scatter
scatered, shall be 11. 4	be scatred	be scattered
See skatered		
sceptre 49. 10	cepter	scepter
se 31. 5 (3 times)		see
—, to 42. 9		to see
44. 23	shall se	shall see
—, do 45. 12		see
18. 31 (2 times)		behold now
1. 29 (3 ,,)	lo	,,
— that thou eate not	shalt thou not eate	thou shalt not eate
2. 17 (2 times)		
6. 20 (2 ,,)	*omit*	*omit*
15. 3 (6 ,,)	beholde	behold
— thou eate 2. 16	shalt eate	mayest eate

	C	A
se that ye eate not 3. 3	eate not ye	shal not eate
— that ye touch not 3. 3	touch not	neither shall ye touch
— that ye eate not 9. 4	onely eate not	shall not eate
— thou kepe 17. 9	kepe	thou shalt keepe
19. 21	beholde	see
—, will 21. 16	can se	let see
— thou take 28. 1	take	thou shalt take
28. 6	thou shalt take	„ „ „
28. 12	beholde	beholde
that ye speake 32. 4	saye	shall ye speake
—, „ „ 32. 19	speake ye	„ you „
37. 32	loke	know
39. 14	lo	see
41. 7	sawe	behold
45. 24	*omit*	see
— that thou burye 50. 5	bury	shalt thou bury
— that ye carye 50.25	cary	ye shal carie
See see		
seall 38. 25	signet	signet
searched 31. 35	sought	
—, hast 31. 37		
See serched		
season 40. 4		
37. 34		dayes
21. 2 (3 times)	tyme	time
42. 16	*omit*	*omit*
seasons 1. 14		
seate, kynges 4. 40		throne
Seavan 36. 27	Seauan	Zaauan
Seba 10. 7 (3 times)		Sheba
26. 33	Saba	Shebah
Sebulon 46. 14	Zabulon	Zebulon
second 41. 5	seconde	
41. 32	„	twice

	C	A
seconde 1. 8 (6 times)		second
7. 11	second	,,
45. 6	two	two
secretly 31. 27	secrete	
secrets 9. 23	secretes	nakednesse
See secrettes		
secrett, kepe 37. 26	hyde	conceale
secrettes 49. 6	secretes	secret
sede 26. 3		seed
26. 24		seede
See seed		
see 18. 24		
—, to 2. 19 (3 times)	to se	
—, will 32. 20		
—, coude 48. 10	coude se	
43. 3 (2 times)	shall se	shall see
1. 26 (8 ,,)	see	sea
11. 6 (2 ,,)	beholde	
1. 10	See	Seas
— thou rule 4. 7	wilt thou rule	thou shalt rule
9. 7	*omit*	*omit*
9. 9	beholde	behold
12. 12	se	shall see
—, the LORde will 22. 14	the LORDE shall prouyde	Iehouah-ijreh
—, coude 27. 1	*omit*	
—, to 34. 1	to beholde	
37. 14	loke	
—, let 37. 20	shal it be sene	shall see
42. 22	*omit*	behold
—, maye 44. 26	darre loke	
—, shulde 44. 34	shulde se	see
See se		
seed 1. 11 (40 times)	sede	
1. 29 (11 times)	,,	seede
3. 15	the same	it
47. 24	*omit*	
See sede		

	C	A
sees 1. 22		seas
seeth 44. 31	se	
—, totehill which the	*omit*	Mizpah
lorde 31. 49		
See seith		
seyth		
seinge 6. 27 (2 times)	seynge	seeing
—, well of the lyvinge		
and 25. 11		well Lahai-roi
See seynge		
Seir 14. 6 (7 times)		
seist 31. 43		seest
seiste 13. 15	seist	,,
seith 16. 13	,,	,,
—, well of the lyuynge	well of the liuinge	Beer-lahai-roi
that 16. 14	that sawe	
seke 37. 16		seeke
—, fell 25. 17 (2 times)	fell sicke	gaue vp the ghost
31. 32		discerne
48. 1	sicke	sicke
Sela 38. 5 (5 times)		Shelah
selfe same 7. 13		
17. 23	same	
17. 26	one	
selfewill 49. 6		
sell 25. 31 (2 times)		
Sem 5. 32 (3 ,,)		
9. 18 (9 times)		Shem
11. 11	*omit*	,,
seme, shal 27. 12	shulde seme	
— cruel 45. 5	† think	† bee angry
Semeaber 14. 2		Shemeber
semed 29. 20		seemed
19. 14	toke	,,
21. 11	displeased	was
semeth 19. 8	liketh	is
Semnon 46. 13	Semron	Shimron

	C	A
sence 44. 28	*omit*	since
send, wyll 7. 4	wil sende	will cause it to
24. 12	mete	
26. 29	let departe	haue sent
—, may 37. 13	wil sende	will send
43. 8	let go	
43. 14	let haue	may send
45. 5	sent	did send
sende 38. 17 (2 times)		send
—, shall 24. 7		shall send
—, will 27. 45		will „
(2 times)		
—, wilt 43. 4 (2 times)		wilt „
—, wyll 24. 40	shall sende	will send
24. 56	let go	send
— for 26. 9	called	called
—, wold 42. 4	wolde let go	sent
sene, haue 7. 1		haue seene
(3 times)		
—, had 33. 10		had „
—, haue 32. 30	sawe	haue „
(2 times)		
—, was 5. 24		was
—, haue 16. 13		haue looked after
—, will be 22 14	shall prouyde	shalbe seene
—, had 24. 30	sawe	saw
—, to haue 48. 11	haue sene	to see
senow 32. 22 (2 times)		sinewe
senowe 32. 25		hollow
sent 20. 2 (14 times)		
41. 8	sente	
— forth 8. 7 (3 times)		
—, hath 19. 13		
—, haue 32. 5		
—, had 45. 27 (2 times)		
28. 5 (2 times)	let departe	sent
— out 8. 10		sent foorth

C	A

sent 19. 29 — conueyed

26. 31 — let go

—, haddest 31. 42 — haddest latten go

32. 18 — sendeth

32. 23 — caried

32. 23 — came ouer

38. 23 — haue sent

— for 47. 29 — called — called

sentence, hath geuen — — hath iudged
30. 6

separat 49. 26 — separate — separate

separate 30. 32 — „ — remoouing

Sephara 10. 30 — Sephar — Sephar

Sepho 36. 23 — — Shepho

sepulchre 23. 6 — sepulcre

sepulchres 23. 6 — sepulcres

Serah 36. 13 (3 times) — — Zerah

46. 17 — Sera — Serah

serche, to 42. 30 — *omit* — *omit*

serched 31. 34 — searched — searched
(2 times)
See searched

Sered 46. 14

serpent 3. 1 (6 times)

seruant 18. 3 (6 „) — seruaunt

44. 30 — *omit*

seruaunte 9. 25 — seruaunt — seruaut
(34 times)

— borne 17. 13 — eny other — he that is borne

24. 53 — *omit* — seruant

25. 23 — shall serue — shall serue

27. 40 — shalt „ — shalt „

29. 24 — mayde — handmayd

29. 29 — mayden — mayd

32. 17 — *omit* — *omit*

44. 19 — seruauntes — seruants

seruauntes 9. 25 — — „
(36 times)

	C	A
seruauntes 12. 16	*omit*	seruants
(2 times)		
17. 23		*omit*
—, be thy 27. 29		serue thee
17. 12	houszholde folkes	he that is borne
serue, shall 15. 14		
—, will 29. 18		
—, shuldest 29. 15	shalt serue	
—, dyd 29. 25	haue serued	
—, shalt 29. 27	shalt do seruyce	
—, to 45. 23	for	for
serued 29. 20 (2 times)		
—, haue 30. 26		
(3 times)		
39. 4	was his seruaunt	
40. 4	might serue	
Serug 11. 20 (2 times)		
11. 21	*omit*	
seruyce 29. 27		seruice
(2 times)		
—, haue done 30. 29	haue serued	haue serued
set 35. 14		
41. 43	made him ryde	made him to ride
See sett		
sette		
Seth 4. 25 (4 times)		
5. 4 (2 times)	*omit*	
sett 18. 8 (9 times)	set	set
—, hast 21. 29	hast set	hast set
—, haue 41. 41	haue „	haue „
24. 33	set	was „
30. 36	made rowme of	set
— his face 31. 21	wente	„
—, haue 31. 51	haue set	haue cast
— eyes, maye 44. 21	wil se	may set eyes
—, by, was 34. 19	was holden in	honourable
	honoure	

	C	A
sett vp, haue 28. 22	haue set vp	haue set
— vp 35. 20	set vp	set
sette 19. 16	,,	,,
—, shalt 6. 16	shalt set	shalt set
—, wyll 9. 13	will ,,	doe ,,
2. 8	set	put
3. 24	,,	placed
— in aray to fyghte 14. 8	prepared to fight	ioyned battle
14. 15	deuyded	diuided
See set		
sett		
sevenfolde 4. 24	seuen tymes	
4. 24	*omit*	
seventh 2. 2 (3 times)		
7. 10	seuen	seuen
seventie 4. 24		seuenty
severall, with a 49. 28	with a sundrye	according to his
sexte 30. 19	sixte	sixth
seynge 18. 18		seeing
—, lyvynge and 24. 62		well Lahai-roi
28. 8		seeing
See seinge		
seyth 16. 5		saw
See seeth		
seith		
shadow 19. 8	shadowe	
shame 34. 14		reproch
—, to do vs 39. 14		to mock vs
—, to do me 39. 17		,, ,, me
shamed, be 38. 23		
shaved 41. 14	let be shauen	
Sheba 10. 7	Seba	Seba
shed 37. 22		
—, shall haue bloud 9. 6	bloude shall be shed	shall blood be shed
shedeth 9. 6	sheddeth	sheddeth

	C	A
shefe 37. 7 (2 times)		sheafe
shepardes 46. 32	kepers of catell	sheapheards
shepe 12.16 (12 times)		sheepe
4. 4 (3 times)		flocke
13. 5 (7 ,,)		flocks
22. 7 (2 ,,)		lambe
30. 32 (2 ,,)		cattell
30. 32		*omit*
31. 19	flocke	
31. 38 (2 times)		ewes
30. 32 (2 ,,)	flockes	flocke
30. 36 (3 ,,)	flocke	flocks
30. 38	they	,,
30. 41 (4 ,,)	flockes	cattell
31. 8 (5 ,,)	flocke	,,
37. 2 (2 ,,)	catell	flocke
37. 14 (2 ,,)	,,	flocks
37. 16	*omit*	,,
— and beastes 45. 19 (2 times)	small and greate catell	flockes
— and oxen 46. 32	small and greate catell	flocks
—, that feede 46. 34	† haue dealt with catell	shepheard
—, feaders of 47. 3	kepers of catell	shepheards
shere, to 31. 19	to clyppe	to sheare
sherers 38. 12	*omit*	shearers
sheves 37. 7	sheeves	sheaues
—, they made 41. 47	*omit*	the earth brought forth by hand- fuls
shewe 40. 14		shew
24. 12	shew	,,
—, wyll 12. 1	will shew	will shew
—, shalt 20. 13	shew	shalt ,,
—, will 22. 2	shal shew	will tell of
—, to 32. 5		to tell

	C	A
shewe, doth 41. 25	sheweth	hath shewed
—, doth 41. 28	,,	sheweth
46. 31	tell	shew
shewed, hast 24. 14		
(2 times)		
—, hath 41. 39		
22. 9		had tolde of
30. 21	had	
—, hath 48. 11	hath caused me	
	to se	
—, myght be 46. 28	to shew	to direct his face
44. 24	tolde	told
—, haue 21. 23	haue done vnto	haue done vnto
shewest 19. 19	hast shewed	hast shewed
shilde 15. 1	shylde	shield
shippes 49. 13		ships
shope 2. 7		formed
shortly 41. 32		
shote 19. 6	shut	shut
See shott		
shytt		
shoters 49. 23		archers
shott to 19. 10	shut to	shut
40. 10	bare	shot
See shote		
shytt		
shoulachet 14. 23	shue lachet	shoe latchet
shrancke 32. 32	*omit*	shranke
shranke 32. 25	shrancke	was out of ioynt
shronke 32. 32	*omit*	shranke
shrubbes 2. 5	twygg	plant
shulder 24. 15	shulder	shoulder
(2 times)		
shulders 9. 23		shoulders
21. 14		shoulder
shyne to 1. 15		to giue light
—, to 1. 17	might shyne	,, ,, ,,

	C	A
shytt 7. 16	shut	shut
See shote		
shott		
Sichem 33. 18		Shechem
(12 times)		
—, of 34. 8	Sichems	of Shechem
34. 18	*omit*	
See Sychem		
Sichems 33. 19	of Sichem	Shechems
34. 26		,,
sicle 24. 22	sycle	shekel
Siddim, vale of 14. 3	brode valley	
(3 times)		
Sidon 49. 13	Sydon	Zidon
See Sydon		
sighte, oute of my	by me	out of my sight
23. 4 (2 times)		
— of, in 43. 14	in sight of	before
See syght		
syghte		
Sillem 46. 24		Shillem
Silo 49. 10	the Worthye	Shiloh
Silpha 30. 9 (4 times)	Silpa	Zilpah
Simeon 34. 25 (6 times)		
29. 33 (4 times)	Symeon	
simple 25. 27	symple	plaine
Simram 25. 2		Zimran
Sineab 14. 2		Shinab
Sini 10. 17		Sinite
sir 43. 20	syr	
See syr		
Sirian 25. 20 (2 times)	Syrian	Syrian
Sirians 22. 21	Syrians	Aram
Sirien 25. 20 (2 times)	Syrian	Syrian
28. 5	Siria	,,
sister 12. 13 (16 times)		
24. 30 (3 times)	syster	

	C	A
sister 34. 26		*omit*
See syster		
sisters 24. 30 (2 times)		
Sitena 26. 21	Sytena	Sitnah
skatered 11. 8	scatred	scattered
11. 9	„	did scatter
See scatered		
skynnes 3. 21 (2 times)		skinnes
slaughter 14. 17		
slayn, haue 4. 23	haue slayne	haue slaine
—, haue 4. 23	„ kylled	*omit*
slee, to 42. 37	slaye	slay
See sley		
slepe 28. 16		sleepe
31. 40		sleep
—, to 28. 11		to sleepe
—, to 39. 10		to lie
39. 12		lie
—, let 30. 15	let lye	shall lye
slepest 28. 13	lyest	liest
slepte 2. 21 (2 times)		slept
30. 16		lay
—, to haue 39. 14	to slepe	to lie
slew 38. 10	slewe	
slewe 4. 8 (6 times)	slew	slew
36. 35	slewe	smote
sley 37. 20 (2 times)		slay
37. 26	sleye	„
— to 18. 25 (2 times)	to slaye	to slay
—, wilt 20. 4		wilt slay
—, will 27. 41	wil slaye	will „
34. 30	shal „	slay
—, shulde 20. 11	shall sleye	will slay
—, shall 12. 12	shal slaye	„ kill
See slee		
sleyeth 4. 15	slayeth	slayeth
slomber 2. 21 (2 times)	slepe	sleepe

	C	A
slyme 11. 3 (2 times)		slime
small 19. 11		
smell 27. 27 (2 times)		
smelled 27. 27		
smylled 8. 21	smelled	smelled
smoke 19. 28		
smokynge 15. 17	smoked	smoking
smooth 27. 11		
(2 times)		
smote 14. 5 (3 times)		
19. 11	were smytten	
32. 25	touched	touched
32. 32	was touched	,,
smyte 32. 8 (2 times)		smite
so 1. 7 (28 times)		
3. 13 (18 ,,)		*omit*
9. 6 (4 ,,)	*omit*	
16. 10		exceedingly
20. 17	for	
22. 8 (2 times)	and	
25. 34 (2 ,,)		thus
29. 28 (2 ,,)		then
29. 30 (5 ,,)		and
32. 19	thus	
36. 7		more then
43. 34	more	
1. 5	then	*omit*
4. 15 (5 times)	*omit*	,,
3. 14	this	this
11. 3	and	and
27. 38	,,	*omit*
— much more, twice	other	double
43. 15		
44. 7	eny soch thinge	according to this thinge

See so that

Sobal 36. 30 (3 times)   Shobal

C

A

	C	A
soch 27. 9 (3 times)		such
27. 4	*omit*	,,
44. 7		these
See such		
sod 25. 29	dight	
Sodoma 10. 19		
13. 10		Sodome
Sodome 13. 12		
(11 times)		
14. 10 (4 times)	Sodoma	
18. 26 (2 ,,)		Sodom
Sodomeward, to 18. 22	towarde Sodome	toward Sodome
soeuer 31. 16 (2 times)		
30. 33		euery one
31. 32	*omit*	
31. 39	,,	which
softly 33. 14		
sogeorne, to 19. 9	as a straunger	soiourne
26. 3	be thou a straunger	,,
—, to 47. 4	to dwell with you	,,
See soiourne		
sogeorned 20. 1	was a straunger	soiourned
35. 27	were	,,
sogerned 32. 4	*omit*	,,
soiourne, to 12. 10	to kepe himselfe as a straunger	
See sogeorne		
sold 25. 33 (3 times)	solde	
solde 41. 56		
37. 36 (4 times)		sold
—, hath 31. 15		
— not 47. 22	neded not to sell	,, not
—, to be 42. 1	*omit*	*omit*
(2 times)		
some 19. 19 (3 times)		
37. 20 (2 times)	a	
42. 4		lest peraduenture

	C	A
some 43. 18		*omit*
42. 38 (2 times)	eny	,,
43. 12	an	an
somere 8. 22	sommer	summer
so much as 14. 23	so moch as	euen to
43. 34	more then	
sonde 22. 17		sand
sondrie 40. 5	his	according to the
41. 11	,, owne	,,　　,,　,,
sone 11. 31 (2 times)	sonne	sonne
19. 23	,,	sunne
See sonne		
sones 37. 32	sonnes	sonnes
10. 7	children	,,
See sonnes		
sons		
sonne 4.17 (130times)		
15. 12 (5　　,,　)		sunne
10. 15 (9　　,,　)		*omit*
15. 2		steward of my house
17. 25 (4 times)	*omit*	
4. 25	sede	seed
38. 2 (5 times)	childes childe	daughter
— in lawe 19. 12		sonne in law
See sone		
sonnes 5. 4 (72 times)		
6. 2 (37 times)	children	
10. 4	,,	sons
46. 7	childers	
— name, his 21. 3	his sonne	name of his sonne
— of Heth 23. 3 (4 times)	Hethites	
23. 11 (2 times)	*omit*	
See sones		
sons		
sonnes in law 19. 14	sonnes in lawe	

	C	A
sonnes in lawe 19. 14	*omit*	sonnes in law
sons 16. 15 (2 times)	sonnes	sonnes
See sones		
sonnes		
soon as, as 12. 14	whan	when
soone as, as 18. 33	,,	
4. 8 (2 times)	,,	,,
9. 24	so whan	*omit*
18. 10 (2 times)	*omit*	according to the time
24. 30	and that came by the reason that	when
27. 5	*omit*	*omit*
30. 25	now whan	when
34. 7	and	,,
39. 5	and from the time for	from the time
39. 18	whan	as
41. 15	,,	that
44. 31	shall it come to passe that yf	when
sore 19. 9 (4 times)		
41. 56 (2 ,,)	*omit*	
41. 57	mightie	
50. 10	bytter	
47. 20	mightie	*omit*
sorow 3. 18		
3. 17	sorowe	
44. 29 (2 times)	,,	sorrow
sorowe 42. 38		,,
5. 29		toyle
27. 41	shal mourne	mourning
sorowed 6. 6		grieued
37. 34	mourned	mourned
so that 19. 11		
(4 times)		
9. 15 (9 times)		and

	C	A
so that 17. 7 (3 times)		*omit*
9. 14		and it shall come to passe
27. 1	*omit*	
28. 21	yf	
48. 10	and	
49. 17	that	
6. 17	*omit*	and
50. 9	and	„
See so		
sothsayers 41. 24	soithsayers	magicians
See soythsayers		
sotyller 3. 1		more subtill
soughte 43. 30	sought	sought
37. 15	sekest	seekest
soule 2. 7 (9 times)		
34. 8	hert	
See soull		
soules 46. 18 (3 times)		
36. 6		persons
See soulles		
soull 27. 4 (2 times)	soule	soule
See soule		
soulles 12. 5 (5 times)	soules	soules
14. 21		persons
46. 15	*omit*	
See soules		
south 13. 1 (4 times)		
southcontre 20. 1	south countre	South-Countrey
southward 13. 14	southwarde	
southwarde 12. 9		toward the South
sowe 47. 23		sow
— the feld, to 47. 24	to sowe the londe	of the field
1. 11	beareth	yeelding
1. 29	beare	„
1. 29	„	bearing
sowed 26. 12		

	C	A
sowed 3. 7		sewed
sowenge 1. 12	that beareth	yeelding
sowynge tyme 8. 22		seed-time
soythsayers 41. 8		magicians
See sothsayers		
space 32. 16		
29. 14	*omit*	
6. 3	respyte	*omit*
spake 8. 15 (12 times)		
9. 8 (2 times)	sayde	
23. 13 (5 „)	talked	
15. 4		came
18. 29	proceded to speake	
31. 29	saide	
45. 17		said
spakynge 24. 15	speakynge	speaking
See speakynge		
spare 18. 24		
—, will 18. 26		
spared, hast 22. 16		hast withheld
speach 10. 5		tongue
speak, to 18. 31	to speake	to speake
speake 31. 24 (4 times)		
—, to 18. 27		
18. 30 (2 times)		will speake
—, shall 44. 16		
32. 4	saye	shall speake
45. 12		speaketh
See speke		
speakynge, had made an end of 24. 45	had spoken	had done speaking
See spakynge		
speckled 30. 33	spotted	
spede, to 19. 15		hastened
24. 12	*omit*	speed
speke, coude 37. 4	coude speake	could speake

	C	A
speke 23. 8	speake	entreat
See speak		
speake		
spende, to 42. 25	expenses	*omit*
(2 times)		
spent, was 21. 15	was out	
—, is 47. 15	are without	faileth
spicery 37. 25	spyces	
spied 42. 27	spyed	espied
spies 42. 9 (2 times)	spyes	
See spyes		
spirite 1. 2 (2 times)	sprete	spirit
See sprete		
spoke 27. 5	sayde	spake
spoken, hast 19. 21		
—, had 21. 1	had sayde	
sportinge 26. 8		was sporting
spotted 30. 32 (4 times)		
31. 10 (2 „)		speckled
30. 40		ring-straked
31. 8 (2 times)	partye coloured	speckled
spoyle 49. 27		spoile
49. 9		pray
spoyled 34. 27		spoiled
sprange 2. 5	grew	grew
10. 18	are dispersed abrode	were spread abroad
spreade, shalt 28. 14	shalt spreade	shalt spread
sprete 41. 8 (2 times)		spirit
See spirite		
springe, shall 17. 16	shall come	shall be
25. 23	„ be deuyded	„ „ separated
See sprynge		
springynge 25. 19	lyuinge	springing
sprites 45. 27	sprete	spirit
spronge 41. 6	come vp	sprang
2. 10	wente	wente

	C	A
sprynge, to 2. 9		to grow
—, shall 17.6 (2 times)	shal come	shall come
41. 22	growinge	came vp
41. 23	spronge	sprung
See springe		
spyces 43. 11		spices
24. 53		precious things
spyes 42. 30 (2 times)		spies
See spies		
spylled 38. 9	let fall	spilled
stablesshed, haue 27. 37	haue prouyded	haue sustained
staf 32. 10	staff	staffe
staffe 33. 18 (2 times)		
stalk 41. 22	stalke	stalke
stalke 41. 5	„	„
starres 15. 5 (4 times)		
See sterres		
statutes 26. 5		
staues 30. 37 (5 times)		rods
steade 22.13 (9 „)		stead
steale, shulde 44. 8	shulde haue stollen	should steale
stere, dare 49. 9	wil rayse	shall rouse
See styrre		
sterres 1. 16	starres	starres
See starres		
still 41. 21	*omit*	
See styll		
stocke, hath made me a laughinge 21. 6	hath prepared a ioye for me	hath made me to laugh
stode 18. 2 (12 times)		stood
18. 16		rose
19. 27	had stoude	stood
28. 12		set vp
37. 7	*omit*	stood
41. 3	wente	„
24. 10	gat him vp	arose

	C	A
stode 28. 18	arose	rose vp
40. 9	was	was
stollen, had 31. 32		
31. 19	stale	
—, hast 31. 30		
—, was 31. 39	were stollen	stollen
—, was 40. 15	was preuely caried	
stonde 24. 13 (2 times)		stand
— vpp 19. 14		vp
— vp 19. 15		arise
stondest 24. 31		standest
stone 2. 12 (10 times)		
28. 11		stones
31. 13		pillar
49. 24	stones	
stoones 31. 46 (2 times)	„	stones
stoore, lay it vp in	shalt lay in stoare	shalt gather
6. 21		
41. 36	found prepared	store
41. 49	stoare	*omit*
stoppe, had 26. 18	had stopte	had stopped
stopped 26. 15		„ „
stopte, were 8. 2		were „
stoupe doune 24. 14	bowe downe	let downe
27. 29	fall „	bow „
—, shall 49. 9		shall bow downe
straked 30. 39	speckelde	
31. 8 (4 times)	„	ring-straked
strakes 30. 37		
stranger 28. 4	straunger	
See straunger		
straunge 35. 2 (3 times)		strange
straunger 15. 13		stranger
(4 times)		
—, art a 21. 23		hast soiourned
32. 4	straungers	*omit*
See stranger		

	C	A
straungers 31. 15 (2 times)		strangers
35. 27		*omit*
17. 12 (2 times)	straunger	stranger
strawe 31. 34		furniture
streates 19. 2	stretes	street
strech forth 3. 22	stretch	put foorth
strength 49. 3		
— vnto him, toke his 48. 2	toke a corage vnto him	strengthened him-selfe
stretched 22. 10 (2 times)		
streyght 31. 21	straight	*omit*
stronge 49.14 (2 times)		strong
49. 7	fearce	cruell
—, were 49. 26	go mightely	haue preuailed
stroue 26.20 (3 times)		
25. 22		struggled
stryfe 13. 7 (2 times)	strife	strife
stryken 18. 11		stricken
21. 4	stricken	,,
strypes 4. 23		wounding
strypte 37. 23	stryped	stript
stryve, shall 6. 3		shall striue
—, dyd 26. 20	stroue	did ,,
stuff 45. 20		stuffe
stuffe 31. 37 (2 times)		
styll 27. 33	still	*omit*
styncke 34. 30	stynke	to stynke
styrre 38. 8	rayse	raise
See stere		
Sua 38. 2 (2 times)		Shuah
Suah 25. 2		,,
subdue 1. 28		
subdued, be 4. 7		shall be his desire
subiecte, were 14. 4	subiectes	serued
submyte 16. 9	submitte	submit

	C	A
substance 13. 6	substaunce	
(4 times)		
31. 18		goods
34. 23	all that they haue	
subtilte 37. 35	sotyltie	subtilty
such 27. 4	soch	
30. 32	the same	
See soch		
sucke 21. 7		
Sucoth 38.17 (2 times)		Succoth
suerlie 50. 24	*omit*	surely
suerly 3. 16	,,	greatly
19. 9	,,	*omit*
See surely		
surelye		
suertie 15. 13 (3 times)	suertye	surety
16. 13	,,	*omit*
18. 13	true in dede	surety
26. 9	*omit*	
—, of a 44. 28	,,	surely
suffred 20. 6	haue suffred	suffered
31. 7	hath ,,	,,
—, hast 31. 28		hast suffered
suffrest vs to dye,		why should we die
wherfore 47. 15		
Suni 46. 16		Shuni
suppose 30. 27	perceaue	haue learned by
		experience that
Sur 16. 7 (3 times)		Shur
sure 23. 17 (2 times)		
—, be 20. 7		surely
surely 28. 16		
2. 17 (4 times)	*omit*	
surelye 42. 14	,,	*omit*
See suerlie		
suerly		
surely		

	C	A
Susims 14. 5	Susim	Zusims
sustenaunce 47. 15	bred	bread
swaged, be 27. 44		turne away
sware 21. 31 (7 times)		
See swere		
swerde 3. 24 (6 times)		sword
swere 21. 23 (4 „)	sweare	sweare
—, wyll 21. 24	wyll sweare	will sweare
24. 37 (2 times)	hath taken an ooth	sweare
50. 6	hath sworne	„
See sware		
swete 3. 19	sweate	sweate
8. 21		sweete
19. 3		vnleauened
swore 25. 33 (2 times)	sware	sware
sworne, haue 22. 16	haue sworen	
swyft 49. 21	swift	let loose
Sychem 12. 6	Sichem	Sichem
See Sichem		
sycles 23. 15 (3 times)		shekels
syde 6. 16		side
2. 14 (7 times)		*omit*
12. 8	side	„
—, see 22. 17	shore	shore
24. 11	besyde	*omit*
—, ryvers 41. 17	water syde	banke of the riuer
Sydon 10. 19	Sidon	Sidon
See Sidon		
syght 18. 3	sight	sight
syghte 19. 19 (8 times)	„	„
2. 9	to loke vpon	sight
4. 14	sight	face
6. 8 (3 times)	„	eyes
6. 11 (2 „)	„	before
21. 11	*omit*	sight
23. 18	sight	presence
38. 7 (2 times)	before	sight

	C	A
syghte 16. 4	*omit*	eyes
—, out of 21. 16 (2 times)	on the other syde	ouer against him
See sighte syght		
sygne 9. 13 (2 times)	token	token
sygnes 1. 14	tokens	tokens
sygnett 38. 18	signet	signet
syluer 20.16 (9 times)		siluer
13. 2	siluer	„
23. 16	money	„
23. 13	„	money
symilitude 1. 26	similitude	image
symilytude 5. 1	symilitude	likenes
5. 3	*omit*	image
Synear 10.10 (3 times)		Shinar
syngynge 31. 27	synginge	songs
synne 4. 7 (3 times)		sinne
18. 20	synnes	„
—, to 39. 9	and synne	and sinne
—, shuld 42. 22	synne	doe „
—, shuldest not 20. 6		held from sinning
4. 13		punishment
19. 15		iniquitie
26. 10		guiltinesse
synned 13. 13		were sinners
—, haue 42. 21	† haue deserued	are verily guiltie
syppe 24. 17	drynke	drinke
syppe, let 25. 30	proue	feed
syr 3. 1	yee	yea
See sir		
syster 4. 22 (3 times)	sister	sister
See sister		
sytt 27. 19	syt	sit
syxth 1. 31	sixte	sixth
syxte hundred and one 8. 13	„ hundreth and one	sixe hundredth and one

	C	A
table 43. 31		*omit*
take 3. 22 (25 times)		
—, will 14. 23 (3 times)		
—, shalt 21. 30 (3 times)		
—, to 24. 48		
6. 21	shalt take	
7. 2 (2 times)		shalt take
—, shalt 24. 3 (2 times)	take	
—, shalt 24. 40	mayest take	
—, se 28. 6	might take	shalt take
—, woldest 30. 15	wilt „	wouldst take
34. 16		wil take
—, let 34. 21	wyl take	will „
—, was 2. 23	was taken	was taken
—, to 12. 19	toke	might haue taken
—, wyll 13. 9 (2 times)		will goe
—, wylt 13. 9	wilt go to	
21. 18		hold
23. 13	receaue	
24. 3	brynge	
—, mayst 24. 7	maiest brynge	shalt take
— hede 31. 24 (2 times)	bewarre	
—, to 33. 11		tooke
—, shall 40. 19		shall lift
43. 12	cary	carie
47. 23	beholde, there haue ye	here is
taken, was 3. 23 (2 times)		
—, haue 18. 27		
—, hast 20. 3 (2 times)		
—, had 21. 25		
—, hath 27. 35 (2 times)		

	C	A
taken, wast 3. 19	art taken	
—, hath 27. 36	taketh	
—, had bene 31. 26		taken
—, woldest haue 31. 31	shuldest haue taken	wouldest take
—, was 12. 15	was brought	
—, hath 31. 1	hath ,,	
31. 9 (2 times)	,, withdrawen	
takynge, in what 30.29	in what maner	how
talked 4. 8 (5 times)		
23. 3 (2 times)		spake
talkinge 17. 22	talkynge	talking
talkyng 27. 6	talkinge	speak
tarie 27. 44	tary	tary
See tary		
tarye		
taried 24.54 (3 times)		
8. 12		stayed
32. 13 (2. times)		lodged
32. 24		was left
tarieng 43. 10	tarienge	lingred
tary 19. 2	tarye	tarie
—, to 19.30		to dwell
19. 17	stonde	stay
tarye 45. 9		tary
See tarie		
Tebah 22. 24	Theba	
teeth 49. 12	teth	
tel 40. 8	tell	tell
tell 15. 5 (7 times)		
—, to 43. 6		
—, can 43. 22		
—, maye 49. 1		
—, can 4.9		know
—, didest 31. 17	toldest	didst tell
—, can 41. 24		could declare
45. 18	shewe	

	C	A
tell 46. 31		say vnto
45. 9	say vnto	„ „
50. 4	saie	saying
ten 18. 32 (2 times)		
tender 29. 17 (2 „)		
tendre 18. 7	tender	tender
tent 18. 1 (7 times)		
9. 21	tente	
tente 12. 8 (2 „)		tent
13. 3 (10 „)	tent	„
31. 35		*omit*
32. 21		company
tented 13. 12	pitched his tent	pitched his tent
tentes 4. 20 (5 times)		tents
tenth 8. 5 (2 „)		
Terah 11. 24 (8 „)		
testament 9. 15	couenaunt	couenant
(6 times)		
testamente 17. 9	„	„
(2 times)		
testifie, dyd 43. 3	sware	did protest
tidynges 45. 16	tydinges	fame
till 38. 17	tyll	
26. 13	„	vntill
tirantes 6. 4	giauntes	giants
Thahas 22. 24		Thahash
Thamar 38. 6 (4 times)		Tamar
Thamar, Hazezon		Hazezon-tamar
14. 7		
than 16. 3 (2 times)		then
3. 1 (27 „)	then	„
1. 3 (47 „)	„	and
26. 26 (3 „)	and	then
9. 15 (6 „)	then	*omit*
13. 16 (6 „)	*omit*	then
13. 18 (4 „)	so	„
14. 8 (2 „)	then	and then
18. 5 (2 „)	„	after that

	C	A
than 5. 11 (9 times)	so	*omit*
5. 24	for so moch as	,,
12. 9	afterwarde	,,
13. 1 (4 times)	so	and
14. 17 (10 ,,)	*omit*	,,
14. 18 (2 ,,)	but	,,
21. 12 (2 ,,)	neuertheles	,,
25. 17 (5 ,,)	*omit*	*omit*
Tharsis 10. 4		Tharshish
that 1. 4 (266 times)		
1. 10 (10 ,,)		and
1. 11 (60 ,,)		*omit*
2. 15 (3 ,,)	the same	
4. 15		lest
4. 20 (2 ,,)		such as
—, after 6. 4	whan	
6. 19 (3 times)	what so euer	
7. 8 (50 ,,)	*omit*	
7. 23 (5 ,,)		which
8. 19		whatsoever
9. 11		neither
9. 18 (2 times)	which	
15. 18 (4 ,,)	the	
17. 13 (2 ,,)	thus	
18. 21 (6 ,,)		the
18. 21		and if not
— dwelled 19. 25		the inhabitants of
20. 9	as	
21. 6	who so euer	
21. 8	whan	
24. 35 (3 times)	so that	and
26. 11	who so	
26. 14		for
27. 41		wherewith
— which 27. 45	what	
29. 28		her
30. 17 (3 times)	and	

	C	A
that 31. 31		peraduenture
31. 32		what
31. 52	yf	
32. 13	soch	
37. 21		it
37. 26		if
41. 5		and beholde
43. 6		whether
44. 5		this
45. 5	because	
50. 14	those that	
1. 7 (5 times)	*omit*	which
1. 9 (68 „)	„	*omit*
2. 11 (3 „)	which	which
3. 15	the same	it
— tyme 4. 26	the same tyme	then
6. 18 (3 times)	and	and
7. 15	in whom	wherin
9. 11	and	neither
10. 9	*omit*	the
10. 12	this	the same
11. 4	whose	whose
12. 2	yee	and
17. 19 (2 times)	*omit*	for
19. 15 (3 „)	which	*omit*
22. 12	and	seeing
27. 24	yee	*omit*
31. 2	and beholde	and behold
31. 25 (3 times)	the	the
31. 50	ye	if
35. 7	*omit*	there
37. 13	„	and
39. 22	„	it
41. 2	beholde	*omit*
41. 6	*omit*	beholde
41. 28	the thinge	which
42. 20	so	so

	C	A
that 44. 20	*omit*	his
45. 29	and	*omit*
theft 30. 33		stollen
Thema 25. 15		Tema
Theman 36. 11 (3 times)		Teman
Themany 36. 34	Themanites	Temani
then 2. 21 (8 times)		
2. 23 (16 „)		and
8. 8		also
12. 6	at the same time	
14. 7 (7 times)		*omit*
23. 19		after this
24. 65		therefore
26. 16	in so moch that	
28. 9	*omit*	
44. 31		when
2. 7 (4 times)	and	and
2. 21 (3 „)	*omit*	*omit*
5. 5	and so	„
12. 1	and	now
21. 10	„	wherfore
27. 30	*omit*	that
30. 3	neuertheles	and
35. 18	but	and it came to passe
41. 19	*omit*	behold
44. 16 (2 times)	„	and
thence 11. 8 (6 „)		
12. 8	from thence	from thence
20. 1 (2 times)		„ „
2. 10 (2 „)	there	„ „
18. 22 (2 „)	*omit*	„ „
42. 2	„	
8. 12 (2 times)	„	*omit*
thense 26. 17	thence	thence
26. 22	„	from thence

	C	A
there 1. 3 (71 times)		
2. 8 (5 „)	therin	
2. 10 (12 „)		*omit*
13. 4 (2 „)	where	
19. 1	in the euenynge	
19. 22		thither
21. 33 (6 times)	*omit*	
28. 2		from thence
38. 22		in this place
47. 23		here
6. 13	before them	through them
7. 14	their	their
22. 13	behynde him	behind him
24. 4 (8 times)	*omit*	*omit*
30. 42	in	„
37. 29	therin	in the pit
therby 24. 14	by the same	thereby
29. 2	therby	by it
thereby 42. 16	thus	*omit*
42. 34	so	„
therefore 12. 12		
(3 times)		
3. 10		*omit*
14. 5		and
17. 5		neither
19. 30	so	*omit*
42. 16	*omit*	„
See therfore		
therein 9. 7 (2 times)		
37. 24	in it	in it
See therin		
there of 40. 10		
41. 8	*omit*	
See therof		
therfore 50. 5		
18. 5 (17 times)		therefore
12. 13 (7 „)		*omit*

	C	A
therfore 26. 21		and
(4 times)		
29. 33 (2 times)	*omit*	therefore
31. 16		then
44. 30	yf	therefore
20. 4 (8 times)	*omit*	*omit*
33. 14	,,	I pray thee
38. 9	,,	and it came to passe
42. 37	but	*omit*
43. 4	so be now that	,,
44. 10	let it so be	also let it be
See therefore		
therin 18. 24 (4 times)		therein
19. 20	there in	thither
23. 17 (2 times)	*omit*	therein
47. 27	in it	therein
23. 6	in his sepulcre	*omit*
44. 5	with all	whereby
See therein		
ther of 2. 21		thereof
3. 17	of it	of it
40. 18	*omit*	thereof
theron 35. 14		thereon
35. 14	vpon it	,,
therwith 45. 5	*omit*	*omit*
Thimna 36. 12	Thimna	Timna
(2 times)		
36. 40	Thymna	Timnah
Thimnath 38. 12		Timnath
(2 times)		
38. 14	Thymnath	,,
thinge 18.14 (4 times)		thing
6. 20	one	,,
22. 16 (3 times)	*omit*	,,
24. 50	this	,,
34. 14	that	,,

	C	A
thinge 34. 19	same	thing
9. 10	creature	creature
24. 8	*omit*	*omit*
—, some 43. 18		occasion
—, cruel 45. 5	eny wrath	*omit*
See thynge		
thinges 20. 8 (2 times)		things
22. 20	actes	,,
24. 28	this	,,
42. 36	it	,,
30. 40 (2 times)	*omit*	*omit*
See thynges		
thinke 40. 14	thynke	
—, wyll 9. 15	wyll thynke	will remember
thinne 41. 23	thynne	thin
See thynne		
third 34. 25	thirde	thirde
thirde 22. 4 (3 times)		third
See thyrd		
thyrde		
thirty 5. 3	thirtie	thirtie
See thyrtye		
thither 24. 6		
39. 1	downe	
See thyder		
thyther		
thornes 3. 13		
thorow 26. 4 (2 times)		in
41. 36	of	through
41. 46		thorowout
— out 7. 22	vpon	*omit*
30. 40 (2 times)	in	in
though 33. 10		
31. 26		*omit*
31. 30	for so moch then as	
17. 12 (2 times)	*omit*	,,
—, what 18. 28	peraduenture	peraduenture

	C	A
though, as 19. 14	neuertheles	as one that
29. 15	because	because
thought 20. 11		
(2 times)		
19. 29		remembered
26. 9		said
—, had 48. 11	thought	
—, me 37. 9		and beholde
31. 31	*omit*	said
—, me 40. 9 (2 times)	dreamed	beholde
40. 16	,,	and beholde
41. 1	*omit*	,, ,,
—, him 41. 3	sawe	,, ,,
thoughte 50. 20	thought	thought
thousande 20. 16		thousand
24. 60	thousande tymes	thousands
thousandes 40. 60	,,	thousands of milli-ons
thre 11. 15 (8 times)		three
threatneth 27. 42	threateneth	purposing
thred 14. 23	threde	threed
threde 38. 28 (2 times)	,,	,,
through out 41. 29	in	
thryd 42. 18	thirde	third
See third		
thirde		
thyrde		
thus 2. 1 (6 times)		
7. 23 (2 ,,)		and
11. 8		so
12. 18		*omit*
21. 32	so	
37. 35	*omit*	
28. 5	so	and
29. 25 (2 times)	this	*omit*
35. 19	so	,,
37. 17 (2 times)	then	and
38. 11	so	then

	C	A
thus 43. 11	this	this
48. 20	and so	and
Thydeall 14. 1	Thydeal	Tidal
14. 9	Thideal	„
thynne 41. 6 (2 times)		
41. 24 (2 times)		thin
See thinne		
Thyras 10. 2		Tiras
thyrde 1. 13 (4 times)	thirde	third
38. 5	yet further	yet againe
See third		
thirde		
thryd		
thyrtye 32. 15	thirtie	thirtie
See thirty		
thyder 19. 22	thither	thither
See thither		
thyther		
thykette 22. 13	breres	thicket
thynge 41. 32	thinge	thing
6. 19	creatures	„
9. 3	*omit*	„
19. 21	poynte	„
9. 12	creatures	creature
See thinge		
thynges 7. 4	thinges	substance
33. 11	„	*omit*
See thinges		
thyther 29. 3		thither
24. 8	thither	„
See thither		
thyder		
thystels 3. 18	thistles	thistles
to 4. 4 (53 times)		
18. 14		too
8. 9 (7 times)		vnto
8. 11	vnto	in to

to

	C	A
to 13. 10	rounde aboute	vnto
13. 12 (2 times)	towarde	toward
14. 4 (9 „)	*omit*	*omit*
16. 6	vnto	with
18. 2	downe vpon	toward
19. 1	„ to	„
— rest 19. 4		laye downe
20. 18	*omit*	vp
24. 57	therto	*omit*
— the eye 26. 7	to loke vnto	„
10. 19	thorow	
14. 10 (81 times)	vnto	
17. 7 (2 „)	of	
18. 12 (4 „)		*omit*
24. 37	for	
24. 53 (13 „)	*omit*	
28. 6 (2 „)	into	
28. 12	vnto the	
29. 23	in vnto	
32. 8	vpon	
45. 9	vp vnto	
34. 19		in
35. 18 (2 times)	towarde	
38. 8 (2 „)	with	
41. 57		into
43. 21	in	
— the syghte 2. 9	to loke vpon	
3. 24 (2 times)	vnto	of
4. 11	vpon	from
6. 13 (15 „)	vnto	vnto
7. 5 (4 „)	*omit*	„
— him, went 27. 27	came nye	came neere
28. 5	vnto	onto
— the 31. 32	awaye	
39. 8	vnder	vnto
—, accordynge 39. 17	euen	
41. 45	a	vnto

	C	A
to 42. 37 (3 times)	into	into
—, accordinge 43. 7	as he axed us	
—, acordynge 43. 15	before	before
43. 24	vnto	into
43. 28	downe to	*omit*
48. 5	hither vnto	vnto
48. 7	towarde	,,
48. 9	hither to	,,
— daye 40. 7		to day
Togarma 10. 3		Togarmah
togedder 3. 7	together	together
to gedder, all 18. 21	all together	altogether
together 13. 6		
(10 times)		
21. 27 (3 times)		*omit*
29. 7 (2 ,,)	*omit*	
8. 19	,,	*omit*
togyther 1. 10	together	together
toke 2. 15 (70 times)		tooke
6. 2		took
2. 22 (2 times)		had taken
— off 8. 13		remooued
— his iourney 12. 9		iourneyed
(3 times)		
24. 46		let
24. 53 (2 times)		brought
27. 36	hath	
— his strength 48. 2	toke a corage	strengthened
3. 12	gaue	gaue
— down 13. 18	remoued	remoued
30. 35	sundered	,,
— councell 37. 18	deuysed	conspired
token 9. 12 (2 times)		
Tola 46. 13	Thola	
told 3. 11 (4 times)	tolde	
27. 13 (3 ,,)	,,	tolde
—, were 27. 42	was tolde	

	C	A
told, had 37. 10	was tolde	told
38. 13	„ „	was told
39. 17 (2 times)	tolde	spake vnto
43. 27	„	„
tolde 24. 66 (4 times)		
9. 22 (9 times)		told
—, was 31. 22		was told
22. 20	was tolde	was told
38. 24	„ „	„ tolde
—, haue 41. 24	haue shewed	told
39. 14	sayde vnto	spake vnto
toldest 12. 18		diddest tell
21. 26	dyddest tell	didst „
tonge 11. 1		speach
11. 6	maner of language	language
11. 7		„
11. 9	language	„
tonges 10. 20	tunges	
to nyghte 19. 5	to night	this night
topp 28. 12	toppe	top
28.18	*omit*	„
toppe 11. 4		„
49. 26		crowne
7. 18	*omit*	face
toppes 8. 5		tops
torne, was 31. 39		
—, is 44. 28		
toward 19. 28	*omit*	
28. 10 (2 times)	vnto	
33. 17	towarde	to
29. 1	in to	into
30. 40	vnto	*omit*
towarde 18. 16		toward
(4 times)		
48. 13		towards
townes 25. 16	courtes	
traveled 38. 28	was in trauelynge	trauailed

	C	A
trauell, to 35. 16	traueyled	traueiled
totehill 31. 49	testimony	† Mizpah
touch 3. 3		shall touch
touched, haue 26. 29	haue hurte	
toucheth 26. 11		
toughtes 6. 5	thought	thoughts
toure 11. 4 (2 times)	tower	tower
35. 21	„	towre
toward 19. 28 (3 times)	towarde	
25. 18	towarde	towards
travelynge 35. 16	trauelynge	*omit*
tre 2. 17 (3 times)		tree
8. 11		*omit*
See tree		
tread on, shall 3. 15	shal treade downe	shal bruise
3. 15	shalt treade on	shalt „
treasure 43. 23		
tree 2. 9 (9 times)		
18. 4	tre	
—, pyne 6. 14	pyne tre	Gopher-wood
40. 19	galowe	
See tre		
trees 3. 2 (3 times)		
1. 11 (6 „)		tree
trespace 50. 17		trespasse
50. 17	offence	„
trespaced, haue 31. 36	haue trespased	„
treuth 32. 10	trueth	trueth
See trueth		
tribes 49. 28	trybes	
See trybes		
tribulation 29. 32	aduersite	affliction
(2 times)		
16. 11	trouble	„
35. 3	„	distresse
trouble 41. 52		affliction
See troubyll		

	C	A
troubled, was 41. 8		
—, haue 34. 30	haue brought it so to passe	
troubyll 42. 21	trouble	distresse
troth 48. 19	*omit*	truely
trough 24. 30		
troughes 30. 38		
truely 47. 29	† faithfulnes	
42. 11 (4 times)	vnfayned	true
trueth 42. 16		
See treuth		
truly 24. 49	† faithfulnes	truely
24. 27	trueth	trueth
trybes 49. 16	trybe	tribes
See tribes		
trybute 49. 15		tribute
Tubalcain 4. 22		Tubal-Cain
Tubalcains 4. 22		of Tubal-Cain
Tuball 10. 2	Tubal	Tubal
turne 19. 2		
—, maye 24. 49		
27. 45	be turned	
31. 3	departe	
—, to 32. 7		*omit*
—, will 30. 31	*omit*	„
—, shall 49. 19	shall hurte	shall ouercome
turned 19. 3 (2 times)		
14. 7 (2 times)		returned
—, was 19. 26		became
31. 32	departed	returned
—, is 30. 8	hath turned	*omit*
38. 16	gat	
42. 24	had turned	returned
50. 20	hath „	meant
30. 40	put	set
turtell doue 15. 9	turtyll doue	turtle doue
tush 3. 4		*omit*

	C	A
twelve 14. 4 (2 times)	twolue	
— moneth 17. 21		next yeere
twenties 18. 31	twentyes	
twice so much 43. 15	other	double
See twyse		
two 1. 16 (7 times)		
twynnes, .ii. 38. 37	two twyns	twinnes
twyns, .ii. 25. 24	two twyns	twinnes
twyse 43. 10		this second time
See twice		
tydinges 48. 1	*omit*	*omit*
tyll 19. 22		till
38. 11		til
10. 19		as
10. 19 (2 times)	*omit*	,,
12. 6		*omit*
13. 12	*omit*	,,
14. 14	vntill	,,
tylle, to 2. 5		to till
3. 23	to tyll	,, ,,
tyllest 4. 12		tillest
tyllman 25. 27	huszbande ˉman	a man of the fielde
tyme 17. 21 (10 times)		time
38. 1	time	,,
2. 4		day
4. 3	daies	time
4. 26 (2 times)		then
6. 9		generations
—, sowynge 8. 22		seed-time
10. 25 (4 times)		dayes
19. 16 (3 ,,)		*omit*
26. 8	season	
30. 33 (3 times)	*omit*	time
38. 12	dayes	,,
—, fyrst 13. 3	*omit*	beginning
— will come 27. 40	it shall come to passe	it shall come to passe

	C	A
tyme, before 28. 19	afore	at the first
32. 4 (2 times)	hither to	now
38. 5	yet further	againe
See time		
tymes 27. 36 (5 times)		times
4. 24		*omit*
17. 7	posterities	generations
17. 9	*omit*	„
—, by 26. 31	„	betimes
— past 31. 2 (2 times)	yesterdaye and yeryesterdaye	before
tymrells 31. 27	tabrettes	tabret
tythes 14. 20		tithes
vnbrydeld 24. 32	vnbridled	vngirded
vncircumcysed 34. 14	vncircumcided	vncircumcised
vnclene 7. 2 (2 times)	vncleane	not cleane
vncorrupte 17. 1		perfect
6. 9	parfecte	„
vncouered 9. 21		
vnder 1. 7 (17 times)		
1. 20		in the open
28. 11		for
30. 29		with
35. 4		in
50. 19		in the place of
32. 25	of	of
32. 32 (2 times)	„	*omit*
— myne hand 33. 13	by me	with me
vndermyned, hath 27. 36	hath vndermined	hath supplanted
vnderstode 42. 23		vnderstood
3. 7	perceaued	knew
vnderstonde 11. 7		vnderstand
vnderstondynge 41. 33 (2 times)	vnderstandinge	discreet
vnknowen 24. 16	vnknowne	neither knowen

	C	A
vnknowne 31. 27	secret	† steale away from
vnknowynge 31. 20 (2 times)	*omit*	vnawares
vnrighte 16. 5	wronge	wrong
unstable 49. 4	thou passest forth swiftly	
until 33. 14	tyll	vntill
untill 27. 45	till	
3. 9	tyll	till
24. 19 (8 times)	„	
10. 30	„	as
vnto 1. 9 (376 times)		
1. 14 (2 times)		for
2. 20 (34 „)		to
6. 2 (8 „)		*omit*
6. 4 (7 „)	with	
8. 9	vnto him in to	
14. 19 (2 times)		of
— heaven 15. 5		forth abroad
18. 6 (25 times)	to	
18. 21	before	
19. 5	*omit*	
20. 13 (4 times)	vpon	
—, greavous 21. 12	displease	
24. 4 (3 times)	into	
24. 38	for	
24. 50	agaynst	
28. 9	his waye vnto	
28. 9	besyde	
31. 18		in
31. 50		beside
32. 4	hither to amonge	
33. 14 (3 times)	in	
33. 16 (2 times)	towarde	
34. 20	vnder	
46. 28	the waye to	
— me, be 48. 5	be myne	

	C	A
vnto 49. 8		downe before
50. 4		in the eares of
1. 30 (10 times)	to	to
4. 5 (6 „)	*omit*	„
9. 2 (3 „)	in to	into
12. 15	before	before
12. 20 (9 times)	*omit*	*omit*
13. 1	towarde	into
14. 3	† into the brode	in
14. 17	in to	at
— them 15. 13	theirs	theirs
17. 19	with	with
20. 16	for	„
24. 17	to mete	to meete
27. 29 (2 times)	downe at	downe at
28. 11	to	vpon
29. 3	in to	in
32. 24	vntyll	vntill
33. 3	to	neere to
34. 30	before	among
39. 1	into	downe to
— the, lyke 41. 39	as thou	as thou art
—, lyke 41. 49	as	as
43. 33	after	to
44. 34	vp vnto	vp to
— this tyme 46. 34	vp hytherto	vntill
—, appoynted the	the people that	to
people 47. 21	went out and	
	in at	
47. 31	towarde	vpon
50. 20	ouer	against
50. 23	of	the children also of
vntyll 8. 5 (2 times)		vntill
41. 49	† yt	„
42. 15	excepte	except
See until		
untill		

<table>
<thead>
<tr><th></th><th>C</th><th>A</th></tr>
</thead>
<tbody>
<tr><td>vp 2. 21 (55 times)</td><td></td><td></td></tr>
<tr><td>6. 21 (11 „)</td><td></td><td>*omit*</td></tr>
<tr><td>19. 2 (13 .,)</td><td>*omit*</td><td></td></tr>
<tr><td>—, rose 19. 33 (2 times)</td><td></td><td>arose</td></tr>
<tr><td>—, stode 24. 10</td><td>gat him vp</td><td>arose</td></tr>
<tr><td>—, rose 26. 31</td><td>arose</td><td></td></tr>
<tr><td>— and sytt 27. 19</td><td>syt vp</td><td>arise I pray thee</td></tr>
<tr><td>—, stode 28. 18</td><td>arose</td><td>rose vp</td></tr>
<tr><td>—, gatt 38. 19</td><td>gat vp</td><td>arose</td></tr>
<tr><td>41. 19</td><td>out</td><td></td></tr>
<tr><td>28. 15 (2 times)</td><td>*omit*</td><td>*omit*</td></tr>
<tr><td>*See* upp</td><td></td><td></td></tr>
<tr><td>vpon 1. 2 (32 times)</td><td></td><td></td></tr>
<tr><td>1. 22 (4 times)</td><td></td><td>in</td></tr>
<tr><td>9. 14</td><td></td><td>over</td></tr>
<tr><td>13. 4 (3 times)</td><td></td><td>on</td></tr>
<tr><td>14. 6</td><td></td><td>by</td></tr>
<tr><td>14. 15 (2 times)</td><td></td><td>*omit*</td></tr>
<tr><td>24. 52 (2 „)</td><td></td><td>to</td></tr>
<tr><td>27. 16</td><td>aboute</td><td></td></tr>
<tr><td>33. 20</td><td></td><td>it</td></tr>
<tr><td>34. 27</td><td>ouer</td><td></td></tr>
<tr><td>39. 5 (2 times)</td><td>in</td><td></td></tr>
<tr><td>26. 22</td><td>„</td><td>in</td></tr>
<tr><td>39. 6</td><td>with</td><td>*omit*</td></tr>
<tr><td>42. 36</td><td>ouer</td><td>against</td></tr>
<tr><td>*See* apon</td><td></td><td></td></tr>
<tr><td>appon</td><td></td><td></td></tr>
<tr><td>vpp 14. 22 (6 times)</td><td>vp</td><td>vp</td></tr>
<tr><td>— apon 8. 13</td><td>vpon</td><td>vp from off</td></tr>
<tr><td>15. 5</td><td>vp</td><td>towards</td></tr>
<tr><td>40. 20</td><td>*omit*</td><td>vp</td></tr>
<tr><td>— to 28. 12</td><td>vnto</td><td>*omit*</td></tr>
<tr><td>vppe 49. 4</td><td>vp</td><td>vp</td></tr>
<tr><td>*See* vp</td><td></td><td></td></tr>
<tr><td>vpper 30. 8</td><td></td><td>*omit*</td></tr>
<tr><td>vppermost 40. 17</td><td></td><td></td></tr>
</tbody>
</table>

	C	A
vesseles 43. 11	sackes	vessels
vexe, shalt 31. 50		afflict
vine 49. 11		
See vyne		
virgyn 24. 43	virgin	virgine
vision 15. 1	vysion	
46. 2		visions
visyted 21. 1	vysited	visited
vitalles 14. 11	vytales	victuals
vitayle 42. 7 (2 times)	vytale	food
42. 25 (2 „)	expenses	prouision
vowdest 31. 13	maydest	vowedest
vowe 28. 20 (2 times)		vow
vowed 28. 20	made	
voyce 3. 8 (11 times)		
3. 10 (11 „)		voice
21. 12	it	
voyde 1. 2		voyd
vyne 40. 9 (2 times)		vine
40. 10	which	
See vine		
vyneyarde 9. 20	vyniarde	vineyard
vysett, will 50. 24	wil vyset	will visit
50. 25	shal „	„ visite
wages 29. 15 (2 times)		
31. 8	rewarde	
walke 17. 1 (2 times)		
13. 17	go	
—, dyd 48. 15	haue walked	
— with meditation, to 24. 63	to his meditacions	to meditate
walked 3. 8		walking
— with god 5. 22	led a godly life in his tyme	
walking, be 12. 19	go thy waye	goe thy way
wandre 20. 13		wander

	C	A
wandred 21. 14		wandered
wandrynge 37. 15	wandringe	wandring
—, must be 4. 14	must be a renne-gate	shall be a fugitive
warde 42. 17		
40. 4 (2 times)	preson	
40. 3		ward
ware 7. 8	*omit*	are
See were		
warre 14. 2		
—, men of 49. 19	a wapened hoost	a troupe
was 1. 2 (118 times)		
1. 7 (3 „)	so it came to passe	
2. 20	was founde	was found
3. 10	am	
3. 20 (5 times)	is	
5. 3 (7 „)		liued
7. 22 (7 „)	*omit*	
8. 11 (5 „)	had	
11. 29 (7 „)		*omit*
12. 19		is
13. 3		had bene
— doune 15. 12	beganne to go downe	was going downe
15. 17		went downe
15. 17		behold
19. 16 (3 times)		being
19. 23	was vp	was risen
— with childe 21. 2		conceiued
— olde 24. 36	in hir olde age	
26. 13		became
— wrooth 30. 2		was kindled
34. 25 (2 times)		were
35. 5 (2 „)	hath bene	
40. 20	behelde	
41. 49	coude not be	
42. 35	founde	

	C	A
was sore 47. 20		prevailed
— full 6. 11	*omit*	was filled
11. 3	take	had
20. 2 (4 times)	is	is
21. 4	*omit*	being
22. 13 (7 times)	,,	*omit*
23. 16	knew	knew
—, the maner 29. 3	they vsed	*omit*
30. 40 (3 times)	were	were
35. 16	came	had
— with him 39. 6	he had	he had
wash 18. 4		
washe 19. 2	let be waszhen	wash
—, to 43. 24	to wash	washed
See weshe		
washed 43. 31		
wast 40. 13		
3. 11	art	
49. 4	passest forth	*omit*
water 2. 10 (22 times)		
1. 2		waters
—, plenteous of 13. 10		well watered
24. 19 (3 times)	*omit*	
24. 44		*omit*
29. 7	geue to drynke	
29. 8	,, drynke	
1. 20	waters	waters
—, to 29. 3	to geue drynke	watered
49. 25	depe	deepe
watered 2. 6		
29. 2	dranke	
29. 10	gaue to drynke	
waters 1. 6 (22 times)		
2. 10		heads
9. 15	floude of water	
watrynge 30. 38	drynkinge	watering
wauered 45. 26		fainted

	C	A
waxe 9. 7	be frutefull	multiply
waxed, was 15. 17	was	*omit*
—, am 18. 12	am	
26. 13	became	
41. 56	preuayled	
— wrooth 39. 19	was wroth	wrath was kindled
— ripe 40. 10	were rype	brought forth ripe grapes
43. 1	oppressed	was
way 3. 24 (3 times)	waye	
waye 14. 11 (18 „)		way
—, great 21. 16	bowe shote of	a good way off
—, on the 24. 59	*omit*	away
—, went their 24. 61		followed
—, went his 24. 61	departed	went his way
—, on the 31. 27		away
—, wentest 31. 30	woldest nedes depart	*omit*
— to turn, wist not 32. 7		was distressed
—, went his 33. 16	departed	on his way
—, went their 34. 26		went out
37. 15		*omit*
38. 21		way side
— myghte be shewed 46. 28	to shewe him the waye	direct his face
wayes, goo youre 18. 5		passe on
19. 2	waye	
24. 55	*omit*	*omit*
—, goo oure 34. 17		be gone
weake 42. 9	open	nakednes of
weapens 27. 3	geer	weapons
See wepons		
weght 24. 22	weight	weight
weighte 43. 21	„	„
weke 29. 27 (2 times)		weeke
weked 18. 25	vngodly	wicked

	C	A
weked 49. 5	deedly	of crueltie
See wicked wiked wyked		
wekedly 19. 7	wickedly	wickedly
wekednesse 6. 5	wickednes	wickednes
44. 16		iniquitie
15. 16	wickednes	,,
See wykydnesse		
welcomed 43. 27		*omit*
welfauored 41. 4	goodly	well fauoured
well 4. 7 (25 times)		
24. 13 (2 ,,)		wel
— of iugmente 14. 7		En-mishpat
16. 7		fountaine
— of the lyvynge that seith me 16. 14	well of the liuinge that sawe me	Beer-lahai-roi
18. 11 (4 times)		*omit*
24. 29	well syde	
27. 36		rightly
29. 14	wel	surely
30. 15	,,	therefore
20. 6	*omit*	*omit*
40. 16	good	good
— fauored 41. 18	goodly	
welles 26. 15 (3 times)		wels
wells 29. 3 (2 ,,)	welles	,,
29. 8	,,	welles
wels 24. 11	well	well
wemen 14. 16 (2 times)		women
See women		
wemanseruaunte 32.5	maydens	women servants
wened, was 21. 8 (2 times)	weened	weaned
wenst 49. 4	hast clymmed	wentest
went 4. 16 (60 times)	wente	

	C	A
went 7. 13		entred
— away 8. 5	wente awaye	*omit*
8. 7	flew	
— furth 9. 20	beganne to take hede vnto the tyllinge of the ground	began to bee an husbandman
11. 31	carried them	
12. 4	wente	departed
12. 6	,,	passed through
13. 18 (2 times)	,,	came
— a pace 18. 6	,,	hastened
— in 23. 18	go out and in	
24. 45	goeth	
— after 24. 61	wente after	followed
— his waye 24. 61	departed	
28. 9	wente his waye	
— vpp and downe 28. 12	wente vp and downe	ascending and descending
— in vnto 29. 23 (2 times)	laye with	
— awaye 31. 20	wente	stale away
31. 55 (2 times)	,,	returned
32. 22	,,	passed
33. 3	,,	,, ouer
35. 3	haue gone	
37. 12	were gone forth	
37. 17	followed	
— in vnto 38. 2	had lyen	
50. 9	take their iourney vp vpon	
24. 30 (6 times)	came	came
— aboute to begyle 27. 12	begyled	shall seeme as a deceiuer
— and fett 27. 15	made	tooke
27. 18	brought	came
— to him 27. 27	came nye	came neere

	C	A
went 33. 16	departed	returned
35. 21	,,	iourneyed
— aboute to 37. 21	wolde haue	*omit*
44. 18	stepte	came
wentest secretly 31.27	kepest that secrete that thou woldest flye and hast stollen awaye fro me	didst flie
31. 30	woldest nedes departe	needes bee gone
wepe 23. 2 (2 times)		weepe
43. 30	wepte	wept
wepons 49. 5	weapens	*omit*
See weapens		
wepte 21.16 (13 times)		wept
wepynge 50. 4	mournynge	mourning
were 1. 31 (4 times)		
1. 7 (6 times)	*omit*	
3. 22 (5 ,,)		*omit*
5. 4 (15 ,,)	was	
6. 4	became	
8. 1 (2 times)		was
9. 18	are these	
10. 32		were diuided
— subiecte 14. 4	were subiects	served
27. 1	waxed	
35. 5	laye	
36. 13 (8 times)	are	
36. 24 (3 ,,)		are
— content 37. 27	herkened vnto him	
— sadd 40. 6	loked sadly	
44. 4		were gone
— but a deed man 44. 22		would die
49. 24	were made	were made
2. 5 (2 times)	was	was

	C	A
were 9. 22 (6 times)	*omit*	*omit*
10. 2 (7 „)	are these	„
10. 20 (4 „)	are	are
10. 22	these are	*omit*
25. 4	are	„
—, as it 25. 25	as	like
— aware 42. 23	knew	knew
46. 32	are	hath bene
— stronge 49. 26	go mightely	haue preuailed
wery 27. 46	weery	weary
weshe 24. 32	wash	wash
—, shall 49. 11	shal wash	washed
See washe		
west 12. 8 (2 times)		
westward 13. 14	westwarde	
wete, to 8. 8		to see
24. 21	tyll he knewe	to wit
wexed 27. 1	waxed	was
See waxed		
weyde 23. 18	weyed	weighed
weyght 24. 22	weynge	weight
whalles 1. 21		whales
whan 6. 1		when
6. 5		*omit*
See when		
what 2. 19 (36 times)		
— another sayeth 11. 7		another speech
what 2. 9	wherfore this	
— and yf 24. 5	what and	peraduenture
— yf 24. 39	„ „	„
24. 57		*omit*
31. 36	*omit*	
33. 5 (2 times)		who
— excuse make 44. 16		how shall we clear
49. 1		that which
— though 18. 28	peraduenture	peraduenture
(5 times)		

	C	A
when 5. 3 (6 times)	*omit*	*omit*
11. 16 (7 „)	and	and
15. 15	in	*omit*
18. 13	and yet	which
31. 8	yf	if
44. 25	then	*omit*
See whan		
whence 16. 8 (3 times)		
3. 19		for out of it
3. 23		from whence
—, from 10. 14		out of whome
whensoever 3. 5	in what daye so euer	in the day
wherby 8. 11	then	so
See whereby		
where 3. 9 (19 times)		
2. 11	and there	
— he was borne 11. 28		in the land of his nativity
—, in all places 20. 13	where so euer	whither
33. 19	there	
19. 29	wherin	in the which
21. 23	„	wherein
— I was borne 24. 7	of my kynred	of my kindred
— thou wast borne 31. 13	„ thy „	„ thy „
41. 38 (3 times)	how	*omit*
42. 13	† awaye	„
whereby 15. 8	wherby	
See wherby		
wherefore 26. 27 (2 times)	wherfore	
32. 32	therfore	therefore
See wherfore		
wherein 17. 8 (4 times)	wherin	
1. 30	that hath	
9. 5	wherin	*omit*

	C	A
wherein 23. 17		*omit*
See wherin		
where of 10. 9	therof	wherefore
wherfore 47. 19		
18. 13 (7 times)		wherefore
3. 13		what is this that
12. 18		why
16. 14 (3 times)	therfore	wherefore
29. 25 (3 „)	why	„
31. 30	„	yet wherefore
38. 10	and	wherefore
38. 29		and
50. 11	therfore	
11. 9 (2 times)	„	therfore
16. 2 (4 „)	and	and
19. 13 (2 „)	*omit*	„
22. 14	therfore	as
29. 25	why	what is
33. 10	*omit*	*omit*
34. 30	yf	„
38. 7	therfore	and
39. 4	so yt	„
40. 15	that	that
45. 7	but	and
47. 15	why	for why
See wherefore		
wherin 6. 17		wherein
See wherein		
wher of 33. 17	therfore	therefore
See where of		
whether 18. 21		
(7 times)		
16. 8 (2 times)	whyther	whither
8. 8		if
17. 27		*omit*
See whither		
whother		

	C	A
whi 26. 10	why	what
See why		
which 1.21 (64 times)		
1. 7 (10 times)	*omit*	
2. 13		the same it is that
2. 14		that it is which
2. 22 (44 times)	that	
3. 12 (4 „)		whom
3. 17 (3 „)	wherof	
4. 1 (2 „)		and shee
4. 17		„ she
6. 2	soch as	
9. 2		they
9. 4 (2 times)	wherin	
10. 8		he
11. 29 (3 times)		*omit*
12. 1 (5 „)		that
12. 7 (6 „)		who
14. 3	where	
14. 13		hee
14. 13		these
16. 14		it
17. 21 (6 times)	whom	
18. 7		and he
19. 21 (2 times)	wherof	
21. 2	like as	
26. 35	both these	
27. 8 (2 times)	what	
27. 17	as it	
30. 40		them
32. 9	thou that	
32. 13	as	
34. 7	the vse	
36. 14		and
48. 7		the same
3. 11	wherof	whereof
5. 5 (2 times)	*omit*	that

	C	A
which 8. 11 (7 times)	*omit*	*omit*
9. 2	,,	they
9. 6	that	who so
10. 1	and they	them
12. 16	*omit*	he
13. 10	that it	that
19. 37 (3 times)	of whom	the same
21. 3 (3 ,,)	whom	whom
24. 5	where	whence
25. 11	and he	Isaac
26. 22	that	and that
28. 13	,,	wheron
28. 20 (3 times)	,,	that
32. 7	what	*omit*
33. 13	yf they	them
35. 20	there	that
36. 8	and	*omit*
36. 19	he	who
38. 30	that	and his name
39. 22	so that he	*omit*
48. 18	*omit*	who
See whoch		
while 25. 6	whyle	
27. 44	,,	a few dayes
14. 1	tyme	dayes
24. 55	at the least ten dayes	a few dayes
See whyle		
white 30. 37	*omit*	
See whyte		
whither 32. 17	whyther	
See whether whother		
whitter then 49. 12	whyter then	white with
who 3. 11 (7 times)		
whoch 38. 10	that	which
See which		

	C	A
whom 2. 8 (8 times)		
46. 18		whome
24. 44	which	
30. 26	the which	
38. 5		and his name
—, with 44. 17		in whose hand
whome 22. 2 (3 times)	whom	whom
4. 20		the father of
43. 29	that	
31. 42	*omit*	*omit*
38. 25	that	whose
49. 10	him	him
whom soeuer 31. 32	whom	
whoore 34.31 (5 times)		harlot
38. 24	whordome	whoredom
whose 16. 1 (8 times)		
whosoeuer 4. 15		
4. 14	who so	euery one that
44. 9	whom'	whom soeuer
whother 28. 15	where so euer	whither
See whether		
whither		
why 4. 6 (6 times)		
26. 9		how
31. 26	what	*omit*
See whi		
whyle 29. 9		while
— to nyghte, great	yet hye daye	yet high day
29. 7		
41. 5	whan	while
46. 29	*omit*	„
whyte 30. 35 (2 times)		white
See white		
wicked 38. 7		
37. 33		euil
See weked		
wiked		
wyked		

	C	A
widowes 38. 19	wyddowes	of her widowhood
See wydows		
wife 12. 11 (28 times)		
17. 19 (12 „)	wyfe	
24. 44	woman	woman
See wiffe		
wyfe		
wifes 36. 39		wiues
45. 19 (3 times)	wyues	wiues
38. 20	woman	womans
See wives		
wyfes		
wyves		
wiffe 30. 9	wyfe	wife
See wife		
wyfe		
wiked 37. 20	wicked	euill
See weked		
wicked		
wyked		
wilbe 43. 14	must be	
wildernes 36. 24		wildernesse
(2 times)		
wildernesse 21. 20	wildernes	
(2 times)		
See wyldernes		
wyldernesse		
will, thy 41. 44		thee
wise, this 50. 17	thus	so
wist 32. 7	wyst	*omit*
31. 32	knew	knew
44. 15	knewe	wote
See wyst		
with 4. 8 (72 times)		
2. 21		instead
3. 6	therof	
— child 3. 16		† conception

	C	A
with 3. 16 (3 times)		in
4. 25 (7 „)		*omit*
9. 12	amonge	
12. 18 (4 times)		vnto
16. 6 (2 „)		to
17. 12 (12 „)	*omit*	
— child 21. 2 (2 times)		conceiued
21. 14		of
21. 23 (4 times)	vnto	
24. 10		in his hand
— child 25. 22		thus
— all 27. 41		wherewith
31. 32 (5 times)	by	
— me 31. 42	on my syde	
33. 8		by
— yonge 33. 13	are yet but yonge	
38. 12 (2 times)		and
38. 16 (2 „)		in vnto
40. 2 (2 „)		against
42. 26 (2 „)	vpon	
— you 43. 12		in your hand
(2 times)		
— them 43. 15		in their hand
48. 6		after
49. 28		according to
3. 24 (3 times)	and	and
19. 5 (6 „)	*omit*	*omit*
24. 40	by	by
25. 13	*omit*	„
29. 25 (2 times)	vnto	vnto
30. 2 (2 „)	at	against
—, laden 37. 25	which bare	*omit*
38. 24	by	*omit*
— him, was 39. 6	medled withe nothinge	he had
42. 28	vnto	vnto
44. 17	by	in

	C	A
withe 6. 3	with	with
See wyth		
within 18. 24		
25. 22 (2 times)	in	
40. 13	ouer	
See wythin		
without 19.16 (4 times)		
41. 16		*omit*
— nombre 41. 49	coude not be nombred	
— money, yf 47. 16		if money fail
24. 8	discharged of	cleare from
See wythout		
witnesse 31. 48		witnesse
See wytnesse		
witt 24. 57	axe her	enquire
wives 28. 9 (3 times)	wyues	
See wifes		
wyfes		
wyves		
wod 22. 3	wodd	wood
wodd 22. 6 (4 times)		,,
21. 33	trees	groue
wold not 48. 19	wolde not	refused
49. 33	*omit*	*omit*
wolfe 49. 27		
woman 2. 22		
(16 times)		
womans 20. 3		woman
wombe 25.23 (4 times)		
wombes 49. 25		wombe
women 24. 11	wemen	
See wemen		
womenseruauntes	maydens	womenseruants
20. 14		
wondred 24. 21	marueyled	wondering
woordes 39. 19	wordes	words

	C	A
woordes 44. 10	as ye haue spoken	wordes
See wordes		
worde 15. 1 (5 times)		word
—, kynde 37. 4	frendly worde	peaceably
wordes 24. 30 (3 times)		
24. 52 (12 „)		words
4. 23		speech
43. 7	as he axed	words
21. 11	worde	thing
See woordes		
worke 2. 2		
5. 29	workes	
worker 4. 22		instructer of euery artificer
workes 2. 2 (2 times)		worke
world 6. 4 (3 „)	worlde	earth
6. 4	*omit*	*omit*
9. 19	londes	earth
10. 32 (2 times)	earth	„
worlde 18. 25		„
49. 26		euerlasting hils
worme 6. 7		creeping thing
wormes 1. 24 (5 times)		„ „
1. 25		thing that creepeth
7. 23		creeping things
7. 14	crepynge thinges	„ thing
worse 19. 9		
worshepped 24. 48	thanked	worshipped
See worshipped		
worshippe 22. 5	worshipped	worship
worshipped 24. 26	thanked	
See worshepped		
worth 23. 15		
—, as moch money as it is 23. 9	a reasonable money	
worthy, not 32. 10	to litle	
wotest 4. 7	is it not so ?	*omit*

	C	A
woteth 39. 8	knoweth	wotteth
— not where he is 49. 13	he is awaye	one is not
wounded my selfe 4. 23		to my wounding
wrastled 32. 24	wrestled	wrestled
32. 25	wrestlinge	„
—, hast 32. 28	hast stryuen	hast power
wrath 27. 45 (3 times)		anger
—, his 32. 20	him	him
wretchednes 44. 34	mysery	euill
wronge 40. 11		pressed
wrooth 31. 36 (2 times)		
30. 2	wroth	anger
39. 19	*omit*	wrath
44. 18	displeased	anger
wroth 4.5		
wrought, had 24. 7		
wydow 38. 11	wyddow	widow
wydows 38. 14	wyddowes	widowes
See widowes		
wyfe 3. 8 (19 times)		wife
2. 24 (34 „)	wife	„
3. 20		wiues
24. 39	woman	woman
See wife		
wiffe		
wyfes 20. 11		wiues
See wifes		
wives		
wyves		
wyked 13. 13	wicked	wicked
18. 23	vngodly	„
See weked		
wicked		
wiked		
wyker 40. 16		white

	C	A
wykydnes 39. 9	euell	wickednesse
See wekednesse		
wyld 44. 28	*omit*	*omit*
wylde 16. 12		wilde
wyldernes 21. 14		wildernesse
16. 7	wildernesse	,,
wyldernesse 14. 6	wildernes	,,
See wildernes		
wildernesse		
wynde 8. 1		winde
41. 6 (2 times)	*omit*	eastwind
wyndow 6.16(3times)		window
wyndowes 7. 11		windowes
(2 times)		
wyne 9. 21 (11 times)		wine
27. 37	wine	,,
wynter 8. 22		winter
wysdome 41. 33	wyszdome	wise
(2 times)		
wyse 3. 6 (2 times)		wise
See wise		
wyst 9. 24	perceaued	knew
21. 26	knewe	wote
See wist		
wyth 6. 14 (35 times)	with	with
2. 1 (2 times)	,,	and
4. 1 (,,)	,,	*omit*
— god, walked 5. 22	led a godly con-uersacion	
— god, walked 6.9	led a godly life in his time	
9. 11 (2 times)		by
14. 8 (3 ,,)	*omit*	
20. 5		in the integrity of my
39. 14	by	
— fyre 11. 3	*omit*	thorowly

	C	A
yee 24. 58	yee I wyll go with him	I will goe
24. 14 (2 times)	*omit*	*omit*
28. 13	„	behold
See ye		
yer 27. 7		before
24. 15	or euer	„
45. 28	before	„
yere 7. 11 (6 times)	yeare	yeere
5. 3 (48 times)	„	yeeres
5. 5 (8 „)	yeares	„
5. 11 (4 „)	„	yeres
11. 10 (6 times)	yeare	yeres
See yeare		
yeres 5. 8 (14 times)	yeares	yeeres
31. 41 (3 „)	„	yeres
5. 6 (5 „)	yeare	yeeres
47. 28	yeares	yeres
41. 50	*omit*	yeeres
47. 9	tyme	„
See yeares		
yeron 4. 22	yron	iron
yes 18. 15	it is not so	nay, but
yesterdaye 31. 29 (2 times)		yesternight
yesternyghte 19. 34	yesternight	„
yet 6. 3 (22 times)		
2. 5		*omit*
18. 22 (5 times)	*omit*	
20. 12	„	and yet
29. 34	yet agayne	again
33. 15		now
40. 8		I pray you
2. 5	*omit*	*omit*
6. 8	neuertheles	„
18. 27	howbeit	which
19. 29	for	*omit*

	C	A
yet 29. 35	the fourth tyme	*omit*
42. 13	*omit*	this day
yf 4. 7 (32 times)		if
15. 5	*omit*	
17. 14		*omit*
24. 14 (2 times)		and
—, but and 24. 40	yf	*omit*
— it be so that 24. 42	„	if now
46. 33		and it shall come to pass when
47. 16	seynge	if
18. 24 (5 times)	peraduenture	peraduenture
19. 12	*omit*	*omit*
— and yf 24. 5	„	peraduenture
—, what 24. 39	what and	„
42. 33	that	that
45. 28	that	*omit*
See if		
ymages 31. 19 (2 times)		images
ymaginacion 6. 5	imaginacion	imagination
See imagynacion		
ynough 24. 25		
33. 9 (3 times)		enough
—, haue dronke 24. 19		have done drinking
—, had lvved 25. 8		was full of yeeres
30. 15		a small matter
34. 21	brode of both the sydes	enough
yocke 27. 40	yock	yoke
yonder 22. 5		
37. 30		*omit*
yonge 14. 24 (9 times)		yong
44. 20		*omit*
— children are fedd with bread 47. 12	euen as yonge children	according to their families